Allegheny International in Am
Fermenta in Sweden . . . must w
of control, or that they cannot b
stories, just the latest stories in a long series of less-publicised abuses
of corporate responsibility.

Meanwhile, as individual investment bankers continue to receive
20, 50 or 100 million dollars per annum apiece for advising
companies on how to make acquisitions, the comparative performance of American and British companies has continued to decline.
The long bull market of the 1980s, which fuelled the fever for
making such acquisitions, disguised a collective loss of competitiveness, and a consequent loss of market share in both home and
overseas markets.

CONTROLLING COMPANIES proposes fundamental but
simple changes to corporate law and practice. Originally published
as ON THE BOARD, the contents of this highly acclaimed business
classic have now been greatly widened and deepened in detail in
order to address all the institutional shareholders, bankers, accountants, consultants, managers and directors who are able to
influence, control or improve company performance.

The problems met within companies are universal and the solutions provided within this book are international. Practical,
purposeful and professional . . . *'there can be little doubt of the
potential impact were Geoffrey Mills' comments accepted and
implemented'*.

Geoffrey Mills has worked in chairman, chief executive, non-
executive or consultancy roles for public and private companies.
After early experience as a diplomat and overseas administrator he
had been a manager and director, working in varied industries and
countries.

Controlling Companies

GEOFFREY MILLS MBE

UNWIN
PAPERBACKS

LONDON SYDNEY WELLINGTON

First published in Great Britain, under the title *On the Board*,
by Gower in association with the Institute of Directors, London in 1981.

Second edition published by George Allen & Unwin (Publishers) Ltd, 1985.

Third revised edition, under the title *Controlling Companies*, published by
Unwin® Paperbacks, an imprint of Unwin Hyman Limited, in 1988

UNWIN HYMAN LIMITED
15/17 Broadwick Street, London W1V 1FP

Allen & Unwin Australia Pty Ltd
8 Napier Street, North Sydney, NSW 2060,
Australia

Allen & Unwin New Zealand Ltd with the Port Nicholson Press,
60 Cambridge Terrace, Wellington, New Zealand

British Library Cataloguing in Publication Data

Mills, Geoffrey, *1937*–
    Controlling companies. —— 3rd rev. ed.
1. Directors of corporations
I. Title   II. Mills, Geoffrey, *1937*–
On the board
658.4′22   HD2745

ISBN 0–04–440205–8

Set in 10 on 12 point Garamond by Getset (BTS) Ltd, Eynsham, Oxford
and printed in Great Britain by Cox & Wyman, Reading.

Contents

Introduction

While a few very visible organisations report rapid growth in size and value, the sum total of British and American companies produce a progressive decline in both domestic and international market share. In Britain, the home of the Industrial Revolution, the import of manufactured goods now exceeds the export of British-made equivalents. In America, the home of the technologies which opened the Post-Industrial Age, the import of high technology products, as well as the import of computer-related products and services, now also exceed American exports in these fields.

National performance results largely from the sum total of company performances, and comparative improvement or decline is most clearly indicated by trends in market share. When companies choose to raise reported earnings by retreating from markets, or by decreasing share selectively, they can only maintain this chosen 'strategy' to a point at which both earnings and market share suddenly disappear together in a puff. In Britain and America, and in other industrialised countries which follow their example, many complete sectors of industry have already disappeared in a puff.

Meanwhile, acquisition and divestment, the buying of business created elsewhere and the selling of businesses which have not been managed successfully, has been turned into an artificial new business sector of its own. Akio Morita, chairman of the Sony Corporation of Japan, one of the most successful companies in the most successful industrial nation in the world, believes that British and American managers fail by focusing short term on chasing quick profits from such 'strategies' of acquisition and merger.

Organisations which can control or influence individual company performance include:

- *the board of directors*, which is the body legally responsible, the body in charge of operations, and the body today most visibly flawed;
- *the shareholders*, who have the power to hire and fire the board of directors;

- the *lenders*, who have the power to stop lending; and
- the *advisers*. Once led by the *merchant and investment bankers*, the income of these bodies has lately become so heavily centred on their 'corporate finance' advice related to acquisitions and mergers that they should today be considered as professional aids rather than as independent advisers. As skilled aids they can certainly be helpful to companies in specific financial functions but, having moved so far from clinical independence, they should no longer be considered for appointment as 'independent' directors to the boards of client companies. While *management consultants* are also increasingly engaged for specific advice on new systems or techniques, they are seldom invited to comment on the composition of the board of directors, or on its style of control, and their strategic influence therefore remains very limited. Which leaves the *accountants*, who as auditors, and now also as the leading consultants to companies, have become today the main potential source of independent external advice to client boards.

Earlier editions of this book concentrated 'on the board', with contents addressed primarily to those who hold legal responsibility for controlling companies. Recent boardroom trends and scandals, which are considered in the following new chapters, have since served to confirm that improvements in total company performance will only be achieved in the future from a more informed, more involved cooperation between the insiders who 'control' and the outsiders who can 'influence'. This will require a more purposeful alignment of their currently very diverse objectives. Many of the outsiders, including institutions, lenders and accountants, are skilled in their own fields and are privately sceptical, sometimes also publicly disdainful, about the apparent objectives of company managements. Yet many profess that they are uncertain how, or on what grounds, they can question the managers and evaluate their objectives. Two new closing chapters can be helpful to them. The book has been greatly widened in scope, and the original chapters have been revised and enriched with numerous new international examples and cases, in the belief that most of those outsiders do now agree the urgent need for their more active influence.

1 Who controls companies today?

The concept of companies with limited liability was first introduced in the nineteenth century to enable the providers of capital to measure and limit in advance the extent of the risks they would be taking. The company managers and the providers of capital were carefully separated by the new legislation, but a man was still allowed to be both. Thus the corporation eventually became, in one irreverent opinion, *'an ingenious device for obtaining individual profit without individual responsibility'* (Bierce, 1911). The managers and the providers of capital, or shareowners, had to be kept apart, but they also had to be closely linked, and for that linking *'the mass of owners is connected to the corporate pyramid by an archaic, creaking contraption at the top called the board of directors'* (Geneen, 1985). Through the years, and particularly during the most recent years, that contraption has become *'the Achilles heel of the American corporation'* (Dayton, 1984). Through the years the voice of the individual shareowner has been overwhelmed by the objectives of financial institutions, which today hold around 70 per cent of the votes.

The institutional shareowners

The range of institutions is wide, their potential power to influence performance is very great, yet their levels of expertise remain very variable. It is not their wit but their focus which is too often foggy. A British study of the ability of stockbrokers and institutional shareowners to understand company accounts (Lee/Tweedie, 1981) covered a weighted sample of 225 professionals who were sufficiently confident of their expertise to take part. Many fared little better than lightly informed laymen:

1

70 per cent had only a 'vague' idea of what depreciation meant;

47 per cent had only a 'vague' understanding of what profit meant;

24 per cent never read the auditor's report; and few of the respondents considered that visiting the companies in which they invested had any importance.

Without visiting companies, and thus without making the opportunity to evaluate company managements, the institutions concerned remain unable to exercise their potentially productive influence. And by such inaction they can allow themselves to be carried away on a bright bubble. Carrian Investments, for just one extravagant tropical example, began as a property company in Hong Kong in 1979. Within a year or so its market capitalisation had reached HK$6 billion. Within two more years it was involved in almost every kind of business activity short of sending rockets to the moon, creating subsidiaries with tell-tale names like 'Extra Dollars', 'Smart Money' and 'Eager Earnings Limited' – yet moments later net assets were negative and the organisation evaporated under a swelter of civil and criminal court actions. Every step in its breakneck progress had been marked by an institution buying its stock.

Problem is that rapid-fire activity and related apparent growth seem to set the institutions' adrenalin a-pumping, and deaden sensitivity to pain. In the 1980s the institutions also supported the management of Guinness under a new chief executive, first praising it for selling off or closing 140 companies acquired by the Guinness family in an unsuccessful attempt to diversify away from its famous branded drink; then praising the same management for acquiring new subsidiaries outside the drinks business; then again, when the Guinness company had become burdened by scandal, praising the company for beginning to sell off all the non-drinks business. Alas the managers, as well as the institutions, also get carried away by all this, and they too lose sensitivity – but it was not the managers, directly, who multiplied the share price six times.

Comfortable conventional wisdom has it that share prices, and therefore the Dow Jones and FT Share Indices, rise when company performance is improving and earnings are increasing. But consider the arithmetic for the FT-SE 100 Share Index (first introduced in

1984) during the relatively low-inflation period from autumn 1984 to autumn 1987. It doubled from 1100 to 2200. In the same period the average price-earnings (P/E) ratio recorded by the FT-Actuaries Indices increased from 11 to 18. If we adjust that increase by the treadwater effect of the UK's compound inflation of *c*. 20 per cent in the period, we arrive, again, at a multiple of precisely 'double'. Meanwhile, in some industrial sectors, for example Packaging and Paper, the sector average P/E itself had trebled in this short period.

In the 1970s a P/E as high as 14 was only 'allocated' to a very successful high growth company which was working in expanding markets. Just before the stock market collapses of October 1987 all industry sectors in the FT's wide sample of 500 companies had average P/Es above 14. From the mid-1970s to October 1987 most average P/Es had quadrupled or quintupled. The conclusion to be drawn is clear and uncomfortable. Share values had not been rising primarily as a result of real increases in average or total performance or earnings, but as a result of brokers and institutions allocating, or accepting the allocation of higher P/Es across all sectors. By doing so they had facilitated the switch in company strategies away from growth by improved competitiveness towards much simpler short-term programmes of apparent growth through acquisitions. And they had given the executive directors their huge stock option bonuses 'on a plate'.

If we choose to analyse individual companies, rather than sector average P/Es, we can also find cases where a company's share price had been marked up sharply by brokers and institutions when it sold off failed subsidiaries and had to be moved into another category in the FT Index where P/E ratios were 'traditionally' higher. This could happen even when asset backing per share had actually decreased. All the modern machinery of 'the market' is not yet helping to hone our judgement, and Lord Keynes had already cautioned us back in 1935 that '*we are concerned not with what an investment is really worth but with what the market will value it at, under the influence of mass psychology*'.

When they hold themselves at a distance from company managements, the institutions' judgement of the roles of key men can become worse than their judgement of corporate performance. For example, when deciding in general meeting whether the chief executive of Guinness should also become the chairman of the board, despite that board's earlier written promise to the shareholders that a new separate chairman would be appointed, the institutions supported the motion by the embarrassing majority of twelve-to-one. Shortly thereafter the scandals broke surface, and that newly elected combined chairman/chief executive left the company. The case provides stark evidence of the damaging quality of the relationship between the providers of capital and the managers of companies today. It cries out the need for the institutions and their appointed directors to establish new styles of common objectives, based on survivability, then on consequent growth, not on the 'easy' criterion of apparent gain in a rising stock market. It cries out the need for the institutions to get to understand the nuances of company behaviour and the reasons, often shameful, why boards of directors compose themselves as they do.

These are described through the following chapters, and are summarised in the guidelines in Chapter 14 'Dos and don'ts for institutions, bankers and accountants'.

The bankers

Bankers, individually, have a greater stake risked in a company than any single shareholder and they have, individually, the power to pull the plug. In Japan the bankers are very closely involved with the practical control of local companies, operating as lenders and shareholders, as well as advisers, confidants and 'colleagues' in commercial – industrial keiretsu groupings. Similarly in Germany, where the bankers are also frequently shareholders, and can have their representatives on the upper tier supervisory board. In Britain and America, the relationship between companies and their commercial bankers is more distant, often almost adversarial. Yet the bankers, when operating as lenders only, should have simpler, more uniform objectives than the mix of shareholders – namely, survivability, and thus the ability to repay, without any of the added complications of levels of yield obtained, or of capital gain, on shares which may have been purchased at very different prices by the different shareholders.

It is anomalous that the criterion of 'ability to repay' has been applied most stringently by commercial bankers to the smallest loans to individual borrowers, less stringently to corporate borrowers, and then almost not at all to the largest loans to the less developed countries (LDCs). In reviewing the dormant power of the primary lenders to influence company performance, and in exhorting them to play a more active role, we cannot avoid recording such anomalies because they currently limit the credibility given by corporations, and by individuals, to banking opinion – the LDC debt crisis could still just manage to lay low the Western system of enterprise which was originally created on the back of the banking process.

It began in the 1970s when too much was lent without controls on usage, security or stewardship: *'the commercial banks were even sillier than the development agencies'* (Prowse, 1987). When Mexico triggered public awareness of the problem by threatening to default in 1982, its debts totalled US$65 billion. By 1984, the figure had, nonetheless, been allowed to reach $89 billion; by 1987, it was around $110 billion, with plans afoot to add another $15 billion to the sums which the country could not repay. In the same five-year period the total of LDC debt had doubled to $1,000 billion: *'the whole banking system was going on la dolce vita.'* But not quite the whole banking system. As we shall note several times through this volume, in connection with several widely differing situations, the exception has been Japan; Japanese banks were scarcely involved in LDC lending.

Eventually the US and UK banks began to write off parts of these loans, which meant that the whole mass of taxpayers, generally, as well as the banks' shareholders, specifically (but not the banks' directors, individually), now had to carry some of the costs of these banking judgements. It provides poor example, and damaging precedent, to the directors of industrial corporations that so very few of those responsible for LDC overlending have not been quietly removed, uncompensated, for their massive misjudgements. It provides worse example that losses on LDC lending are being handled, accounting-wise, in different ways by different banks, either 'below the line' or 'above the line' as 'extraordinary items' or 'exceptional provisions'. One of these fundamentally different treatments allows

'profit', on which the profit-sharing schemes for the benefit of the
executive directors are based, to be reported at an unrealistically high
level, with the directors consequently receiving undeservedly high
bonuses.

Yet banking criteria have still not been universally revised; now
overlending by foreign banks to *British* companies begins to cause
concern (Jay, 1987). Criteria applied remotely can prove to be remote
from reality. *'Mexico and Venezuela had oil, Argentina had wheat –
Chile had confidence, and the bankers liked that particular product at
that time'* (Kaletsky, 1983). Lending to companies, or to individuals
when protected by the limited liability Companies Acts, is also
judged largely on 'confidence'. William Stern went bankrupt owing
more than £100 million without ever, in his own words, putting a
'penny' of his own money into his companies. He was later discharged
from bankruptcy for less than a ha'penny in the £, or for 0.005 of his
debt, so that, in the court's words, the business world would not be
deprived of his skills any longer. Herbert Towning was discharged
from his £19 million bankruptcy for 0.00055, while the Registrar
remarked that *'the banks never enquired about his circumstances'*
(DT, 3.2.83). The banks also had confidence in Laker Airways. When
Sir Freddie Laker left the employment of another airline to set up on
his own he stated that his objective was to have a company with six
planes and 120 staff, and if it got any larger *'you can kick my xxxx'*.
When the company was eventually put into receivership it had
fourteen planes and a staff of 2,500. It had been sunk by new
borrowings to finance the purchase of eighteen more aircraft, at a
time when the company was already largely funded by debt, was only
just in reported profit, and was operating in a market already constrained by severe overcapacity. We could choose other or later cases,
but Sir Freddie was an enterprising man, a folk hero, and justifiably
so; his company was not killed by any one of his managerial limitations, alone, but by the failure of advisers, directors and, particularly,
bankers to observe, understand, check, allow-off for, batter down or
help overcome those limitations.

British *primary* commercial banks, which are few and national,
seldom make losses or go bust, being protected by a unique ability to
take both fixed and floating charges on a company's assets. American

banks, in contrast, are numerous, often very localised in their operations, and increasingly frequently make losses or go bust; 138 failed in 1986 and 200 are expected to fail in 1987. Bizarre cases abound, but would be unfairly cited here because *'greed and poor judgement are clearly more widespread than downright criminality'* (Gilbert, 1985). The cumulation of this looseness in judgement and control was illustrated in 1987 when the International Monetary Fund (IMF) reported that in the first half of the 1980s, in just five years, no less than US$388,000,000,000 of the world's money 'went missing'. That is the figure by which the world's debits exceeded national credits. Certainly the money had vanished, but the IMF could not explain why or whither.

While a banker's lending to a single corporate client may be far smaller than its lending to a single LDC, and far larger than to any individual borrower, its working contact with the corporate client is always a great deal more frequent. In times of difficulty it can be daily; in times of crisis several times daily. Yet the banker cannot give operating instructions to company managements, even in times of crisis. It should not need to. If the banker has maintained a policy of regular contact with several of the directors, including several of the non-executives, through all the good times, it will find that any advice it gives during the occasional bad times will carry more weight than remote, disinterested instruction.

The accountants

Almost as close to the daily operations of client companies, and on a much wider front, are the accountants. As appointed auditors, with the unique ability to read the minutes of board and board committee meetings, their responsibilities are to analyse and report on the accuracy, under prevailing law, of the accounts presented. While they cannot control the actions of the managers, they are expected by the courts to advise, and they are certainly increasingly well placed to influence corporate behaviour. They have most cannily extended their relationship with the near-captive market of clients whose books they audit by first moving into management consultancy, a field which they now dominate, and then moving further into the field of recruitment consultancy, both overt and covert. One of the largest international accounting firms today advertises itself as 'Accountants. Advisers. Consultants'. It cannot be surprising that the accountants have become the primary target for legal action by disadvantaged shareholders and others when the companies they audit get into trouble. But it can be surprising, and disturbing, that the value of suits outstanding against the major accounting firms now totals many hundreds of millions of dollars. Most actions still centre on the alleged failure to detect fraud, though allegations of failure to spot weaknesses in companies which are acquired become more frequent. On top of which '*there is a feeling that accountants were getting too cute*' (Sorkin, 1985). The Securities and Exchange Commission (SEC) is among those filing actions against the accountants, as firms, partners or individuals, but has itself occasionally provided cosmetics for cuteness. In 1983, it unanimously approved an accounting device which allowed companies to buy government securities, reduce balance sheet debt by an equal amount, and thereby beautify financial condition and create opportunity for instant, unrealised profits. The very name of the device, called 'in-substance corporate defeasance', should give pause.

One can hardly blame even the most experienced and respected accountants if such passing cuteness deflects concentration. Allegheny International had five company jets, and it lent $30 million at 2 per cent to some of its officers, and all of that was visible. Bryanston Finance, an umbrella organisation for a secondary bank based in the Bahamas, had two principals; it also had separate subsidiary companies established for the purchase of jewellery for the third wife of one of the principals, for the purchase of two jets and six Rolls-Royces for his use, for a Scottish hotel in which he was the only guest, a yacht for the company's chartering business which he alone used, and for eighteen gun dogs, eleven greyhounds, several race-horses, personal laundry, and the manipulation of some other millions which had disappeared unaccounted. Most of which had also been visible. The auditors to Bryanston Finance, a major accounting firm of the highest standards, had not been blind to the situation, and had eventually withdrawn from their contract with the client, but they were chastised in the subsequent court actions for failing to brief properly the auditors who replaced them, *and for not having advised the non-executive directors of their observations*. In the latter, the writer submits, lay their simplest and most serious omission, which had prevented any opportunity for an active cooperation between those who 'influence' and those who 'control'.

There is continuing debate whether the accountants' primary duty is to the board of directors which initially appoints them as auditors, or to the shareholders who then formally agree or renew that appointment at each annual general meeting. The legalities may be obscure, but the practicalities are clear enough; in any country, under the local Companies legislation, it can be clumsy or even counter-productive to bring every problem before the shareholders en masse. Thus the accountants' first responsibility must, in practice, be to the board of directors.

A 'dissenting' director can face precisely the same dilemma as the auditor when worried, for example, by evidence of a chairman's abuse of the board, or by his abuse of legal board processes, or by his unbalanced personality and actions, or by worse. Either can reasonably decide to avoid bringing such matters before a full general meeting – but neither the director nor the auditor can avoid presenting them to the board itself. When doing so they will probably find that, as in all human groupings (see Chapter 4, 'Groupthink'), the board will act by 'closing ranks', despite the mass of evidence that they should act very differently indeed. In such likely event the director or the auditor can resign, having acted responsibly – but any lesser action by either would be culpable irresponsibility. From the record, few directors dare to shoulder this responsibility; even fewer accountants know that they must also carry part of it.

The accountants have an additional strength from working closely with the bankers, particularly when a company weakens. It is the bankers who normally decide, following an accountant's report, to put in a receiver, and in the UK the receiver himself is always an accountant. They are numerous. Per head of population, the UK has twenty-two times as many chartered accountants as the Germans. It has twice as many as the rest of the EEC countries added together, plus a range of other qualified but non-chartered variations. Yet in a survey of 425 senior professionals in 1981 (*The Accountant*, 1981), carried out in conjunction with the Stock Exchange, it was found that half considered British management was 'less than competent or poor', while the other half considered it was 'competent, good or very good'. This could be taken as indicating the same average level of practical judgement on company managements as the shoe-shine boy could achieve by flipping a coin, heads or tails.

The patently frequent failure of institutions, bankers and accountants to judge or influence company performance stands in embarrassing contrast to the equally patent skills of many of the individual members of those organisations. The anomaly arises because they do not exercise themselves in probing through to the realities of corporate behaviour; they do not trouble to evaluate the level of reality behind the reasons given by the directors for their actions. The guidelines in Chapter 14, 'Dos and don'ts for institutions, bankers and accountants', will be helpful. The pages in between set out in detail why such guidelines have needed to be defined.

2 What needs controlling?

Buying up and buying out

Without active or effective external control or influence today from institutions, bankers or accountants, most corporate executive directors are free to pursue those policies which most attract them, corporately or individually. A common characteristic of British and American boards has become the replacement of strategies for business development by much easier programmes for acquisition. The more successful Japanese corporations do not pursue such programmes. They have two words for acquisition and take-over, 'baishu' and 'nottori', which are the same words as they use for 'bribery' and 'hijack'. They view groups of subsidiaries as cooperating companies, whereas Americans and British view them as financial hierarchies. The Japanese are business-oriented; the Americans and British have become figures-oriented. In a rising stock market it is much easier to make 'good figures' by making bigger companies than by making better businesses.

It is true that large companies can demonstrate both higher profits and higher rates of profitability than small companies (Luffman/ Reed, 1985). They have greater financial and organisational flexibility. They can sell or close without troubling to try to improve performance in weaker subsidiaries, and can then borrow and buy something else which looks bigger – or better, because it is at the time working in markets which are softer. The net result is 2 + 2 = 3. Then 3 + 3 = 5. Then 5 + 5 = 8. The original aggressor company grows from 2 to 8 while the national total of 12 declines to 8-plus-whatever-else is being kept alive by new parents. In America and Britain, the two countries most fevered by the fashion for mergers, the greatest losses of market share are within their own home markets. It is critically important, but little known, that while Britain continues to

11

move too rapidly out of manufacturing into services, it is losing market share in services twice as fast as in manufacturing (Harvey-Jones, 1986). In contrast, the Japanese place the winning of market share as second in their list of planning objectives, and second only to a unique overriding priority to ensure that individual corporate moves will serve collective national interest. Contrast also Germany, where hostile take-overs are almost unknown.

In this volume we are considering corporate performance, not the morality of merger mania, junk bonds, poison pills, stubs, greenmail and related. Those are financial phenomena, largely created and nurtured by operators and intermediaries with little or no practical involvement with the businesses of the corporations whose shares they handle. We must note, however, that:

> *Every study has shown that polygamous companies grow no faster, in terms of e.p.s., than firms that stay resolutely single.*
>
> HELLER, 1986

> *. . . some estimates put the failure rate for acquisitions of all sorts at around the 60 per cent mark.*
>
> LESTER, 1985

> *Nine times out of ten two companies are better than one. Many of these take-overs are devoid of industrial logic . . . Some of them amount to little more than a cynical City exploiting vain manage-ments set on their own aggrandizement* (Linaker, 1986), or, in the opinion of the chairman of the Council for Wider Share Owner-ship, some are just: *personal megalomania masquerading as corpo-rate efficiency.*

> *The boom* [in take-overs] *is much more about protecting the jobs of directors than about efficiency or shareholders' interests.*
>
> HARRIS, Feb. 1986

> *There is little evidence of cost reductions or efficiency gains following mergers.*
>
> SMALLWOOD, 1986

The institutions, bankers and accountants are well placed to acknow-ledge the accuracy of this short selection of conclusions, and to judge what proportion of take-overs are engineered to facilitate private or insider dealing.

The raiders and traders and merchant bankers, in contrast, will naturally claim that take-overs are based on an essential 'corporate restructuring' to make assets more productive and to shake up idle managements. Maybe sometimes. But claiming that it's all a question of improving long-term management is deceptive.

There are in fact *two* simultaneous, yet wholly contradictory fashions, which are both claimed to be based on 'management' considerations. One proclaims that performance is improved by bringing companies into larger corporations which will be smarter at managing their resources. The other tells us that managers perform much better when removed from the shackles of larger corporations – hence the parallel fashion for buy-outs. The two trends move in diametrically opposite directions. They are based on diametrically conflicting management hypotheses. Their only common feature is that it's the same intermediaries who benefit from them. In buy-outs the investment and merchant bankers, for example, can obtain: equity interest in the new company; fees for putting the deal together; fees for advising the portfolio companies; fees for watching over the pooled funds of investor clients before the funds are committed; fees as a share of the profits of the pooled funds after they are committed; fees as directors of the portfolio companies (Lowenstein, 1986).

We can conclude, with few qualifications, that these fashionable trends no longer have very much, if anything, to do with the controlling or competitiveness of companies. We can observe, also, that managers themselves can benefit from the results of these fashions much more easily than they can by exercising smarter management. As aggressive bidder corporations grow, so do the incomes of the managers; salaries and options simply rise in step with size. And as management- or leveraged buy-outs begin their independent life, the purchase price financed to greater or lesser extent by tax-generated cash flows, their share prices can rise rapidly to a level which must highlight the question of just what the managers were doing before they were cut loose. Reality is that: *'Too many people are just doing deals; they're not doing companies'* (Ross, 1984), and, in at least one informed conclusion: *'the leveraged buy-out is intrinsically a scam'* (Klein, 1984). Fashions change. The mini-skirt could only rise so high. From the abundant evidence on these two exaggerated financial fashions it is clear that:

- some, but only the minority, of shareholders, obtain short-term benefits from take-overs and buy-outs;
- these fashions can only continue with levels of banking support reminiscent of their lending to LDCs; and
- it is *only* the executive directors of bidding companies (whose salaries and options always increase), plus the executive directors in targeted companies (who land on their golden bustles), plus the investment and merchant bankers who gain without fail.

Executive control

Trends in buying up and buying-out have so dominated investor and lender attention in recent years that they have disguised the effects of, and have thus facilitated the growth of, a number of damaging trends *within* companies.

Senior executive pay, perquisites, and pay-offs have risen far beyond reason, and quite possibly beyond a politically dangerous flash-point. The reasonable, and productive concept of excellent reward for excellent performance has been replaced by the assumption of the right to excessive reward, based on company size, irrespective of real, personal performance. Further, the executives' security of tenure has strengthened. While the number of chairs in the senior recruitment game of musical chairs may in total be decreasing steadily, and while there may be an occasional well-publicised sacking or two, the use of the chairs is being restricted carefully to the existing players in the game. Even those sacked for patent mismanagement can get back into the game if they are nimble, and most of them do. If T. Boone Pickens is only half right in his belief that *'80 per cent of America's top executives are incompetent'*, then it's easy to see the developing problem.

Hand in hand with the growing protection and covert recruitment of top managers, and related to it, is the frequent combining of the roles of chairman of the board and chief executive officer in one person. Contrary to all logic, the practice is more common in large corporations than in small. It grows apace, despite the accumulating weight of evidence against it. Both executives and non-executives are well aware of the dangers in the practice; domination can lead to autocracy, and then easily to bullying manipulation of men and board meeting minutes. Yet more often than not, when the signs develop, they will shrug them aside, perhaps making a mumble or two over drinks after the board meeting, but never a murmur within the boardroom itself. In theory the executives, with the protection of their multi-year service contracts, should have been made more courageous, and thus better able to raise and pursue the abuses which they meet more frequently in their daily duties than the part-time non-executive can experience. In practice, however, those very service contracts provide a warm womb-like environment which the executives become even more fearful of leaving. Consequently the value of the executives as directors, as opposed to their value as managers, decreases steeply.

The participation of prevalent types of non-executive director, dissected in detail through the following chapters, has failed to prevent the development and dominance of these trends. Board directors, whether executive or non-executive, can often remain blind to the realities of top management objectives, or to management relationships which can affect performance. Some observers conclude that activities and advancement of all beyond middle management level *are purely and simply dependent on how well the person pleases and submits to the wishes, whims and idiosyncrasies of the boss*, adding that control must therefore lie firmly with the board as a whole in order to guard against the chief executive's possible: *laziness, extreme selfishness, lack of creativity and leadership . . . and manipulative practices* (Aggarwal/Aggarwal, 1985). Laziness may be seen in different forms, and may be disguised quite easily by frenetic activity and lots of late night sessions. It's a biological characteristic of humans, and can lead to reducing active judgement, and then to a slackening of control. It's seen less often in smaller companies, which demand a great deal more work, wider detailed skills and more frequently exercised judgement from their decision-makers, but it might be deduced in some large corporations where the top men are surrounded by layers of in-house experts, and have countless outsiders on tap against the payment of fees. Perhaps it could be deduced in pre-scandals Guinness? Was it just an extra large dose of due diligence which led that company to use no less than 120 outside advisers when bidding for Distillers? Said a Guinness director, '[there were] *even people to advise us on the advice we were given*'. Was it also great diligence which engaged around fifty staff from the American consultants Bain, in different parts of the organisation against the payment of fees, of £8 million in one year? Who was doing the really productive working and thinking and deciding? Whatever the proper answers to the questions, and the writer does not know or seek to suggest them, the fact is that there was indeed a slackening of control in that particular company. While some of the board and others were receiving fees measured, most strangely, in millions of pounds for their part-time, short-term, limited involvement in the bid process, the board, as a whole, was clearly not involved, nor even informed about what was going on.

In the controlling of companies, a commonly repeated pattern has been allowed and encouraged to develop. Full-time executive directors are in control, not the board (see also Mizruchi, 1983). The chief executive is allowed to dominate and the board becomes a rubber stamp (see also Weidenbaum, 1986). The dominant chief executive 'buys' and maintains the passive 'loyalty' of subordinates with the security of service contracts, and with more money than they have really earned, using an equally passive non-executive remuneration committee to 'push it all through'. The non-executives are there to prevent all this from happening, and occasionally a board does reshape itself after a drop in performance and a burst of savaging by the media. But that is almost always 'after the event'. Many non-executives, including both the powerful and successful as well as the second-order make-weights, fear the imagined results of making visible boardroom changes. They sit mum while the chairman allows himself to manhandle or mouth at a dissenter, even when they also dissent. They funk firing the chief executive who is held in contempt by his subordinates, even when they share the same conclusions. They convince themselves that the short-term need to avoid the possibility of unsettling the brokers and institutions, and the bankers and auditors, is really worth the greater risk of medium-term harm to the corporation. In fact those organisations are usually a little more streetwise than that, and can read between the lines, given the chance. But most non-executives, like the least courageous of the executive directors, don't dare to put that to the test. Harold Geneen (1985) confirms the phenomenon. The directors are '*concerned, too, with the "talk" it will cause among the securities analysts, the bankers and lending institutions, and investors . . . The chief executive is the chairman* [sic] *. . . if they fail to persuade others they can expect retribution. . . He would act to remove them from the board . . . In the end the dissident board members might rationalise . . . Now the directors have joined in a conspiracy of mediocrity.*'

Just occasionally the process of removing an inadequate CEO really does get under way before the company gets too deeply into visible trouble. It can take two to three years of quiet lobbying to achieve, and the company may last that long, but once started the process never reverses (Alderfer, 1986). It is not such a difficult process when the hat of the chairman and the hat of the chief executive are on different heads. As Geneen, however, cautions from his own experience: '*I wore both hats at ITT and it felt great . . . But it was not fair to the interests of the stockholders . . . nor did it serve the purpose of the board of directors . . . as things are presently constituted, there are few, if any, real checks or balances upon the power of the chief executive within our large public corporations. That's the presumed job of the board of directors, and it is not doing it.*'

Nor are the institutions, lenders and accountants checking to see that they are doing it. They are not even checking the most readily obvious abuses by the board, or by individual directors. Consider a commonly repeated example. A company working in established, non-political, non-controversial domestic markets has no adequate business-experienced non-executives on its board; agreeing the need to have some – at least the cosmetic need – it chooses to appoint either

- a retired foreign service diplomat, the highlight of whose career had been a spell in Kiribati, or

- an aged politician without business experience, and without any other achievement by which the world can remember him, or
- a long forgotten ex-captain of industry who is obviously too ill or too tired to say a word, or
- a remnant from a failed company, recently acquired, who will clearly agree with everything, or
- the full-time chief executive of another company who will equally clearly attach as much importance to this part-time role as he does to the other four or five which he squeezes in.

Looking aside from the question of what kind of personal standards these men apply to their own behaviour when accepting such appointments, it is obvious to the one-eyed that the chairman, or the chief executive, is stuffing the board with passive votes. The men appointed may be, or may once have been, decent and capable in their other roles, but they do not have the understanding, or the energy, or the health, or the wit, or the time, to do anything remotely useful to the company concerned. This happens every day.

The institutions, bankers and accountants let the abuse be confirmed without even token query or comment. Consequently the directors, particularly the full-time executive directors, are left free to use public listed corporations as private playthings, with the board's collective responsibilities being surrendered to a single dominant director. That single director may be a management giant, or, at the other extreme, he may be both managerially incompetent and mentally unbalanced. There are visible examples of either extreme at the head of listed corporations. From the evidence – namely, from the observable fact that the inadequate are not always removed – it is clear that many of the other directors do not mind which extreme presides in their particular board. But can we really expect otherwise when the institutions who own most of the shares, and the bankers who lend most of the money, do not themselves appear to mind?

The legal concept of a board of directors, consisting of several persons making collective decisions, was introduced to take account of, and thus to help remove, the harmful effects of the weakness, madness or sinfulness of individuals. But what is the board? How does it interrelate with those external organisations? What is it doing, and how well? What should it be doing, and how? Let us now examine these questions, root and branch.

3   The board

The board is . . .

The board is . . . responsible. Those who appoint it enjoy the protection of a most lenient limited liability. The board itself has no similar legal life-belt.

It is an anomaly in law. The directors are agents of the company, but are neither agents nor servants of the shareholders who appoint them. They are bound by the company's own articles, and by a widening shelf-ful of national legislation, which describe the extent to which the board is responsible.

The board is an entity separate from the sum of its individual directors which makes single, collective decisions. It can evolve and change as an entity in step with the changing demands of its company's growth stages and business environment. It will perform more wisely than its wisest director, or fail more foolishly than its weakest, in accordance with how well it does evolve and change to meet those demands. The life-span and vigour of its company become good, or bad, or depressingly mediocre, in accordance with the wisdom and intent with which the board makes and monitors its decisions. The board alone has ultimate responsibility for corporate standards of performance.

It is the company's top manager, appointed to control the company, which means to direct and manage the management, who in turn control the sum of its business operations. Its prime responsibilities must therefore be:

- to evaluate, define, and when necessary redefine, the businesses in which the company will operate, the resources which will be allocated to each, and the timing and rates of return which are required from each;

- to select, monitor, and hold responsible the managers to whom the daily control of these operations is entrusted – particularly, but not exclusively, the chief executive.

Companies fail when their boards do not discharge effectively either one, or both, of these overriding responsibilities. Which occurs when:

- the board itself is poorly led or uniformly composed, seeks rest rather than a continuing restlessness, looks comfortably inward rather than critically outward and forward; or when
- the selection of, or subsequent failure to remove, inadequate managers is based on dominant individual objectives, not corporate objectives; or is based on blinkering, or blindness, or both.

The board is a counsellor. It does not wait passively to evaluate the operational or planning proposals which come up to it in neat packages but actively advises and assists where possible in their compilation. There is no law nor article which states that it must do this. There are no regulations or precedents which prescribe limits on how much or how little the directors can be charged by the board to undertake, or how deep or shallow these undertakings can be. As the body responsible for controlling the company it should not need legislation to explain that it must be active rather than acquiescent.

It is the keeper of the company's conscience and the measure of corporate morality. By setting the standards of corporate courage it delimits the management's morale. From the boardroom to the shopfloor, both productivity and performance are most closely affected by morale, which is itself most closely affected by visible morality. The effective company meets its creditors on time, especially the small ones; does not abuse its suppliers or maltreat its physical environment; is clinically correct with its customers, employees, auditors, analysts, shareholders, lenders and taxmen.

While there is little room or requirement for altruism within the competitive corporation, there are very few corporate employees who find it satisfying to break any of the rules.

Most importantly, the board is a group, programmed with the psychology and dynamics which govern the behaviour of all human groupings, from humble to great. In this it is as far removed from the psychology and dynamics of its individual directors as an ant-hill is from its ants, or a coral reef from one of its polyps.

Boards can fail, and so companies can collapse, when these characteristics are ignored, not known, or denied.

And the board is . . . performing poorly. Both in home as well as in overseas markets, and both in mature business sectors as well as in developing high technology fields, American and British companies continue to lose market share. The wealth and flexibility made available to Britain by major new gas and oil resources off-shore have not altered these trends. In the British machine tool market, now definable both as a mature business and an increasingly high technology field, Japanese share rose from 10 per cent to over 40 per cent in just two years against a rapidly falling £ sterling; since then their share has continued to rise as the £ has continued to fall against the yen. Meanwhile, Japanese sales to the 'neutral' Chinese market rose to 25-times the British volume achieved, and a Chinese minister observed that the British no longer seemed able to think 'in the long term'. In the USA the dynamism which had long been powered by its own more abundant resources is beginning to falter under pressure from competitors which do not have such natural advantages. Out of abundance the USA developed mass production and designed the quality control procedures for monitoring such production. It invented air conditioning for its comfort and microcircuitry for its safety. Yet by the 1980s the mass-produced American air conditioning equipments were proving many times more fault-ridden than Japanese equivalents, and American microcircuits for military systems were being supplied without adequate quality control. High technology products had accounted for more than 40 per cent of all US manufacturing exports in 1985, yet within two years the US trade in such products had fallen into deficit. Comparative corporate performance had declined.

A national performance is essentially the sum of corporate performance, which is itself a summing of individual board performances. The performance of a board can be very different from the intrinsic quality of its company's businesses, or from the professional quality of its individual directors. Witness the major corporate disasters of recent decades, where boards magnificent with men of undeniable quality have dropped into the rubble of their companies, almost before they detected that something was wrong with the edifices they so splendidly straddled. Germany in the 1930s, the USA in the 1950s and 1960s, Italy, UK and Japan in the 1960s and 1970s, worldwide in the 1980s – there is no lack of well-publicised examples, as well as a whole host of smaller dissolutions which never triggered public comment. The directors were splendid, but their companies crumbled with as much dignity as the walls of Jericho because their boards had collectively failed. The directors had proved no more effective as a board than any dozen of their least experienced shareholders or junior managers could have been, given the chance.

Every time you find a business in trouble, you find a board of directors either unwilling or unable to fulfill its responsibilities.

DAYTON, 1984

To put a scale on the problem:

Of the top five hundred American industrial companies, I would estimate that approximately 95 per cent of their boards of directors are not fully doing what they are legally, morally and ethically supposed to do. . . They are not doing their jobs.

GENEEN, 1985

More important than the major corporate disasters of the past is the progressive decline in comparative performance of the thousands of companies which continue to survive, their declining progress disguised by a long period of inflation, then by a long bull market, which have buoyed up their apparent results. Many subsidiary companies are, in practical terms, insolvent, but are carried along by their parent companies with guarantees or loans which no external lender would ever countenance. Others are sold off, treated to a management buy-out, or quietly dissolved as a kind of washing-of-hands which has no more credibility than Pontius Pilate's public display.

The board is an entity with many powers, but with declining power. Declining not because the quality of directors or managers decreases – though it has been argued that most of the business schools in the world are not producing better businessmen. Declining not because directors and managers work less hard – though it is quite evident that many lose heart, sit tight, keep mum, and develop such a low profile that it is not just their heads which go under the sand. Others indeed work harder than they need, travel a very great deal more than they should, and burn more midnight oil than is good for them. But declining because the manner in which most boards define what needs deciding and doing, the manner in which they monitor the achievement of what they have decided, and, most critically, the manner in which boards compose themselves in the first place, is a hundred years behind the demands of the present increasingly competitive business environment.

The decline of the board is a universal phenomenon of this century.
PETER F. DRUCKER, 1974

Decision-making by the board is one of the few aspects of present-day management which cannot be computerised. The board's collective work is all done in the minds of individual people. The quality and suitability of its work depend not only on the quality of the directors, but on how the various members of that group of people react with, stimulate, hold back, add to or subtract from each other. The board is a group.

Psychology of groups

Current knowledge of the psychology and dynamics of groups, in which the individual subdues a part of his individuality in order to contribute to the collective activities of the group, is still limited.

Management aspects of group processes, even the humdrum question of how to make committees more generally productive, have been little researched in comparison with all other aspects of management.

But a number of consistent conclusions about group effectiveness have been reached in studies conducted in several countries, and they do provide strong guidelines for composing and controlling board-room groupings which can best meet the variety of responsibilities that are placed on the board. If the reader who is also a director compares these rather dry experimental conclusions with the details of his own boardroom's behaviour, he will find all manner of parallels with features which disturb him about that behaviour.

Broadly:

- Groups produce better solutions to problems or tasks than individuals.
- Heterogeneous groups produce better solutions than homogeneous groups, than groups composed of people of similar styles and backgrounds. They are measurably more creative when the tasks to be achieved are complex.
- However, for maximum effectiveness, the size of groups must be as small as can cover the variety of contributions required.
- The members who arrive at the best solutions to problems or tasks are most often in an initial minority. The success of a board, as a group, must therefore lie in the facility and freedom with which members can influence each other, and with which the initial distinctions between majorities and minorities can be made to disappear, or become unimportant.
- The effectiveness of the group increases if it contains a clear leader, by character a self-confident decision-maker. His natural role within the group is to ensure that individual members contribute what they can to the formation of a common decision. This requires him to trim back those who seek to domineer, including himself. Many a chairman in a board, and many a chief executive in a management committee, finds difficulty in differentiating between domineering and leading. Many an executive director can recall with discomfort those management meetings which always proceeded as a monologue.
- The leader's ability to influence is closely correlated with his ability to be influenced. The leader who seeks to make all the decisions himself, rather than to maximise performance of the group, will

produce progressively worse decisions as the potential contribution of his colleagues is withheld in frustration.

- There is a marked difference in the effectiveness of different styles of leadership. The 'domineering' leader produces a temporarily firmer behaviour within the group, but individual contribution declines. The group becomes less able to make collective decisions, works poorly together, loses morale. These may indeed be the very characteristics which satisfy the personal preferences of the natural autocrat, but they do not meet the requirements and responsibilities of the group as a whole. The 'retiring' leader, who only offers his own opinions when asked for them, induces other members to show more initiative, but the group slowly loses both morale and its feeling of common responsibility. The 'democratic' leader actively helps individual members to focus on group objectives. Collective involvement develops, and the group becomes an effective entity.

- In groups where cohesion between the members is based on personal attraction or similarity, discussion turns to gentle pleasantry. Where cohesion is based on the maintenance of the group's prestige or standing, then the group strains to avoid any damage to its status or acceptability. Other objectives become subordinated to the pursuit of this non-productive aim. One member comes to dominate, and the others become submissive.

- On the other hand, where cohesion is based on the primary objective of task-achievement, then the conduct of affairs becomes more goal-oriented and businesslike. Thus the cohesiveness best suited to the enjoyment of, say, club membership, is quite different from the type best suited to the productive direction of a competitive enterprise. In the former (and many boards are run on the principles of the nicest clubs) a drive to maintain cohesiveness will soon enough cross purposes with a drive to improve performance, and the objective of apparent cohesion will be sustained at the expense of effectiveness.

- Pressure for conformity (which most directors will immediately recognise as being a characteristic of their own boardroom) can rob the group of original contribution. Where the issue on which there is strong disagreement is subjective, for example when it concerns individual people and their positions, the pressure exerted on the minority, or on the individual, becomes very great. Every executive director with any length of experience will remember, with embarrassment or pain, a number of occasions in his career when he felt forced to acquiesce in a decision which he knew in his mind and in his bones to be 'wrong' – and which the passage of time has certainly demonstrated to have been wrong.

- In the homogeneous group of similar members with similar backgrounds, such pressure will normally whittle down the minority to one, and he will then have to choose whether to row in or to ride out. Prolonged non-conformity, particularly if seen normally in one member, is viewed by that kind of group as a threat. The greater the extent or the length of the non-conformity, the progressively less tolerant the other members become. Pressure grows from patient discussion, through terse comment, to impatience, to gentle ridicule, and then to abuse. (It happens like this in all groups, not just in the boardroom.) Non-conformity creates anxiety, and the uniform group does not like the boat to be rocked – even though the boat be becalmed, or sinking.
- The uniform or homogeneous group can produce effective decisions both rapidly and smoothly when the problems concerned are not particularly complex – in a business sense, when the trading environment is relatively stable. Thus the uniform board was able to play its role with broadly adequate success in past decades. But the competitive environment is no longer stable, and never will be again. It will continue to exhibit increasingly rapid change. The tasks which face the boardroom will continue to be complex and conflict-ridden.

Compatibility is not always a boon. In competitive situations it is measurably a disadvantage.

The board as an effective group

In the knowledge that most, or all, of these characteristics apply as much to the board as to any other human group, we can sketch the outline of a board which has the best chance of remaining effective in a changeful competitive environment.

The effective board is . . .

- heterogeneous; composed of people of markedly different styles and backgrounds;
- flexible; composed primarily of people who are independent within the board, and who are not bound by any firm allegiances inside it – either to chum, or to boss, or to loyal subordinate. There will thus be no permanent majority or minority, and discussion will be characterised by the ad hoc grouping and regrouping of directors to argue whichever case happens to make best sense. In practical terms, this means having a sufficient number of 'active' non-executive or outside directors, who can detect when minority proposals are being suppressed, and who can 'side' with the non-conformists at least long enough for the board to determine whether the minority proposal is 'better' or not;
- task-oriented; discussion being centred on achieving specific and common objectives, not simply on reaching broad-brush political or policy conclusions. Such conclusions will always prove sterile unless followed by the definition of related action and perform-ance goals. These enable the directors to identify with the board's measured objectives, to become committed to its measurable success, and eventually to feel that success or failure is their own success or failure. It is not enough that directors are legally responsible. They must both feel, and want to be, responsible;
- performance-oriented; achievement must be regularly analysed, explained, redirected. The knowledge of real success improves morale, which in turn improves productivity;
- free of all non-combatants. It has been experimentally determined (though every director already knows this in his toes) that the regular non-contributor has a distinctly unsettling effect within small groups;
- small. A board of more than about ten directors will become stiff with non-combatants;
- led democratically – so that each director's opinion may be freely presented and impartially judged;
- a clique, not a claque.

The board is not . . .

The board is not . . . a club.

Companionship and convenience do not feature in its objectives.

A study published in 1974 (Whitley, 1974) recorded some striking data regarding the composition of the boards of twenty-seven of the largest City of London companies. While the high correlation dis-covered between actual club membership and Oxford and Cambridge College background might well have been expected, the high level of interwoven directorships between the twenty-seven companies, of interwoven blood relationships between the twenty-seven boards, and of common schooling among the directors must cause considerable surprise.

No fewer than forty-six of the directors of the boards of the eight leading insurance companies in the sample had been schooled at Eton, an average of almost six Eton directors apiece. And 34 per cent of the whole sample of 341 directors on whom data were available had been educated at that same school. However excellent one school and its products may be, the statistical odds against such percentage composi-tion resulting from any criterion other than clubbability are remote.

The board is empowered and entitled to compose itself in any way which it judges fit, and which the shareholders in general meeting will endorse. And the boards covered in the Whitley study, which included the largest clearing banks, merchant banks, discount houses and insurance companies, had succeeded in earlier years in preserving the international pre-eminence of the City of London in their parti-cular fields of activity. But by 1982 the London branches of American banks controlled the same amount of money as all of the London clearing banks combined, while the London branches of Japanese banks controlled even more. By 1986 Japanese banks accounted for roughly a quarter of the gross banking assets in the UK, nearly twice the share of the Americans. Thus in the heartland of British financial expertise, Japanese, American and other foreign banks have taken such large shares of the market that the native British organisations are left in the role of minority participants.

The first edition of this book suggested that '*it will be interesting to observe whether the composition of the boards of these large financial institutions will shift significantly, and whether British market share in these fields will continue to be preserved* '. On the evidence of the record, some of these institutions have *already* lost credibility and comparative competence as the composition of their boards leaves them understimulated and overcomfortable. And worse with the unincorporated associations concerned with commodity trading and insurance. In the case of the City of London's once universally respected Lloyds insurance organisation, recent years have seen scandal follow scandal, to the point at which Mr Albert Lewis, the insurance superintendent of New York State, could write that:

> *Lloyds has lost credibility and insurance business is now looking for other markets. You would have thought that an outfit such as Lloyds would have an accounting system that works, an internal security system and a credit support system to prevent all that has happened.*

FINANCIAL TIMES, 1982

Several years later a local expert observer could add that:

> *The British insurance industry has a notable reputation for poor management. Inert, incompetent, and lacking in any sort of imagination are just some of the charges that are levelled at the management of this important financial sector, which has a singularly undynamic image.*

MOORE, 1987

Clearly 'chum's honour' had *not* proved a good enough standard of control.

Clubbability can have more ridiculous aspects. Consider the case of a publicly quoted Group which was expanding in good markets. A succession of head-hunting organisations had strained unsuccessfully to search out a new chief executive designate to take over in a short period from the ageing incumbent. Eventually, through the expedient of once traditional recruitment advertising, an appropriate man was located and selected by the committee of directors. But before the die was cast by the man concerned, the chairman of the board took him aside and advised bluntly that the ageing incumbent would never let him succeed because he was not a Freemason, or one of the American equivalents made jolly in the minds of the public by the antics of cartoon character Fred Flintstone of the Raccoon Lodge of the Royal Order of Water Buffaloes. (The less public but real-life antics of the P2 Freemasons in Italy and Argentina, for examples, are not so jolly.) So several more headhunters and advertisers had to be brought in before another year's passage located someone who gave the right sort of handshake. A bar-room ballade? A snippet of pub gossip? Not at all. The writer of this volume was the 'man concerned'.

In a small private organisation one might almost understand, though not freely accept, this level of required clubbability. In a significant publicly quoted corporation it smacks of the very grossest irresponsibility. And yet, dig a little and you will find many similarities. There are many kinds of clan and club and coterie among men.

Each country has local variations, some helpful or harmless, some vicious, and some exportable. The 'old boy network' is as common in the boardrooms of egalitarian Denmark as it is in class-ridden Britain. East Africa has 'age mates', formed from initiation groupings, and West Africa has 'home boys', from the same regions. Japan has habatsus (Chapter 7). But Japan also has the Yakuza; Naples has the Camorra, Calabria the 'Ndrangheta, and Sicily and America have the Mafia. Just one characteristic is shared by these widely ranging examples of collective interest groupings; they were originally based on concepts of honour and cooperation. The Yakuza, who are active in drugs trading, extortion, bribery, loan-sharking and 'white slavery', also claim that they stand for the preservation of democracy and capitalism, and they were allowed by the American Administration to regroup after World War II for that reason. The danger with all such clans and clubs and coteries is that concepts of honour can be abused by misinterpretation, and concepts of cooperation can lead to criminality. In a corporate context, and in the context of this volume, their greatest danger is that they can induce in their members a limited or deceptive view of their external environment.

The board is not . . . a committee.

Committees are set up by other bodies, which give them terms of reference. The board continuously defines and redefines its own terms of reference. It should not, therefore, accept and trot through the agenda presented to it on the sole initiative of the chairman, or of the chief executive, or of the two in tandem. It should, on the initiative of the directors as a whole, combine in compiling its own agenda. This is the least awkward way of defining detailed terms of reference, without having to repeat to the chairman, or chief executive, or both, that they must not seek to cover only those questions which they are personally prepared to cover.

The board must not acquiesce on the nod. It must not, committee-wise, conceive camels of compromise through comfortable consensus.

The board is not . . . a formality.

It is not a programme of ten or twelve meetings per annum (worse, three or four) at which a series of tidy agenda are tidily despatched.

It is not a rubber-stamp for decisions in practice already made, or worse, for actions already taken, though it is often treated as such – particularly in those countries which apply a two-tier system of board in which the 'upper' tier can have little other practical purpose. This is also true in the USA and UK where many a chairman or chief executive in a unitary board will take it as a personal affront when directors express disagreement with a predigested decision which is dropped onto the board table for rapid ratification. Among the many detailed characteristics of boardroom behaviour in less than successful companies, this is perhaps the most prevalent. At least it is the most visible.

Which is surprising if we pause to consider that even Karl Marx was able to determine that life is all about 'conflict'. The very essence of business life, in particular, is complexity, competition, and conflict. If it was not absolutely inevitable that there could be significant disagreement in the boardroom on one item or another on the agenda about every second or third meeting, then one would not need the board at all. If there is no air of tension as one enters the boardroom about every second or third meeting, then one can safely conclude that the board is becoming too remote from the conflict of the arenas in which its corporate performance is being determined. Certainly the boardroom should not become a battlefield where the factions sally out from under their respective banners, fighting for what each banner represents and then rallying back to it after every skirmish. But if it does not experience a painful skirmish every now and again, it is probably already dead.

The board is not an ivory tower, remote from or largely uninterested in its managers and their managing.

The success of the board's decision in the field depends as much on the managers' ability or opportunity to implement as on the wisdom of the original decision. The field failure of a board policy, whether because it is badly implemented or because it was a bad decision to begin with, can seldom be exposed to the board in sufficient time to make suitable adjustments if the board works to a watertight separation from management. It has been demonstrated that, in many of the major corporate collapses of recent years, the problems of the companies concerned were not clearly known to their boards until very shortly before, or sometimes after, they sank. A few months before Rolls-Royce collapsed, its board stated publicly that *'The company is in good shape'*. Only three months after telling shareholders and trade unions that it remained strong in tyre manufacturing, the board of Dunlop was selling its main tyre manufacturing businesses to a Japanese company. Only two months before the collapse of the leading Danish computer corporation, Christian Rovsing International, through undercontrolled overexpansion, the Danish newspapers were covered with advertisements placed by the corporation to obtain more staff to carry out *further expansion*.

The smaller the company, the less distinct the borderline between policy and management, and there is precious little difference at all when the unit contains less than 300–400 employees.

Remoteness from management at any size will mean that the practicality of board decisions will be about as dependable as doing the football pools with a pin.

4 Groupthink

The board, the cabinet, the president's team, the general's staff; each is a group composed of individuals who are charged with reaching the best possible decisions for the organisations which they represent.

But all individuals carry within their own 'information processing systems' one or more of a set of common flaws. No individual mind is completely 'open'; we all have a few deeply held opinions which inhibit our decision-making, and we all have personality characteristics which can prejudice our judgement. When we act within a group the weaknesses in our individual judgement can be compounded by 'groupthink'.

In America, Europe, Britain and most industrialised societies, important decisions are taken 'at the top' and are then passed downwards for action. It is at the top where the dangers of groupthink are strongest and where its harmful effects are most destructive. In Japan, by contrast, important business questions are viewed and reviewed, again and again, as they work their way upwards through an organisation. This avoids the growth of groupthink in precisely the same way as the rolling stone avoids the growth of an insulating layer of moss.

Individuals see themselves as parts of groups. We need to belong and we blinker our objectivity in order to convince ourselves that we do belong. We limit our vision of the environment outside our group. We automatically attribute our group's values and beliefs to 'all other sensible people' and we then scorn any who chance to disagree. We simplify the messages from the external environment and filter away facts which we should be facing.

Within the kinds of group which are considered in this book, the personality characteristics which most strongly affect decision-making are:

- power seeking, as opposed to pursuing what is sweet and true;
- emotionality, as opposed to active objectivity;

- creativity, as opposed to 'common sense'; and
- a drive to be active rather than being contemplative.

Consider the first of these characteristics. The power seeker, driven by a belief in the overriding importance of holding power, or by a less worthy lusting for it as a substitute for other qualities which he lacks, will view any deviation from his group's beliefs as equivalent to treason. Many political leaders exhibit this characteristic – irrespective of Party because ideology per se is not held in importance. In Germany in the 1930s the Leader arranged that any deviant was shot; in the UK of the 1980s a similar political deviant can only be riddled with scornful condemnation as a 'wet', or with public humiliation before the television cameras. In a boardroom where the leader of the directors, whether chairman or chief executive, is driven by this particular characteristic, and in all boardrooms where the chairman is also chief executive, the deviant director is going to have an unpleasant time, as long as he lasts. It won't be much solace to him as he straggles along with the rest of the dole queue that:

Those who have left the greatest improvement are the ideo-logically-oriented, not the power-seekers who move on, leaving nothing but now irrelevant personal power structures.

KATZ & KAHN, 1978

Witness the collapse of numerous major companies when the dominant director dies or retires; he created little and left nothing behind him of permanent value.

Formal psychological experiment has demonstrated that people have a defensive mechanism which can shut out unpleasant or threatening facts by denying, ignoring or distorting those facts. Most of us use it to overcome extreme traumas which might otherwise overwhelm us – that is doubtless the purpose for which Nature intended this protective mechanism to be used. Others apply the mechanism as a routine, weakening not only their own judgement but also that of the group within which they operate, because:

Organisational executives whose defensiveness results in their avoiding certain types of unpleasant information may be reinforced in their blindness by subordinates who keep such facts from them . . . One great weakness in an autocratic structure is that defensive mechanisms among its top leaders will receive institutional support rather than corrections. Subordinates protect their own positions by screening facts to accord with the emotional biases of the chief. The whole institutional environment may be modified to confirm the pathological [sic] tendencies of the people on the top . . . In the autocratic organisation so modified, social realities now reinforce fictions, false perceptions and erroneous beliefs. Criteria for the evaluation of organisational performance will be avoided under these circumstances, because they threaten the present comfortable way of life of the authorities by intruding with objective facts. Its leaders become incapable of changing policy, and unless these leaders can be replaced the organisation faces disaster.

KATZ & KAHN, 1978

Which is a concise description of what has happened in countless cabinets, councils and committees in the past and will happen, alas, in the future where ministers and managers do not have the understanding or the courage to risk disturbing their own 'comfortable way of life'.

The description 'skilled incompetence' was introduced by Professor Argyris of the Harvard University Graduate School (Argyris, 1986) to cover managerial behaviour of this kind. Points of view are expressed in a way which avoids giving offence or disturbing that collective comfort – thereby ensuring failure to resolve the underlying problems. The inability to confront the truth leads to communication gaps, and then to defensive, collective cover-ups.

Individuals, like gnus, will herd with other gnus unless some external influence is driving and re-sorting them – like a 'listening bank' which really does listen, a merchant bank adviser who really does advise, or an institutional investor with more sense than money. The bankers and investors have created for themselves a continuing conflict. They wish to continue to profit from funding companies which will remain in business and thus be able to refund the monies. With rare but well-publicised exceptions, they do not wish to have any involvement with the management of those companies, or with any effective review of that management. A conflict between wishes and needs will become unbearably stressful unless some of the conflicting variables are removed or rationalised away.

> *Rationalisation is so prevalent a reaction to situations involving conflict that it cannot be regarded as abnormal.*
>
> MUNN, 1972

The first formalised description of the mechanism for avoiding conflict was in Leon Festinger's *Theory of Cognitive Dissonance* (1957). This recorded that the individual seeks to reduce uncomfortable inconsistency, or dissonance, either by changing his opinions ro by giving up one role which conflicts with another. The individual may seek to reduce such discomfort by filtering out the facts which produce it. He ends by believing that he has solved the problem, or that it never existed, or that he never really disagreed with the chairman, or that he really has discharged all his responsibilities . . . or that whatever else used to trouble him no longer does so.

Every two or three years in the USA and UK, which tend to keep in step in such matters, there is a spasm of surprise in the media about just how badly most companies do perform, usually triggered by a new boardroom scandal which is a little riper and ranker than most. The spotlight turns onto the bankers and institutional investors to see what they are going to 'do about it'. Last time it happened in the UK the institutions reacted by reducing dissonance and discomfort. Together these financial giants laboured mightily and they brought forth a mouse. They formed something called PRO NED. Together the massed battalions of the Bank of England, The Accepting Houses Committee of all the major merchant banks, The Stock Exchange, the Confederation of British Industry, *all* the London and *all* the Scottish clearing banks, the Institutional Shareholders' Committee, toss into the pot the British Institute of Management – they all clubbed together to establish a tiny head-hunting office. This joined the handful of other tiny head-hunting offices which dabble in finding non-executive directors for companies which approach them. The funders had rationalised their problem out of sight and mind. Only slowly, after the passage of years and the accumulation of commercial scandals, does the new office attain more visibility.

To describe the characteristics of group decision making, American psychologist Irving Janis coined the word 'groupthink' (Janis, 1972). By analysing a number of major historical blunders he demonstrated that the errors of the groups of policy-makers concerned could not be explained by weaknesses in the training, intellect or personalities of the individuals within those groups. The decision-makers concerned were qualified and undoubtedly competent. In the case of the attack on Pearl Harbor in 1941 the decision-makers, Admiral Kimmel and his staff, failed to act reasonably on the facts available to them. They had been told on 27 November that the Japanese were certain to declare war within a few days time (which they did on 6 December), but the Pacific Fleet was still kept huddled together within the harbour, most of the aircraft were similarly positioned as mass targets for air attack, surveillance was inadequate and many of the troops were on leave.

Janis (Janis & Mann, 1977) concluded that, within groups, individual irrationality is magnified by groupthink, and that irrational processes can take over in the decision-making of the group members, just as they do in the case of *abnormal* personalities. This exaggeration of individual weaknesses leads to a number of defects. For example:

- Group discussion covers too few alternatives.

   Choice is always exercised with respect to a limited, approximate, simplified model of the real situation . . . the chooser's . . . definition of the situation.

                                                          MARCH & SIMON, 1958

Recruitment of senior staff provides an example. The group may 'decide' it should not recruit women, or men over 45 or 40 or some other unscientific cut-off point – or blacks, the unemployed, the self-employed, or those employed in any position in any other kind of industry but their own. This leads to the progressive conformity, and thus to the progressive weakening, of the group.

- The group fails to examine sufficient relevant information from experts and tends to select only that information which supports its original position.

The information search by policy-makers is not for all the relevant and valid information possible but for the data that will be useful to implement their own basic values.

KATZ & KAHN, 1978

Something which every management consultant will be able to confirm.
- Once launched on a course of action, the group does not re-examine its original assessment, particularly the extent of the risks involved.

One of the most common norms appears to be that of remaining loyal to the group by sticking with the policies to which the group has already committed itself, even when those policies are obviously working out badly.

KOLB/RUBIN/McINTYRE, 1979

Closely related are two other defects:

- The group fails to re-examine the alternatives available to it, and fails to prepare contingency plans and to allow for probable hindrances (such as political opposition or bureaucratic inertia). Plans are usually far too optimistic about the time-scales required to achieve the plans' objectives.

Janis called groupthink '*a collective pattern of defensive avoidance*'. The most fertile ground for its development is a group with high cohesiveness and close similarity between the backgrounds and styles of the individual members (same schooling, 'up at Cambridge together', fox-hunting, Freemasonry). Without methodical routines for obtaining and evaluating information on alternative policies, the group becomes insulated – the inert stone, as compared with the rolling stone.

He described eight symptoms of groupthink:

- **An illusion of invulnerability**
  It can lead to excessive optimism and undue risk-taking. Admiral Kimmel was observed to laugh at the suggestion that the Japanese aircraft carriers might be sailing towards Pearl Harbor, yet he already knew that those carriers had been at sea for several days, that American Intelligence had lost contact with their location and direction, and that war with Japan was certain to begin at any moment.

- **Collective rationalisation**
  The collective discounting of warning signs and anomalies. Companies in decline may go through several years of successive refinancings, during which period the board and the bankers could and should have concluded instead that reorganisation, replanning and new management were the primary needs.

- **A belief in the inherent morality of the group**
  This leads the members to ignore ethical, legal and commercial consequences, as though they are inconsequential. Illegal collusive tendering and price-fixing have been, and doubtless still are, extremely widespread practices in some British, American and European industries. The main mechanical engineering contractors in one European country used to apply this practice and produced poor or negative financial returns. In contrast, in the same country through the same period, serving the same markets and customers, the electrical engineering contractors did *not* follow that practice but competed legally. They managed to maintain a consistent, positive level of profitability. Yet with these and similar hard facts known to them, many leading British companies in this field not only pursued the practice but promoted its 'virtues' to other industry members.

- **A stereotyped view of rivals or out-groups**
  The outsiders are normally characterised as weaker or less good than the members of the in-group.
  The music hall scale of the Bay of Pigs invasion was based on a gross underestimation of Cuban troops. At the beginning of World War II many European military decision-makers really believed that the Japanese could not see at night.

* **Pressure against any member who dissents**

  The crucial factor is isolation . . . The group . . . put pressure on the individual simply by isolating him.

  KELVIN, 1970

Shopfloor workers will send a colleague to 'Coventry' if he disagrees with them about striking. This means that no one talks to him, even though he stands beside them. Boardrooms have less physical but equally painful methods for achieving the same objectives of conformity or departure. The greater the difficulty of the problem or decision faced by the group, the greater the pressure within it for conformity, quite regardless of the potential value to the group of the dissenting voices.

  The autocratic chairman/chief executive will lean only lightly against the director who disagrees with his choice of colour for the new carpet, but will produce his heaviest bullying for the director who disagrees with his choice for a new directorship. The bully will normally get his way in 'difficult' situations because the more difficult the problem the easier it becomes for the doubter to submerge his doubts and accept the rest of the group's judgement.

* **Self-censorship**
  Silence helps the individual to relieve his doubts, and to remove the discomfort of doubting. Which leads to:

* **A shared illusion of unanimity**
  Dissent does not come to the surface and silence is taken to imply consent.

* **The emergence of self-appointed mind-guards**
  These are members who protect the group from alternative or contrary information which might break their collective complacency about the rightness of their decisions. They can include a high-profile chief executive or a low-profile company secretary, but the role is the same whoever performs it. 'We do all agree with everything you say Adrian, but not with *the way* you say it' is the most common kind of protective deception used to enable the group to go on doing what Adrian disagrees with, even though they know they agree with him . . .

The starkly Orwellian terms used by Janis – 'groupthink' and 'mind-guards' – might suggest to the reader that the dangers of groupthink are greatest, and its effects most harmful, in austere, barrack-like boardrooms and councils of little cheer. In fact:

> . . . *members of decision-making groups become motivated to avoid being too harsh in their judgements of the leader's or their colleagues' ideas . . . The more amiability and esprit de corps there is among the members of a policy-making group the greater the danger that independent critical thinking will be replaced by groupthink.*

JANIS, 1972

The harmful effects of the pressure for conformity in a company board, for example, are seldom seen in one big, rapid bang such as at Pearl Harbor, but they can be seen quite clearly in US and UK companies. It is not their wit but their decision-making which is failing. Harvey's Abilene Paradox states that a man sitting on a committee will often vote for a decision which he knows is absolutely wrong, and an American university has confirmed the reality of the Paradox by formal scientific process. An experiment was devised in which the subject had to judge the lengths of different lines. He sat at the end of a row of people, all of whom, unknown to him, were part of the research team. Several lines were projected onto a screen and each person was asked to judge which lines were of the same length as a standard line. For the first few judgements everyone agreed. Then each member of the research team began to make some obviously wrong judgements – but 50 per cent of the subjects agreed with that erroneous judgement on at least two occasions. Those subjects who resisted the 'pressure' to agree to a wrong judgement were observed to experience real discomfort. But when the subject had *just one* ally who shared his correct judgement, the rate of erroneous conformity dropped dramatically.

The length of a piece of string is most commonly what your group would like it to be, which may bear no relationship to its measurable dimensions.

Jerry Harvey, a psychologist at George Washington University, cited as a practical example of his Paradox the case of a US company which nearly bankrupted itself by continuing with an expensive research project, despite that the company's president, the relevant vice-president and the manager in charge of the project all knew it was hopeless. The president would not admit this because he feared it might provoke the vice-president to resign; the vice-president and the manager kept silent for fear of dismissal (Dixon, 1986). The reader will be able to recall his own examples, both inside and outside the corporate environment.

During the 1970s attempts were made by experimental psychologists to investigate specific unexplained flaws in human information processing and decision making. For example:

- the ease with which decision-makers can be diverted by irrelevancies;
- the manner in which they can be swayed by the format in which information is packaged for their consideration; and
- their illusion of control over matters which are in fact pure hazard.

These are familiar flaws if we take political examples, but they are just as common in the boardroom or council chamber. The assumed objective of such groups is to choose courses of action which give optimum results; in practice the courses selected, and the criteria against which they are selected, are almost always smaller, easier and less effective. If the criteria applied are so often second- or third-order, then the objectives set, and the results achieved, are most unlikely to optimise or maximise. Herbert Simon found an explanation; the group does not in fact optimise or maximise, it *satisfices*.

For example, when a board is faced with several investment alternatives the group will readily select one which is 'good enough', rather than rigorously analyse all alternatives to find the best of all available. Even in situations where the group really has worked its way through to a likely best alternative, it may feel such uncertainty about the future results of its choice that it falls back to a more conventional second-best, which may in fact be the umpteenth-best – but is a choice which will create no ripples, which will cause no disapproval and which will be readily acceptable to superiors and peers (Johnson, 1974). Another study (Cyert & March, 1973) has established that the greater the uncertainty about future results the greater the tendency to make policy decisions on the basis of short-term acceptability within the organisation.

Satisficing is as common to the housewife choosing items in the supermarket as it is to a minister or manager faced with more weighty decisions. But the housewife is responsible only to herself and has only to meet her own requirements, the most important of which on any one shopping day might be thrift, or generosity to guests, or just personal curiosity about a new product on the shelf. The minister and manager are paid to override any such personal motivations. But their groups do not normally search about purposefully until they find the best possible balance between pros and cons. They move stepwise, in small discrete steps, until they find a solution which is *readily acceptable to all members without dissent*. Most change is seen to occur in such small incremental steps. The first guns fired arrows. Later models fired stones, then round lumps of metal. The first motor cars were literally horse-less carriages which very closely resembled the carriages which were still being drawn by horses on the same roads; they did not incorporate any of the design advantages which the absence of horses made possible.

Thus we simplify problem solving by reducing or rationalising away alternatives. Then, having committed ourselves to a conclusion, we become much less objective about the weight we attach to the alternatives (Festinger, 1964). We 'bolster' the decision because we are aware that it has negative arguments against it and that the rejected alternatives had positive arguments in their favour. We bolster in order to minimise the stress that could grow from doubting the correctness of our decision. We then deny any negative feelings and we minimise our feelings of personal responsibility . . . 'anyway no one will know'.

As Mephistopheles said to Faust, '*That's so far ahead you can forget about it.*'

Irving Janis has suggested a number of procedures which could help to counteract groupthink:

- The leader of the group must act impartially, without pressing his own preferences.
- The leader should ask the members to raise objections and thereby stimulate dissent. He should encourage criticism, especially of his own judgements. While this may seem to be common sense it is most unlikely to happen under the autocracy which makes so many boardrooms less effective than the sum of the directors present.
- Whenever policy is evaluated, one or two members should play devil's advocate.
- The group should occasionally divide, discuss and then regroup.
- If the matter for decision concerns rivals outside the group, then much time should be given for reviewing the rivals and their possible intentions.

  In a company context, each business operates in an environment which consists of its competition. It is affected less by the state of the market than by what the competitors are doing about the state of the market.
- After seeming to reach the best conclusion, the group should attack that conclusion from all viewpoints.
- One or two experts or qualified colleagues who are not members of the group should be invited to meetings to challenge the viewpoints being expressed by members.
- Each member should discuss the group's decisions with *his* external colleagues and report back on *their* attitudes.
- Different groups, under different chairmen, should be established to review the same facts.

Clearly, time and the need for secrecy preclude the exercise of all these suggestions in all cabinets, committees and boards. Hence the importance of composing the group to minimise groupthink by including the maverick and the court jester (see Chapter 8). Boards seldom do. Some still take pride in their apparent ability to 'muddle through'. 'That's all right old chap, we'll muddle through' is viewed as a resourceful answer to many impending crises, whereas most outsiders can recognise it as being only a demonstration of unpreparedness.

In 'The Science of Muddling Through' (Lindblom, 1959), the process was described as '*satisficing by taking small incremental steps*'. And if that sounds like progressing with the waddle of a clockwork duck, then let the decision-makers look to their dignity.

5 Types of board

Keeping in mind these characteristics of group decision-making, we can consider the functions of different kinds of board and the factors affecting performance.

A brief note about comparative terminology may first be helpful. The *memorandum* in the UK includes the company's objects, powers and share capital details, and is equivalent to the *articles of incorporation, certificate of incorporation*, or *charter* in the different states of the USA. The *articles*, or *articles of association* in the UK are equivalent to the *bylaws* in the USA. Together the charter and bylaws, or memorandum and articles, are sometimes called the company's constitution or statutes (which should not be confused with the use of the word 'statute' to describe an Act or specific piece of legislation). Through this volume we will use 'articles' in the British sense, meaning bylaws, both because that usage has widest international currency and because 'bye-laws', with an 'e', has a very different meaning in many countries and could be confused. Regarding men:

- *chief executive officer*, or CEO (USA) equates with *managing director*, or MD (UK), and overlaps with the usage of *president* (USA). Current trends indicate that president and MD are used more often for executive heads of subsidiary or independent companies, while CEO and chief executive (now common in the UK) are used for heads of Groups. Through most of this volume we will use chief executive as it best describes the role;
- *vice-president* (USA) equates with *executive director* (UK);
- director in both countries covers both executive and non-executive directors, the latter often called 'outside' or 'part-time' directors;
- *officer* (USA) equates with *executive* or *senior manager* (UK).

A word of caution about the quaint UK usage of the term 'president'. The title means absolutely nothing, and has no legal basis. It is usually given to an aged chairman/chief executive by a board which could find no other way of telling him that he should now get out of the way and stop trying to run the show. The board will always explain that the title, and the pleasant 'consultancy fee' which usually goes with it to supplement the old man's pension, has been given in recognition of the man's past services – for which he had already been handsomely paid. The whole fiction is quite unnecessary and does not provide the company with a pennyworth of new business, or generate an ounce more loyalty.

All boards

The management of a company is separated in law from the ownership of its shares. The rights of the shareholders (also called shareowners, stockholders or members) are few in number but potentially powerful if resolutely exercised. State and national legislations vary around a recognisable pattern, which in countries with unitary boards similar to those of the USA and UK includes the rights:

- to ensure that the company is properly administered;
- to elect or remove directors;
- to receive information in accordance with the Corporation or Companies Act;
- to appoint the auditors;
- to approve the accounts;
- to wind up a solvent company voluntarily.

Given a significant majority, often 75 per cent:

- to alter the articles and re-define the powers of the directors.

Even a minority of shareholders who feel they have been unfairly prejudiced may, through the court:

- require the Department of Trade to investigate the company;
- take legal action against the directors;
- petition for a winding-up of the company by the court.

The fiduciary and contractual relationships of all the directors are primarily to the company, *not directly* to the shareholders. They operate in accordance with the powers and responsibilities defined in the company's articles, and in the Companies Acts, and they exercise them collectively, not individually, within the boardroom.

Within these broad definitions, the board may determine what types and limits of action and decision it will reserve to itself, and what it will delegate to whom, always bearing in mind that no functions or powers can be delegated without express provision in the articles that this may be done. No managing director can be appointed without similar provision.

The company will change over the years by size and markets, and by structure and strength, and the board's priority of responsibilities will need to change in step. At any stage of development the board will not be able to control the company without exercising the responsibilities:

- to select or remove individual directors, including the chief executive and the chairman of the board; to alter their mix and compose the board itself as a productive entity;
- to define the limits of authority of the chief executive in terms of expenditure, appointments, businesses, contracts and functions. To define similar limits of authority for other directors and top managers, or alternatively to approve those defined by the chief executive. Without clear definition of precisely what is delegated and what is expected, there can be little blame attaching to subsequent inaction. In particular, to describe what is required from each non-executive in terms of time and type of contribution expected;
- to approve the appointment or removal of top managers immediately below the board. It is sensible policy at all levels in the company to ensure that appointments or dismissals are referred, for prior approval, one notch above the man's immediate superior;
- to define, or approve similar limits of authority for subsidiary companies, and for their senior executives;
- to compile and communicate company policies, covering: style of operation; external and internal relations; markets and businesses;

required return on capital (ROC) and performance standards; growth and change policies; planning and budgetary procedures;

- to review the business alternatives open to the company on an ongoing basis, and arrange that meaningful plans are produced at all levels, covering the longest realistic time-scales. For large companies, this may be twenty years at corporate level, but only three years at subsidiary level. With smaller companies, quantitative planning is difficult to stretch beyond about three years, but qualitative planning needs to look further ahead. Out of which process comes the sacred one-year budget;
- and through this process, to determine the total resources of the company, both actual and potential, in men, money, methods and market position. To allocate these by unit and time-scale, defining closely what returns, and when, these resources are required to generate;
- to advise management in the compilation of plans and strategies, and to assist, where this would be helpful, in their implementation. Active non-executives can often contribute outside the boardroom, particularly in smaller or subsidiary companies;
- to structure and organise the company, determining that units and key individuals can interrelate productively, and that the good ones can grow without hindrance;
- to map out the mechanism for internal liaison, upwards, downwards and sideways between units;
- to describe a similar mechanism for external communication, determining which directors will be responsible for each category of liaison. The external world includes customers, suppliers, lenders, the media, government bodies, and sometimes the local community – not just actual or potential shareholders and city analysts;
- to develop a mechanism for employee participation at all levels, to the extent, and in the style, which both the board and the employees agree is most suitable to the company. To determine from time to time that participation is real, alive, and treated as an asset, not a nuisance;
- to define how the board itself will operate, what routines it will adopt, what it will look at and decide monthly, quarterly and

annually. To determine in careful detail how, and with what data, it will monitor the performance of management and the financial progress of the company;

- to monitor management performance against both one-year budgets and longer-term plan figures. If performance against budgets is widely astray, there may be something wrong with management. If performance against the plan progression is widely astray, there may be something wrong with the policies or strategies on which the board has relied;
- to close, and keep closed, the loop of analysis, evaluation, decision, planning, implementation, monitoring, adapting, monitoring . . . One of the strongest arguments in favour of the unitary board system is that the company's top decision point in this continuous process lies within the loop, not outside or tangential to it;
- to monitor its own performance as a board, at least annually. To place an item on the agenda at which each of the directors really feels that his contribution is in the spotlight, including the chairman and each of the non-executives. If each has contributed with energy and value, he will feel no discomfort. The board represents the most important of the company's investments. The performance of that investment should be as closely reviewed as the returns on any other expenditure.

Holding boards

The holding board (or 'main' or 'Group' board) is to its subsidiaries as the independent company is to its individual businesses. They both decide what resources they will allocate to each of the activities for which they are responsible; determine what returns they require from each; appoint managers to operate each; decide how they will monitor each; then control the corporate whole by monitoring the returns which the managers generate from those resources.

The holding board's first decision is whether the subsidiaries are to operate as real companies. If so, the subsidiaries will need real boards of their own, operating freely within a set of limits of authority. If not, the holding board's management responsibilities become very great, and the responsibilities of the managers, or the let's-pretend directors of the subsidiaries, become very much less. The holding board cannot 'have it both ways'.

There is no rule of thumb applicable to all Groups at all stages of growth which can describe when centralisation of responsibility and control will be more effective than decentralisation; which is one reason why some Groups are observed to organise and reorganise periodically from one extreme to the other, apparently willy-nilly. Nor is there any rule which suggests that the holding board must handle each of its subsidiaries in the same way. Different units at different stages of growth, or with different problems or opportunities, can be controlled differently. The board can handle one at arm's length, and then rootle into the smallest details of another, at the same board meeting.

The best guideline is that the board should select for its chief executive a man who is by nature primarily people-oriented, rather than primarily figures-or machinery-oriented; who can readily accept that his main role is to engage people for positions below him who are good enough to operate entirely without him. Many chief executives cannot 'stand back' from their position to this extent, or will not take the risk which this might seem to involve. But only this will enable the board to push authority downwards, with any confidence. Without confidence, it has to retain a heavily centralised structure and control.

As the Group's top manager, the holding board has a number of responsibilities, either in law or in practice, which interface or overlap with those of management below it. The board has to describe to management where it will interface, and where it should choose to overlap. In setting these boundaries it must be ready, and be seen to be ready, to take advice from management as to where a proposed interface should be an overlap, or, more likely, where management feels the opposite should be preferred. The board will make its own decisions, but will acquire credit and credibility by at least seeming to share this kind of decision. When there is any doubt, the board should settle for a closer, rather than remoter, involvement. Subsequent complaint from management that the board 'interferes' too much may be valid. Or it may signal that management has something to hide. Or that it has nothing of significance to expose.

During the 1960s and 1970s, fashion yo-yoed between centra-lisation and decentralisation rather as the contemporary hem-line rose and fell, to some extent in accordance with what the haute consulting houses were promoting that season. Any reader who has walked into the shambles which often followed one of those freshly introduced 'broad strategic concepts' of centralisation or decentralisation (it matters not a jot which of the two) will know that the concept seldom got down to looking at how things would actually have to work in detail in areas a notch or two below the holding board.

The fault for the futility of many of these expensive manipulations did not lie wholly with the haute consulting houses. Too often the board which commissioned and briefed them for the reorganisation project had been well bitten by the bug of change, but had not known its company well enough to know where it really needed to scratch.

Structural change demands close understanding of how the smallest parts of the company's businesses are pursued and com-pleted; where the company is strong, and how in practice it is weak; which managers are effective and which are misplaced. Structures only work if the theoretical ideal is first calculated clinically, and is then adapted a little to suit the peculiarities of those markets and managers judged to be most valuable to the company.

The board's role in determining the optimum structure becomes more onerous as the Group diversifies. A natural objective in the plans of most holding boards is steadily to increase both the size and the variety of their businesses, at least partly as a defence mechanism to dissuade predators which might find 'size' quite easy to swallow, but 'diversity' more difficult to digest. The process can get out of hand. By the 1980s the fashion for take-overs was forcing large corporations to make larger and larger acquisitions in order to be able to indicate 'growth'. Most acquisitive Groups today, including smaller multi-activity organisations with ambitions to expand, main-tain few central resources of expertise, apart from financial researchers and financial controllers. They have little or no ability to assist acquired subsidiaries in any practical way. Their spread of businesses becomes too wide for the directors themselves to encompass. Thus the holding board is having to push large portions of policy-making down line, while tightening the machinery for central monitoring. The reality and effectiveness with which the holding board then keeps control of its total business becomes dependent, first, on the quality of the reporting and monitoring system and, secondly, on the quality of the chain of individuals linking that board through to the lowest operating levels.

While it is always partly true that 'management is all about people', this is always entirely true in relation to how, and how well, the holding board manages its Group.

Private companies

The roles and responsibilities of public and private company main boards differ only in secondary detail. The public company, shares in which can be traded freely, and which may be Stock Exchange listed and quoted, has more onerous external communication commitments. It has to satisfy the enquiries of analysts, brokers, journalists and corporate shareholders. It is under greater pressure to preserve an appearance of unity and calm within the boardroom, as a demonstration of its ability to handle its affairs smoothly.

British public companies are on average larger than equivalents in Europe. (As an aside, the average size of factory or production unit in Britain is also larger than in any other country, including Germany, Japan and America.) More than 40 per cent of employees in British industrial companies are in Groups employing more than 40,000, and the proportion increases as mergers multiply. The equivalent figure for America is 30 per cent, also increasing; for France and Germany it is around 20 per cent; and for Japan just 4 per cent. Of the one million registered companies in Britain, more than half of the total in the whole of the European Economic Community (EEC), only a quarter of one per cent are listed public companies. Nonetheless there are more domestic listed companies on the London Stock Exchange than there are domestic listed companies on all the other Exchanges in the EEC put together. It might be argued that this motley of facts and comparisons describes a situation of developing imbalance.

In the USA, early practice favoured the limited partnership for small business organisations, reflecting the use of that format in parts

of Europe. For similar small businesses the British preferred to
establish limited liability companies which restricted the transfer of
shares to named or agreed persons. Sizes and proportions may differ,
but each of the industrialised nations has now developed two kinds of
limited liability corporation:

- the UK's plc and Ltd
- West Germany's AG and GmbH
- France's SA and Sàrl
- Denmark's A/S and ApS
- Japan's Kabushiki Kaisha and Yugen Kaisha.

The USA originally had only one kind of stock corporation, but some
states have now legislated for a 'close' corporation, equivalent to the
European private limited liability company.

Governments in America, Europe and Britain have sought to
stimulate the creation of more small private businesses, but the
argument that 'small is beautiful' does not always accord with the
facts. A recent study (Burns, 1985) indicates that small business
profitability is now declining in Britain (though rising slightly in
Europe), and it questions whether governments should concentrate
their support on this sector. Certainly an increasingly competitive
environment will make it difficult for small new companies to survive,
except where they operate exclusively in limited, localised service
fields. There are a number of qualitative factors which contribute to
the lesser performance of the small company. Broadly:

- 'small' normally means 'private'. Private companies are allowed to
  keep very private indeed, and their filed returns, while meeting
  the law's requirements, still manage to describe very little;
- the leaders of small companies take pride in working from the seat
  of the pants, except in countries such as Denmark where they
  commonly operate to the same, or similar, professional standards
  as large local companies. They do not correlate size with sophis-
  tication;
- the skilled European executive will work readily in a smaller local
  company which pays him well and gives him the kinds of challenge

and role he likes to undertake. The equivalent American or British executives know that it damages their cv's to move 'down' from a larger to a smaller company, which therefore has difficulty in attracting good staff. And then in keeping them; the head-hunters know that they can be seduced out to join a larger organisation;

- the smaller company therefore lacks expertise, either because some of its key people are lightweight, or because it has gaps in the skills employed. It has considerable need for external doses of expertise, in the form of traditional consultancy, or for internal professional support for its managers in the form of 'active' non-executive directors. But the smaller company commonly considers both categories of support to be close to parasitic, and seldom uses either, however great the demonstrable need. But always better the 'parasitic' consultant than the saprophytic receiver;

- as a consequence, management and accounting techniques are clumsy, reporting is primitive, monitoring is hit-and-miss, resources are often unproductive, planning is rudimentary or absent;

- the few dominant shareholders, who are normally also the dominant directors, even in large private companies where their combined stakes represent a minority, find it difficult to divorce shareholding from directorship – as the law requires them to do. Too often 'private' still means 'personal', despite the fact that the company is registered under national legislation;

- in the private company, often also when they are large, the board is commonly composed of one or two families and their nominees, plus perhaps a sprinkling of retired executives and a few chums. The power struggles in the boardroom, in the absence of truly professional and independent outside non-executives, can come to resemble the family feuds once common in the 'Old West', and still common on the North-West Frontier – conflicts quite irrelevant to the business in hand;

- with the main shareholders already inside the board, and the main lenders almost always passive till the very moment the company is sick unto death, there is no source of external pressure to improve board composition and company performance. There is no external pressure for change, no inclination to engage external expertise to assist with change, and often no internal recognition of the need for change. Small companies consistently run into trouble, or go into liquidation, when they grow through a 'change step' without recognising it, and the size of the business overtakes the board's ability to manage it.

Harold W. Fox, Professor in Business at Muncie, Indiana, has suggested that the solution for providing small companies with supporting expertise is the 'quasi-board'. He argues that leaders of small companies, who are usually the owners or controlling share-holders, feel 'threatened' by independent non-executive directors or external consultants, and thus need counsel from men of equivalent experience who hold *no* position of authority within their companies. In cases of family squabbles or disagreement between the directors, the quasi-board can give independent advice which is not seen to 'automatically' override that of any of the shareholder directors. Fox suggests that there should be two–four formal meetings of the quasi-board each year, with each quasi-director providing about thirty hours during that period, compared with the average of 120 hours per annum provided by directors in large corporations. To support his interesting proposals Fox advises that he himself sits on a number of quasi-boards, each of which plays a successful role.

The present writer's opinions are that: thirty hours per annum is far, far less than useful; most men appointed by the owner-managers are unlikely to say much which disturbs that individual; quasi-directors without the power to dismiss the president are without one of the main weapons of control; and few suitably qualified men will take on a role in the prior knowledge that no one will have to act on their advice, and where they have no decision-making responsibility. Another American proposal (Castaldi/Wortman, 1984) suggests the formation of 'colleagial' (sic) boards in small companies, meeting weekly as colleagues of the CEO, or as 'near-peers' with similar rights and responsibilities. They would vote on motions, revise recom-mendations, and monitor the CEO, thus acting like directors; they would also furnish ideas and expertise, thus acting like consultants. The present writer believes that, because small companies are created and constrained by broadly the same legal requirements as large corporations, they need directors with full legal responsibility, internally, plus the ad hoc help of professional consultants, externally. They should not be given alternative soft options.

Governments can mistake the key features of small company weakness. When they try to help the establishment and growth of small companies they concentrate on improving sources of *funding*, the one problem which the owner-manager *is* prepared to admit having. Governments would achieve a hundred times more by concentrating on improving the provision of expertise for small companies, and improving the mix of decision-makers required within their boardrooms. Till they do, we shall continue to see that most small new companies collapse within a few years of their birth.

Divisional boards

A division can be real or apparent. In larger Groups it is normally real. It has Company Limited status, owns all its subsidiaries, operates like its own 'holding board' within widely defined limits of authority from its parent, and has a board of directors which functions as such, non-executives and all.

Lower down the size scale, a divisional company is often little more than an extra level of management committee, producing less active contribution than its own subsidiaries.

And as the size of the Group decreases, the incidence of the apparent division increases. Subsidiaries with similar characteristics are collected into divisional groupings as much because this looks good in corporate sales literature as because it might occasionally help to put together into one pot the related problems and opportunities of like-working companies. There is a divisional committee with one of a dozen alternative names, intended to be a forum for airing those related problems and opportunities, and for reaching improved conclusions. It seldom satisfies either intention.

The instinct of territorial protectiveness among subsidiary company executives will always be stronger than the instinct for collective survival, unless the mechanism imposes a collective responsibility by giving the members a level-pegging directorship status.

When the division is apparent, cooperative liaison can become a formality and a frustration. Even the first step of inducing the constituent subsidiary MDs to review each others' figures is seldom worth the hassle, and they will never get round to exposing their innermost concerns.

In a divisional committee the competent manager will use his skills to shield his own unit from scrutiny, drawing attention away from it by adept reference to problems known to exist in other units.

In a divisional board, with real teeth and real business objectives, the competent manager, who is now also a divisional director, will in contrast use this forum as an enlarged arena in which to exercise his strength. This can only be for the collective good, as the parent company must always be searching for ways of developing the confidence and experience of its best managers, and thus for growing its own future successions.

Good subsidiary company MDs can be vulnerable to dissatisfaction, being at the same time halfway up the management hierarchy and halfway down to the hard surface of the shopfloor. They are among the men most easily located by head-hunters out on a 'search'. They may be better than their boss thinks they are, or better than he wants others to think they are. So give them a proper divisional Company Limited pool to swim in, and watch.

Composing divisional boards can generate more heartache or resentment than composing the holding board. How many and which of the subsidiary MDs to include is always a dilemma, and the selection of the most appropriate functional specialists can be equally tricky. It is an activity which the Group chief executive alone can seldom carry out to everyone's satisfaction, and is a good reason for requiring the parent company non-executives, who are accepted as being 'independent', to get to know and evaluate down-line management. In this they can greatly assist the Group chief executive, especially when he is suppressing a good man or two for personal or irrational reasons, and everyone else, including the independent non-executive, can see this.

The larger the Group, the more instances there are of such conscious or subconscious suppression. The queen bee will naturally suppress the development of other queens, and the chief executive will have as much trouble as anyone else in restraining his own queen bee instincts.

The larger the Group and the wider the division in its content of subsidiaries, the more vital to the effectiveness of parental control is the nature of the human linkages from one level to the next. Where the linkage is through a single-man chain – Group chief executive/ divisional MD/subsidiary MD/subsidiary executive – each operating as a direct-line boss over subordinates, the parent board has to work with severely limited vision. The key people in the chain will each be covering so much other detailed ground that they, too, will 'see' but a part of the whole.

No man alone is wise enough.

PLAUTUS

More effective is to duplicate or triplicate the linkages, with the board at each level requiring one or two of its other directors also to exercise an active interest in the affairs of the next level down. The finance director or business development director may be charged in this way with a defined role to review and assist, and indeed quite frequently are. They are sometimes called 'non-executives' when they sit on the next board down, but cannot truly perform as non-executives because they inevitably represent 'higher authority'.

Much less common, though of great potential value, is the placing of a parent non-executive on each divisional board, alongside divisional non-executives who are not on the holding board. The mechanism can be repeated downwards onto the boards of the main subsidiary companies. In any Group, the responsibilities of controlling and assisting without undue interfering, could be most productively achieved by a planned overlap in board membership at each adjoining pair of board levels, including the line boss, a non-executive and a relevant executive director.

If it is still controversial to recommend that real non-executives should sit on divisional and subsidiary boards (and there are very few who do), and if it is quite novel to recommend that some of them should overlap onto two levels of board, then it must be close to heresy to recommend that the divisional board should not be chaired by the Group chief executive. But if the line boss of the divisional executives is chairing their board meetings, then they might well be forgiven for sitting silent from 'Matters Arising' to 'Date of Next Meeting', simply waiting to be told what to do by the man who is their line boss and their board chairman rolled into one.

The almost universal arrangement whereby the Group chief executives does chair the divisional boards is not helpful in 'bringing out' the executives, or in extracting their maximum contribution. Further, it keeps the Group chief executive rigidly 'in line' where he could benefit more, and could himself contribute more freely, if he were sitting elsewhere than at the head of the table.

Let a non-executive chair the divisional board. Let the Group chief executive sit among his colleagues, observing, weighing. No one is going to deny that he really is the boss just because he does not do all the talking. Heresy this may seem, but it goes to the core of the problem of composing a structure for achieving contribution, and thus perform-ance, in a diverse organisation.

If the divisional board, or divisional committee, is to be nothing more than a mechanism for past performance review, then it is not needed at all. If boards below the holding board, because they are weak or small or new, really are to be viewed as management committees, then call them that and avoid the Company Limited status.

But if a grouping of subsidiaries with common markets, technologies or management processes is to benefit from an interchange of ideas, opportunities or men, then it must feel that it is structured and truly empowered to do so. If the parent does want the divisional board to take initiatives within defined but uninhibiting limits, to make suggestions, disagree, present better alternatives, evaluate, plan, decide and then implement with the wholehearted commitment of its directors, then it must create a divisional entity in which the directors concerned can do all these things with a feeling of excitement, not formality, and with the knowledge that their contributions not only will be visible but will actually be seen.

This will be achieved if the divisional board is chaired by a holding board non-executive, contains also divisional-level non-executives, plus the Group chief executive, another Group executive, and a balanced team of divisional managers.

The divisional board should differ from an independent board in two characteristics only. First, that it does not *choose* its own chairman.

Secondly, that it does not *choose* its MD. These appointments must, in all senses, remain in the control of the parent. The divisional directors are appointed by the holding company, which owns 100 per cent of the shares in the divisional company. While they formally 'elect' their chairman and MD, at their board, there would be much disorder if they did not simply elect the two choices of the parent, whose rights to make these appointments could be found in the articles of the divisional company.

If the size and complexity of the parent are such that it cannot pretend to be able to manage by edict through the Group chief executive – and it normally cannot – then the divisional board must be composed for independent decision-making, not just for receiving and disseminating instructions. If the Group chief executive, on the other hand, believes that he can in fact manage his empire by a straight-down-the-line mechanism, then he may be in need of a sabbatical. If he cannot extract more by prodding from the side than by sitting at the top, then he is just a boss, not a leader.

Subsidiary boards

Subsidiary boards are where it all happens. Where the business is done and the cash is generated. Where the reality of the Group board's judgement is put to the test. Where the Group grows its future top talent, and the square peg in the round hole is most visibly discomfited. Where returns are most realistically measurable and motivation of men most easily achievable, because performance is most clearly attributable.

But where the executive directors say the least and are commonly the most frustrated. Where the board is most frequently a formality, subjected passively to predetermined decisions worked out at a level above, or between the central directors and the local MD without any involvement of the subsidiary company directors. Where unproductive resources or businesses are most frequently retained through a whimsical attachment to decisions made in the circumstances of long ago. Where few employees meet a real live Group director face to face, and where few have any time for, or understanding of, the concept of the non-executive, or of anyone else who is not alongside them with sleeves rolled up.

It used to be believed that the primary motivation of men was money. It may still be with that rare and valuable animal, the 'born salesman', and in some cases with the natural entrepreneur – though he is unlikely to be working for long in the kind of structured environments which we are considering.

But it has been determined that managers are at least equally motivated by 'recognition', and by the opportunity to be recognised. Their greatest needs are often those which are least satisfied: the need for personal growth (not everyone can climb the pyramid); and the need for achievement which the person himself can accept as being real, and as being the fulfilment of what he earnestly believes he is able to contribute.

If subsidiary boards, too, were composed and operated as 'real' boards, there would be an awakening and quickening of contribution from the thousands of down-line directors who currently sit on their hands. In working with subsidiaries as a Group executive director, non-executive and consultant, the writer has concluded in almost every case that the subsidiary company directors had much more to 'give'. Sometimes they volunteer this conclusion themselves, asking if 'something can be done up there' to make their boards more meaningful. Usually it cannot. Holding boards understandably, but wrongly, often believe they would lose a larger element of control if down-line boards actually formulated decisions, rather than just accepted instructions.

There is another major advantage to be gained from giving the subsidiary board a truly independent role. In the prevailing style of subsidiary board, which is a board only in name, the executive director does not have to face conflicts within the boardroom, and so does not develop his ability to handle conflict productively. As he grows, this gap in his experience remains a gap. When he reaches the holding board and detects that conflict is likely to arise on a major topic, he will normally run away from it – he is not exercised in doing anything else. Which is one reason why wholly executive boards, without any outside directors, can become paralytic.

Conflict will always arise at holding board level. It can be funked, or handled productively. The clashing of strong opinions should not be seen as a problem; it can be used as an opportunity.

> *The world is ruled by force, not by opinion; but opinion uses force.*

> PASCAL

The board's horror, or the chairman's horror, of visible conflict stems often from one or two nasty experiences in the boardroom in the past of a kind which it, or he, has sworn never to go through again. Those experiences proved so painful, not because the subject matter was so sensitive but because the directors at that time, through their inexperience of boardroom conflict, handled it so clumsily.

An advantage in having non-executives on at least the more important subsidiary boards is that their presence can help the growing executives to exercise their muscles and their tongues productively, not painfully 'clumsily'. They can draw out the Young Turks, without fear or favour, without crossing their lines of command, and without caring a jot about their irreverence as long as what they are saying actually carries the enterprise forward.

The objectives of the next-up level of board must always be that the subsidiary achieves a set of collectively defined targets by whichever means are most likely to succeed, with the resources which can be made available; then to toughen the targets; thus to obtain more from those resources, and from its senior men. This is not achieved by telling them what to do. They must help work that out themselves. They need to be part of a mix of colleagues which enables, and encourages, them to do so.

> *Art is I; science is we.*

> CLAUDE BERNARD

The optimum amount of autonomy for a subsidiary is simply definable: within the Group board's definition of limits of authority, it should be total. The Group or divisional board can always tighten or loosen those limits for each subsidiary separately, in accordance with its results and the demonstrated performance of its management. With some of their own directors on the subsidiary board, they can ensure that things do not gallop away unbridled.

Remote control, which so often means bureaucratic and form-ridden control, can deaden. But remoteness can be turned into a bonus, without diminishing ultimate control, if each adjoining level of board shares two or three directors in common, including an independent. Sometimes a Group pushes down too much authority. Management failure down line is not just a failure of down-line managers. Incompetence can be created from above. The limits of senior men can be wrongly measured, even by experts. Hence several should measure them.

The ideal composition for an effective board in a major subsidiary is just as described for the divisional level. One or two executives, and a non-executive from the level above; subsidiary-level non-executives; a small team of subsidiary company managers; chaired by a non-executive.

There's a long gradation of skills and duties between the directors and decisions of a Group and one of its small outposts. Naturally. But people contribute most positively in the same sort of environment, whether writ large or small, and they react and interrelate at all levels in accordance with the same laws of nature. Their boards, to be effective, need to be composed to the same patterns. All levels are also bound by the same Corporation Acts. The legal niceties do not normally cause any bother until a subsidiary runs into trouble and a parent decides to liquidate, or to dissolve without liquidation; both of which situations are likely to increase in frequency.

Many a Group has created spurious subsidiaries in order that a large number of senior employees can put the title 'Director' on their visiting cards. In at least one major City of London Group, over 10 per cent of all employees are directors of subsidiaries whose boards meet only once a year, and then only to fulfil the formal requirements of the Companies Acts.

The value of this sales aid, or ego booster, must be balanced against the dangers that a client may view the person with such a position as genuinely responsible for more than the Group wants him to be responsible for, or that at time of subsequent dissolution that person truly is enmeshed in more than he was intended to be concerned with.

The individual director may consider the legalities of corporate relationships irrelevant to daily operations, or that the threat of insolvency is too remote to cause him concern. But his own relationship with subsidiaries, and the attendant responsibilities, may not be so remote. Under the legal concept of the 'shadow' director, a board member has to view his responsibilities by also looking 'downwards', below the level of the board to which he is formally appointed. Parent and subsidiary company directors, for example, can run the risk of being charged with 'conspiracy to defraud' if the parent controls a subsidiary through its nominated directors and they carry on a business which is insolvent. This is not some minor technicality which need cause little concern, as many directors might discover if they tease apart the current situation of all their subsidiaries, including those little nuisance companies which never rate a mention at the board.

Within European countries the law on the relationship between a Group and its subsidiaries is certain to change under pressure from the EEC, and properly so. It must be inherently 'wrong' that the House of Lords could rule in 1980 that, in accordance with current law, despite allegations of illegal trading, Lonrho could not force Shell and BP to disclose certain documents held by some of their subsidiaries on the grounds that these documents were not 'in the power' of the parent companies.

EEC proposals on a new legal parent/subsidiary relationship are likely to conclude that the subsidiary should support its parent, even against its own interests, with the 'contra' that the parent must carry a joint liability for the subsidiary's debts. This would provide an equitable balance between control and responsibility.

Minorities

Minority shareholders in subsidiary companies prove, more often than not, to be an embarrassment which is best bought out sooner rather than later. They arise most commonly when a Group acquires an independent private company, engages a number of the original directors, and allows them to retain a percentage of the shares.

The rights of such shareholders are theoretically the same as the rights of minorities in a holding company, though in practice a new parent with as little as 51 per cent in a subsidiary will take decisions affecting that subsidiary as though it was alone. Otherwise it would not have made the acquisition in the first place.

Occasionally a parent will introduce a minority shareholder into a subsidiary for marketing or technical reasons. This rarely works well. If the expertise desired is in the hands of specific individuals to whom the minority stake is offered, then it would be better to introduce such expertise in a consultancy mode. If the expertise desired is in the control of a company to which the minority is offered, then it would be better to establish a licensing or know-how agreement, and otherwise keep at arm's length.

Introducing any kind of business associate to the boardroom, whether technical or marketing associates, or suppliers or distributors, is bad enough; offering them a minority stake is worse. They reduce the board's independence in business decision making.

If you cannot escape from having minority shareholders in a subsidiary, with or without board seats, or with or without a role in daily management, then agree in advance with them, and record, precisely what information they will receive; when they will receive it; what roles, if any, they are expected to play. This will ensure they are kept properly in the picture, without being able to harass a board which, while acknowledging that in law the minorities must be treated without 'unreasonable prejudice', really just wants to forget about them.

Joint ventures

There can be sounder reasons for establishing new joint venture companies, with shareholdings at 2×50 per cent or 3×33.3 per cent, than for establishing subsidiaries with minority interests. But in the long term the difficulties posed by most joint ventures, particularly when they remain small, are such that once the initial objectives of the grouping have been achieved, then one dominant partner would do well to buy out the others.

The grouping of equal partners is normally based in the first instance on an observed need to marry market and technical expertise, and perhaps financial muscle, which the separate partners do not encompass individually.

After some years of life the joint venture company will have developed all that expertise within its own separately existing organisation, and the need for a single line of control will become apparent. In almost every joint venture, one partner progressively dominates the decisions and actions of the collective unit. The interests of one will progressively differ from the interests and needs of the others. The difficulty is that the board of any company, including the board of a joint venture, is required to base its decision on the interests of that specific company alone. In a joint venture these can come to conflict with the interests of one, or all, of the shareholding partners. The expedient of agreeing, by written contract between the partners, that one will manage and control the joint venture is sometimes used. It will be readily seen that this can only be a temporary expedient; the situation of the joint venture and the interests of its shareholders will change through its history.

A quite typical joint venture history is represented by the case of a 50/50 company in North England, which was established by a UK Group with local market knowledge and a Dutch Group with both technical expertise in a new field of ultra-heavy haulage techniques, plus a pool of expensive capital equipment usable only for such work. In its first two or three years, with a flush market linked to the North Sea activities, when alternative suppliers with the requisite skills and equipment were few, the objectives in marrying the two interests made sense, and made money. As the market declined, and as competition increased, margins available naturally decreased. The joint venture, which by now contained within itself all the necessary market and technical expertise, could not justify the purchase or replacement of the capital equipment needed to service a very seasonal market. Nor could it justify the purchase of equally specialised equipment for extension out of its originally selected sector of that market. But the equipment could be, and often was, hired from the pool held by the Dutch partner. That partner, however, needed discretion over the pricing of hire, which was the main cost item in this particular business. It needed to be able to choose freely whether to marginal cost in quiet periods, or to make up ground during international peaks, when all potential suppliers were charging high. The joint venture was thus not able to make its own decisions about its own major cost item. The costs, and thus the competitiveness, of the joint venture were in practice controlled by one partner. The only workable solution was for the UK shareholder to sell out to the Dutch, and this was done.

Several joint venture companies established with a flush of enthusiasm in the 1970s between Japanese and European Groups have ended in the same way. Toshiba bought out Rank, its British partner in a television manufacturing joint venture, while Hitachi bought out GEC, its partner in another television joint venture.

Most joint ventures reach similar situations of conflicting interest. Their boards, with representatives from each of the partners, and from the senior management of the joint venture itself, usually wait too long to decide on the inevitable concentration of shareholding because of the effect this will have on the individual directors' positions. Top executives in the joint venture may not be happy with being absorbed into one organisation, which can be felt as moving from real independence to simple subsidiary status. And they may not like the idea of working for the 'obvious' buyer, for one of many possible reasons.

Profitability inevitably sinks as the board delays taking the decision. Again this is a situation where the involved but independent non-executive – if the joint venture board contained one, and it seldom does – could take a lead. Only the outsider, who is independent of each of the shareholders, can ensure that the interests of the joint venture itself come first, as long as it is alive, and can ensure that the transfer of control is rational and humane when joint control is put to death.

Associate companies

The Group's minority stake in an associate company is an investment. The performance of its investments is seldom reviewed by the board as frequently as the performance of subsidiaries. If one does not control the decisions of the associate, then there is not much to review except the ROC.

There may be value in having a director or two on the board of the associate; a functional specialist such as the finance or business development director, and one non-executive. Not a general manager, as he could be discomforted when management decisions are not wholly within his influence.

If the Group has several associates, it could be useful to 'group' them together under the watchful eye of the same two directors, who would report regularly to the board on actual ROC achieved compared with planned levels and compared with that achieved by the Group's own subsidiaries. When the Group has dozens of associates, or exceptionally hundreds, as in the case of a transnational corporation which engaged the writer for consultancy on nominee directors, the normal practice is to nominate the local general manager to the boards of the associates in his region. These non-executive roles become part of his routine job description, and when he is transferred elsewhere his replacement automatically takes over the same directorships. The practice produces damaging discontinuity. It also generates conflict as the director of any company, anywhere, has the primary duty to serve the interests of that specific company. The interests of the Group, or of the local subsidiary, can run counter to the interests of the associate, just as we find with joint venture companies. The conflict can be critical in associates operating in countries which have very different concepts of business ethics from those of the Group. It is therefore strongly recommended that Groups with numerous associates should nominate suitably qualified independent, external directors to the boards of their associates, instead of using local managers. For this purpose they can establish their own pools of men of the required experience, with whom they can maintain regular liaison, and from whom they can obtain, with the prior agreement of the associate's board, completely independent advice about the progress of the associates.

It might be found more sensible to sell out, reduce the overdraft, and boost the growth of the subsidiaries; or alternatively to increase one's stake in the associate to a majority, and then boost that new subsidiary. Either way, the stake held is a commitment of Group resources which needs as much monitoring and measuring as any other use of resources.

The EEC's proposals for a Eurocompany, last amended in 1975 and still awaiting approval from the EEC Council, contain some complex rules for situations where the minority stake exceeds 10 per cent. But where the stake is at or below 10 per cent the proposals require the minority holder to sell out to the majority company, or alternatively to take shares in the majority company itself. This is fair confirmation of the thesis that minority stakes, in subordinate companies, are seldom worth the hassle to either the minority or the majority holder.

Diversity and technology

It is simpler to compose, and operate within, a board concerned with a turnover of several hundred millions in a uniform business than it is with a grouping of small companies which each sells a few millions in differing markets and product categories.

Woolworths (UK), before trying to acquire its way out of decline, had just one board covering the activity of 60,000 employees, all in High Street or related retailing. A grouping one hundredth the size may well have half-a-dozen boards, and need them all; it can be more complex to plan and develop, despite the fact that the resources deployed are tiny by comparison.

The measure of the task facing the board is a multiple of the variables of products, markets, competitors, customers, technologies, techniques. Size naturally introduces its own variables, such as the numerous alternative businesses into which the large Group can afford to diversify. But size can also provide a balancing, comforting element of financial flexibility. The smaller, diverse enterprise's problems begin with fitting the best mix of talents into its boardroom, while still keeping the total numbers within workable limits. Specific expertise has to be concentrated in the executives, most of them below the board. Where additional technical support is required, it is best engaged and employed outside the boardroom; the board itself will not have the time or the space to cover all the detailed knowledge to which the diverse units need daily access.

In this environment the most useful kind of outside non-executive director is a generalist; a strategist experienced in multi-unit operations; someone who can balance the pros and cons of the diverse units and help decide dispassionately which should be built up with the limited resources available, and which should be run down to make more resources available; who is not devoted to, or technically enthusiastic about, any one of those units.

This conclusion runs counter to prevailing practice in smaller, diverse enterprises. Technically based companies tend to believe steadfastly, even stubbornly, that only men with from-the-cradle experience in the technicalities of their specific businesses can be of any use in helping to grow them. Engineering company boards, including those of very large engineering-based groups, contain predominantly engineering-trained directors, even when the diversity of specialities is such that no one member can have deep knowledge of more than two or three of the fields covered. They seldom contain broad-based businessmen, strategists, planners, or experienced generalists, either as non-executives, or even as executives.

The problem increases in the 1980s, when the dominant engineering companies are based largely on state-of-the-art electronics. The technologies are so specialised, with their own languages and dialects, that the engineer finds it even easier to out-talk the 'ordinary' business manager, strategist or accountant. Alas, many such companies are collapsing because they believe their dialects contain some kind of personal magic. Even companies of the skill and standing of Denmark's Christian Rovsing A/S collapsed because its non-executives, accountants and bankers didn't or didn't succeed in their efforts to square up to the technologists and *demand* that they begin to count costs, measure markets and weigh probabilities.

Funnies

What about that subsidiary in Panama, or the British Virgin Islands? Its original purpose may have been valid, legal, and even decent. It is always quite proper to minimise the unproductive cash-negative of taxation however one legally can, and it is equally proper to ensure that the company has a sound mechanism for transferring monies in all directions with that, or other, business objectives in mind.

The legal ground rules can change, either happily, as in the case of the removal of UK exchange control regulations, which eliminated the need for many of the funnies, or unhelpfully, as they are likely to do in connection with the taxation of international and multinational enterprises. The board has to ensure that yesterday's mechanism is still the most effective, and is still at least legal.

The wise director will ensure, first, that he knows all about the funnies in detail; who is on their boards, why, and what they are doing. Chances are that the people concerned have forgotten all about those particular directorships. Second, that their activities are reviewed regularly at the board. The mechanism may be intelligent and acceptable. It may have become rusty or inefficient. Or it may have developed, intentionally or otherwise, into a system whereby the directors, or some of the directors, or in a private company some of the shareholders, obtain a higher proportion of personal gain than is equally exposed to all the other directors or shareholders, or which is not exposed to the taxmen in quite its clearest colours.

The wise director will accept nothing which is not freely exposed, or not freely exposable. He will not let any element of concern lie 'on the shelf' until a more suitable moment. The only suitable moment is when the concern first arises. The claim, later, that he did not know or did not understand is neither acceptable nor credible, even if true. If he finds that the law is being broken, and he is unable to have this remedied immediately, he must resign. His personal dilemma on such resignation is that other parts of the law state that he cannot bottle up within himself the knowledge that the law is being broken. He is bound to expose known illegalities. Mentioning this fact to his co-directors should usually do the trick and remedy the abuse. But if it does not, he has to expose it. If one bunch of malefactors is not seen to hang publicly, then others will proliferate.

One major accounting firm has found fraud in 5 per cent of the receiverships which it handles, not always involving overseas funnies, nor, usually, on a scale which contributed to the companies' financial collapse. The accelerating run of corporate scandals on both sides of the Atlantic must now raise the question as to whether the prevalence of illegality is as high, or higher, in continuing businesses which have not yet been subject to the receiver's searching analysis. One estimate puts the annual rate of fraud losses in the UK in 1987 at around £1.8 billion, and a leading international firm of accountants has seen the need to publish a booklet for client companies on how to fight fraud.

The dangers in breaking the law do not need expansion here. It is the borderline mechanisms which can cause greatest harm to corporate health. Borderline operations are always clearly known to a number of the staff below the board who handle the paperwork. A progressive decline in morale seeps out of their offices, spreading and multiplying. It can be felt in the air.

It is not the criminal things which are hardest to confess, but the ridiculous and the shameful.
                                        JEAN-JACQUES ROUSSEAU, 1766

The Greek god Hermes, and his Roman counterpart Mercury, were the gods of speed and the patrons of travellers (before the Christians replaced them in the latter role by the good St Christopher). They were also the gods of trade, 'both honest and dishonest'. From well before their time it has been commonly assumed by the layman that the one always contains just a little of the other, even though every now and again demonstrably upright businessmen, such as the Quakers who contributed so much to the development of eighteenth- and nineteenth-century Britain, were able to belie the general assumption.

The small pressure groups which currently spend their energies on the iniquities of underpaid workers in Sri Lanka or South Africa could one day turn their attention to the local enterprises which they believe overstep the rules.

Don't wait. If your list of subsidiaries and associates includes the Netherlands Antilles and Norfolk Island, start by asking your own questions about these. There is nothing improper about the helpful services provided by these excellent countries. But there may be about the way a company uses them.

Nationalised industries

There has never been any strength of support in the USA for nation-alisation, or government ownership, of industrial and commercial corporations, and there has been only limited support for the concept of centralised control of the social services. European support for these concepts is variable and anomalous. In Sweden, there has long been a high proportion of government ownership among major industrial corporations – yet in neighbouring and equally 'socially conscious' Denmark there has been very little. In Norway, the once numerous but small government-owned industries proved so unsuccessful that they were sold off to private investors; by contrast, in France the nationalised industries have been large and successful in open compe-tition with privately owned corporations.

In the UK, support swings according only to the politics of the governing party. Dogma alone dictates whether the production of steel and aeroplanes should be managed by organisations in which shares are owned by the tax-payer or by organisations in which shares are freely traded in the Stock Exchanges. By the Acts establishing the nationalised industries the categories of control vested in ministers were in theory quite similar to those vested in the sum of the shareholders in a company limited, with the addition of control over major capital expenditure, and over borrowings. The ministers were not empowered to instruct or manage.

In practice the relationship between ministers and nationalised industry management became a 'mess of fictions'. Ministers and officials began to interfere ad hoc. One chairman at British Steel had nineteen different ministers to contend with during his ten-year term, and British Rail faced seven different investment programmes in a five-year period. Within such unplannable terms of reference the directors can scarcely feel responsible for the poor performance of their boards; the eunuch in the harem can scarcely be derided for not even wanting to disport himself lustily.

The mess of fictions disguises reality.

The performance of any organisation, industrial, commercial or governmental, depends always on how well it is managed and directed; on how wisely the objectives of the organisation have been defined and how effectively actual performance is monitored and adjusted against those objectives. Performance levels do not depend, in any way whatsoever, on who 'owns' the organisation. Nor do levels of performance depend *directly* on the presence of competition. British Steel and British Airways, for just two examples, did face foreign competition, but did not prove more efficient than organisations with monopoly status. Their performance levels were eventually raised, while still under government ownership, by the introduction of more purposeful planning and management. And by the removal of executive abuses. When the new management of British Airways reviewed past performance they concluded that their predecessors had run it '*as if money grew on trees . . . the perks and privileges we discovered there were amazing*'. Even in the absence of apparent competition it is possible to create external yardsticks against which management can be measured. In Holland, the telephone system has 200 customer lines per employee; Bell Canada has 185; NTT (Japan) has 151; Pacific Bell 140; monopoly status British Telecom achieved just 90. Three years after being sold out of government ownership, and after the introduction of an element of local competition, British Telecom has not made any significant improvement to that figure – though it has, as an aside, raised the board's remuneration by 132 per cent (*Economist*, 1987).

The real difference between corporations owned by the taxpayer and those owned by a few thousand minority shareholders is that they demonstrate in an exaggerated form the very same weaknesses: bad or non-existent planning; dominating control; emasculated boards.

6 Tiers: one, two, many

Who shall guard the guards themselves?

JUVENAL

Every Group of companies already contains several tiers of decision-making, including holding board, divisional boards, subsidiary boards and all the management committees which are positioned through their structures to review and decide a defined range of questions at each tier.

The debate on 'tiers' within the EEC's own machinery of committees, and within relevant industrial and commercial organisations in member countries, centres exclusively on the holding board level; on whether or not to introduce yet another level by splitting that one into two. The debate always links the question of having two top-level tiers with the question of having employee or union directors on the proposed 'upper' tier, the supervisory board. The two questions are best considered quite separately.

Whether a company's performance can be aided by introducing a supervisory tier, which watches over management, is a perfectly valid question in itself. Whether that supervisory tier or, for that matter, whether any other level of board should contain employee or union directors is also a perfectly valid question. But to avoid confusing structure with composition, or confusing politics with performance, this volume will leave the question of employee representation to Chapter 8, concentrating here on the structure of the holding board level.

Among European nations, Ireland, England, Sweden and Denmark are called 'common law' countries, where court judgements are guided by recorded precedents. Other nations are called 'civil law' countries, where the law, based originally on old Roman law, is largely codified – for example the Code Napoléon. Distinctions between the two systems continue to 'blur' because the common law countries progressively codify by enacting new statutes, and the civil law countries make increasing use of precedents, or 'case law'.

77

British Commonwealth countries, such as Australia and India, have laws and legal systems resembling those of England, and have Companies Acts based on British models (which apply in both England and Scotland). When Australia revised the British models for its own use, the governments of Malaysia and Singapore decided that *their* proposed new Companies Acts would now be based on the new Australian legislation – and so a 'family' of law diversifies in detail, while remaining linked in principle.

American legislation affecting the formation and conduct of corporations includes elements from both English and Continental European practice. As each of the individual states had enacted its own Business Corporation Act, or Law, the American Bar Association instituted a lengthy research project which led to the production of the Model Business Corporation Act of 1969. The objective was to influence the individual states to adopt all or parts of the 'commonised' model, and a few states have already done so.

Overriding the state laws are a number of federal Acts and Codes, many of which were developed during the period of the New Deal. A uniform Commercial Code, and the federal Securities Acts, have been applied in all the states. One of the great contributions by the USA to the development of the principles of law has been the separation of the control of investors' protection (by the Federal Securities and Exchange Commission) from the laws of corporate organisation.

A small American organisation will normally seek incorporation in the state in which its head office is based. A larger organisation will seek its charter in a state which offers the best financial advantages, meaning, primarily, the lowest fees and taxes. Delaware is favoured by many. Americans may understand, from their own limited local conflicts of state practice, the greater problems being experienced in the countries of the European Economic Commission (EEC), where established member countries with similar local practices are seeking to impose their standards on 'new' members, such as the UK.

The company law Directives of the EEC stem from provisions in the Treaty of Rome which were intended to facilitate the freedom of establishment of companies within the EEC, and to protect the interests of members and third parties. Like any other bureaucracy, the EEC machine will go on extending its interpretation of this 'brief', and its subsequent generation of Directives, until such time as the men who control the machine decide to switch it off. Meanwhile, the parliaments of member countries are bound to enact the adopted Directives within their local legislation, against a timetable established by the Europarliament.

The First Directive confined itself to routine matters such as the publication by each company of its memorandum, articles, balance sheet and profit and loss accounts. No local problems arose, and all the EEC countries implemented the Directive in localised formats. The later Directives caused wider differences of opinion, or more direct opposition. The longer the Eurolegislators are left to deliberate, the more detailed their drafts become and the more disagreement will inevitably arise. Maximum disagreement arose, and continues, concerning the Fifth Directive, on which the previously relatively passive acceptance of the main contents of EEC company legislation was abruptly halted. The first draft was prepared by a former German trade union leader in 1972. By 1978, the proposals – for two-tier boards with worker and union directors on the 'upper' or supervisory tier – had come to resemble the current German system (see Appendix II).

As the proposals wandered through the EEC machine, a Dutch Commissioner, Mr Vredeling, added some new proposals which seek to enforce compulsory consultation between directors and employees prior to implementation of board decisions – which would often mean prior to the making of the decisions. The danger in adopting alien practice without dissecting every detail of its local suitability, and rejecting whatever is considered harmful or irrelevant, is that the pressure to adopt increasingly alien practice would itself increase. Consider the example of Sweden, not a member of the EEC, but a strong influence on neighbouring Denmark, which is a member. In 1984 the Swedish parliament enacted a law which required that the proceeds from a new tax on company profits, plus the proceeds from a deduction from wages and salaries at all levels, would be paid into a number of funds with boards of nine members – five of them trade union members. The funds would be used to buy shares in any public company, and within three years they should become the country's largest shareholder. 75,000 directors and managers took to the streets in protest, to no avail. The funds will achieve a controlling interest – an extraordinary mixture of extreme socialism and cold capitalism which will put the control of capitalism into the hands of its natural 'adversary'. Similar proposals are being aired in Germany and Holland.

Consider also the Swedish legislation of 1977 for employee participation in decision-making. An official Swedish publication states that this law '*implies the birth of a new order. Labour and Capital are to be regarded as equals where the right of decision-making is concerned* ' (Swedish Institute, 1979). But the thesis that labour equals capital defies all logic. The assumption that boards and company management represent capital also defies both logic and existing law.

The majority report of the Bullock Committee of Inquiry on Industrial Democracy (a British attempt to produce proposals along European models, which foundered largely because it was given terms of reference which begged the question to be considered) also made the same mistake of confusing capital with the management of companies. It wrote about '*putting the relationship between capital and labour on to a new basis which will involve not just management but the whole work-force in sharing responsibility for the success and profitability of the enterprise*' (Bullock Committee, 1977).

But the content and intent of the law regarding companies is that capital, or shareholding, is separated from management. The board does not represent capital; it represents the company. For it to be able to represent the interests of company, capital and employees, equally and simultaneously, then logic alone dictates that all of the directors must be in one place, at one time, around one table, in a single-tier board.

Proposals from Europe for splitting the holding board's responsibilities between two legally separated tiers have been based on the following beliefs that:

• uniformity in all things within the EEC is a good thing. A neat and tidy concept which the average Frenchman must care for as little as the average Englishman, and which we can put quietly aside;

- two tiers have worked well in West Germany and some other member countries of the EEC, which have all made demonstrably better industrial progress than the British in recent decades; and
- executive boards need to be watched and controlled from without their own boundaries, being too often characterised by too little will and courage, and too much self-perpetuating self-interest.

How much reality is there in the last two beliefs?

There has been a two-tier system in Germany since it was first introduced by Bismarck over a hundred years ago. It has evolved to a stage where the 'upper' supervisory tier contains no representatives of management, not even the chief executive. It consists of down-line employees, union representatives and non-executives such as bankers – all of them, with the best will in the world, quite remote from the work of the senior managers. Its judgement on proposals of almost any kind which come up to it from the management, including investment proposals, can be based on little more than intelligent ignorance. It can only rubber-stamp, or interfere clumsily. Tease out this question with German executives over a lager or two and they will almost invariably admit that this has been precisely the case for years. The system worked well because the management board itself worked well enough for the supervisory board to have no real additional business purpose. The incentives for management success in post-World War II Germany (and in post-World War II Japan) have been stronger, more pervasive, and initially more necessary than elsewhere. Couple this with a natural German ability to plan and methodically implement, and one can conclude that German companies succeeded so well in spite of, not because of, the separation of management from its supposed supervision.

There is something inherently bizarre in creating an extra tier of board in order to examine and keep in line another level of board. Who in turn will examine and keep in line the newly created supervisory tier? The shareholders? The shareholders in committee? (The Danes have a few such shareholders' committees.) The employees? The trade unions? The government? None of these groups can act any more directly on, or cooperate any more usefully with, the supervisory tier than they can with the unitary board.

The implication is that the supervisory tier will not need such external supervision because it will contain two distinct types of person, representing two distinct types of interest, and that each 'side' will not let the other 'side' get away with anything improper. Which means consciously creating adversary roles within a body which, by definition, is intended to have a unified purpose.

Comparing again with German experience, we find that the 'unnatural' dividing of responsibility between two tiers had no ill effects until 1976, when their Codetermination Act was introduced. In this the 'two sides' concept was enshrined in the complicated arithmetic which has been summarised in Appendix II. The motivation behind the arithmetic was clearly political, and it is no coincidence that since 1976 Germany has been experiencing a level and kind of industrial unrest in its major corporations which they had not had to handle before.

In early 1983 the major German employers' association, BDA, commented on the 1976 law through Dr Wisskirchen of its legal department:

> *The experience has not been positive . . . Decisions are postponed or delayed. Management thinks in terms of what it is possible or not possible to get through the board, not what is economically best for the company.*

> LLOYD, 1983

Meanwhile, it has become undeniably true that many of the single-tier boards in the UK and USA are indeed now '*characterised by too little will and courage, and too much self-perpetuating self-interest*'. Directors' pay, perks and pay-offs have grown in volume like bacilli in a sick body. With limited recruitment methods directors can, and frequently do, block the recruitment of any other director, executive or non-executive, who they judge is likely to upset cosy continuity by questioning, or even looking at, their standards and suitability for office (see Clough, 1981, in chapter 10). Should these abuses continue it will become impossible to argue the logical case for maintaining the single-tier system; directors will have to be monitored and marshalled like miscreants. The *logic* of the case is clear enough. Boards fail, however many directors they actually contain, when they do not contain enough directors who are able enough, experienced enough, committed enough or courageous enough to press the right kinds of business decision through any barriers, including through a dominant single director or a placid but permanent majority, or a stubborn self-interested minority.

Dividing the topmost decision-making body must therefore have the very opposite effect to what is needed. It reduces the competences present within each half. It defines precisely what is to be done and decided in each, which is another way of saying that it defines what is not to be done and decided in each, thus impeding the director who is willing to give more. It builds walls between three different kinds of director split between two different kinds of board.

The onus for composing an effective board does not lie solely with the chairman. It lies with each director, executive or non-executive. Each is able to detect when his board is poorly balanced, or is running out of steam, or is dominated by self-interest. There are always a handful or two of directors for every one chairman, so the main impetus for change should come from around the table more frequently than from the chair. It does not. And because it does not, the main impetus for changing boards is coming from a variety of sources which themselves have no experience of operating within boardrooms.

The chairman sits on top of the board. With unusual exceptions apart, the man sitting on the top of any structure is, in the nature of all humanity, the last to decide that true change is needed. He has to be triggered.

The individual board still has time to take its own initiatives to decide and balance its own composition, to introduce courageous objectivity within its existing single tier, and to eliminate any chance for the complaint that it is self-perpetuating, self-interested, or lacking in will or courage.

The guards may still, just, guard themselves. But the Allegheny International affair in the USA, the Guinness affair in the UK, and a host of less-publicised cases in both countries involving boards, collectively, or leading businessmen, individually, have blunted their weapons.

7 Japanese boards

We have considered the roles and characteristics of American, European and British boards and directors. What comparisons can be made with, and lessons learnt from, their Japanese equivalents?

Seen 'on paper', the typical Japanese corporate board combines all the very worst characteristics of the very worst American or British boardrooms. It is:

- too large, often with thirty to fifty directors;
- too executive, usually with no non-executives at all;
- too passive, containing just a hierarchy of managers working their way upwards without treading on the toes of those above them;
- too rigid, with presidents inevitably turning into chairmen at a certain age, and with no one questioning the practice because no one ever questions the president;
- too free from external evaluation and pressure, and keeping itself like that by hiring thugs to man-handle shareholders who dare to query the performance of the directors at a general meeting.

But, seen in 'practice', that typical Japanese board is only a small part of the corporation's decision-making machinery. The dangers of groupthink, or destructive autocracy, are avoided within the corporation through the 'ringi' system of consultation and contribution, which requires that a proposal must work its way sideways and upwards through the whole width and height of the organisation. The Japanese corporation does not 'break' the rules of group psychology described at the beginning of this volume – it simply applies them differently.

There are four categories of Japanese corporation, two of them – the Kabushiki Kaisha and the Yugen Kaisha – resembling the American corporation and 'close' corporation, the German AG and GmbH, the French SA and Sàrl, the Danish A/S and ApS, and the British plc and Ltd, respectively. Under the Japanese Companies Act there must be at least three directors. In practice, boards contain from five to over thirty, commonly fourteen to sixteen, which makes them on average rather larger than American boards and a great deal larger than British boards. A unique feature is that the boards appoint two or three of their number to be 'representative directors', who represent the company to third parties and who sign for it. The representative directors, operating as an executive committee of MDs, commonly meet weekly, while the full board meets only monthly. As other directors are viewed as 'junior', the decisions taken at such weekly meetings will be passed on the nod by the full board.

All directors are elected at general meetings of shareholders. This is normally through proxies vested in the board, so that membership of the board is in practice controlled by the management. As few as 3 per cent of the shareholders can request the court to remove a director they judge to be inadequate, and a majority of only two-thirds of the shareholders can alter the articles under which the directors operate.

However, the position of the small shareholder is much weaker than this might suggest. Changes to the Commercial Code during the post-World War II military occupation, when the giant 'zaibatsus' were broken up, may have been intended to increase the power of the shareholders, but in practice had the opposite effect. While before the war there were numerous part-time non-executives on Japanese boards, today there are few indeed – around one in thirty directors only, having a role equivalent to the 'independent outsider' on UK or US boards. Japanese executive boards are still able to resist any change to their unhindered control of their own operations.

Abuse of this position has extended to the employment of 'sokaiya', or sophisticated toughs, whose role is to cut short any shareholder who complains too much at general meetings. Japanese police estimate that there are around 5,000 sokaiya in the country, and that 3,000 listed Japanese companies pay out close to £100 million per annum to these toughs to perform that role. Corrupt practice of any kind tends to rebound on the user of the practice, and the sokaiya discovered that they could maintain their high fee rates by threatening to blackmail companies, or individual directors, who would not pay. The sokaiya have established networks within companies which keep them supplied with details of the darker deeds of the directors; this they have been able to hold over the heads of the boards concerned. In October 1982 the Japanese authorities revised the national Commercial Code in order to prohibit the making of 'gifts' to professional shareholders, with the objective of eliminating the sokaiya. Freed from this strangely primitive constraint, the shareholders in the very far from primitive Sony Corporation took thirteen hours at the annual general meeting to let the board know of their displeasure with some of the board's recent decisions. Whether the influence of the sokaiya will in fact be eliminated, or whether it will find other ways of resurfacing, remains to be seen.

The small shareholder owns just over 30 per cent of the equity of listed companies, which is roughly the same proportion as is held by individual shareholders in many Western countries. However, composition of the larger shareholders is very different. While institutions, including pension funds and insurance companies do hold sizeable stakes in Japanese companies, the majorities are held by the companies' own bankers, and by trading or other companies with which there are close business relationships. Thus meetings of shareholders are in a sense 'family affairs', and even here the 'collective' character of Japanese enterprise is well demonstrated. The dominant shareholders are much more interested in business cooperation, on a continuing basis, than they are in dividends or capital gains.

The executive board is thus free from 'pressure' from the shareholders. Until 1974 it was also effectively free from any real pressure from its auditors, who were considered till then to be subordinate to the management, and often consisted of unqualified retired directors, or trainees who were being groomed for a directorship – the very last categories to complain about management's performance, or its treatment of its accounts.

In 1974 an Act was passed introducing statutory auditors, elected by the general meeting and reporting to it. They were given increased powers. On the evidence to date, these are about as passive as their predecessors. While they are not allowed to be directors or managers, it is reported that they are commonly treated as normal employees, within a hierarchy. The board continues to be allowed to be strongly self-protective.

Entry to the board is controlled by the chairman, the president, the senior representative director, who may or may not take external advice, for example from the bankers, before promoting a manager to a directorship. With a strictly executive board, directorship is seen as one more rung up the management ladder, not as a wholly separate role. Within the board there is also a pronounced hierarchy, from the chairman of the board (most frequently a retired president) through the president of the corporation, to executive vice-president, senior MDs, MDs, to senior and then junior 'ordinary' directors. These are not legally defined positions, but the terms are commonly used.

Junior directors will never rock the boat, and will never criticise a senior director, even when he is patently 'wrong'. All levels of director fear the loss of face implicit in a sideways move to some ceremonial role, and will not risk it. The wishes of senior directors therefore always prevail.

Senior directors could certainly abuse such a rigid system, but its very rituals contain some safeguards. The unwritten, but generally agreed, qualifications for a board position include:

- success as a manager, which can be judged from the record;
- support from the funders, which can be tested in discussion with a shareholding banker;

and a qualification perhaps unique to Japan:

- support from labour as someone who has demonstrated that he will continue to represent the interests of the employees.

Directors consider themselves as being just as responsible for the interests of the employees as for the interests of the shareholders. They do not need legislation to tell them this; it is common sense, and needs no formal record.

Within the corporation the choice of a new president proceeds as smoothly as the election of a new director. The president, or the *'representative director with the title of president'*, is normally nominated by the retiring president, who will have taken advice from other senior directors and from the main funders, the shareholding bankers. If a president subsequently proves inadequate, the banks and other institutions will have a quiet word or two with him, and he will not stand for re-election. He may or may not remain a director, but in either case there will be no publicity, no publicly visible disagreements.

With few exceptions, the nearest one finds today to the nonexecutive role is in the frequent use of advisers to top management, who work alongside, but outside, the board. They are often retired executives. With no specific shareholder representatives on the board, the major shareholders rely on regular, informal meetings with the president for obtaining information about progress. Such meetings would not be permitted under the USA's SEC rules, or in the UK, where all shareholders are intended to have equal access to the same information. But we have already noted that the individual shareholders 'do not matter' in Japan, whereas major institutional shareholders are 'part of the team'. This situation may change, at least change enough to bring back some pressure for the appointment of non-executives. There has been a noticeable increase in the *proportion* of individual shareholders in recent years and this, coupled with the anticipated effects of the anti-sokaiya legislation, could lead to change. The media, too, are becoming more active in pursuing complaints about abuse of power by some Japanese corporations, following allegations of bribes paid to Arab and European individuals, of American bribes accepted by their own Prime Minister, or large-scale stealing of secret technology from America's Silicon Valley. We shall see.

Meanwhile, though managers and other employees retire at 55 years, there is no retiring age for the board. A small number of companies have introduced their own internal rules for retirement of directors, but there is no evidence of haste to adopt the practice as a norm. The chairman generally goes on for as long as he himself chooses.

With boardroom power concentrated in the hands of two–three men, there can be few individual checks on their performance. But then Japanese companies, through all levels and activities, are concerned with the performance of groupings, not with the performance of individual men. The whole structure of a Japanese company is made up of numerous groups, which can be shaped and reshaped as the immediate needs of the company change. A company structure chart will illustrate these groupings, and will include the title of the group leader, but not his name. The individual manager will not have a job description. His status will be defined by a level, but not by a job. He can be moved about sideways, and frequently is.

The Japanese believe that all tasks must be carried out by groups, and that success lies in the success of the group in achieving the tasks set for it. This may depend to some extent on the skill of the (temporary) leader of the group in eliciting maximum performance, but the success will not be attributed to him individually. This characteristic recognition of the importance of group decision making, and the strong task- and goal-orientation of Japanese groups, will remind the reader of the findings on group effectiveness which were recorded in the earlier chapters. It has given the Japanese company great flexibility and mobility, which have in turn helped it to meet crises, or external business challenge. Coupled with the 'ringi' system, in which all who are able to contribute to a business decision are closely involved at all levels and stages, this has given the Japanese company a commitment to decisions finally made, and thus a concerted drive, which other competing countries have not been able to match. But it has been based on the inborn sense of collective responsibility which is found in Japan all the way from the quasi-kinship relationships of the village to the dealings of a corporation with its bankers, trading partners and government.

Japanese business life is characterised by the presence of numerous interest groups: trade groups, industry federations, professional associations, some growing naturally out of these relationships. Most will, of course, be concerned with protecting the interests, even the excessive self-interests, of their members, but 'collective responsibility' remains stronger than self-interest – an altruism which would not be understood in the City of London or in the lobbies of Congress.

Japanese managers, boards and interest groups share another characteristic which would cause open disbelief in Western countries: they all, and automatically, put the *national* interest first, clearly positioned *before* the interests of their members. Such characteristics will

in time produce their own kinds of problem as the zaibatsus continue
to regroup, as the size of individual corporations increases, and as
structural fragmentation, which results from multi-group operation,
becomes less easily managed. Some Japanese companies are trying to
modernise their structures with Western-style divisionalisation. One
has even skipped over the ringi system in taking a major, and
necessarily rapid, decision – C. Itoh and Co. when, in cooperation
with Sumitomo Bank, it took over the failing Ataka and Co. Others
will be led into, or driven into, taking such Western-style short-cuts in
order to accommodate Western partners in joint venture projects.
There can be a conflict of practice. The concept of general management, of total line management authority being vested in one man, is
still alien to the Japanese. Groupings of senior executives normally
carry out functions which, in the UK or US, would be delegated to a
chief executive, even in down-line companies. This can slow action
and reaction. There can also be a coming together of similar practice,
not always to the immediately obvious benefit of the company. Each
Japanese corporation contains a series of parallel, vertical hierarchies,
or 'habatsus', made up of cliques related by common schooling,
common university, or some other similarly shared background.
Bonds within these cliques are strong, and a man often works his way
up through the organisation by being promoted through the good
offices of his clique-colleagues above him. This system criss-crosses
with the horizontal, task-oriented groupings, and sometimes causes
destructive conflict. Such conflict has, to date, been held to a
minimum by focusing the attention of the groupings on beating some
further afield target, such as selected foreign competitors.

   Stresses are actively developing within Japanese companies, stimulated by the disruptions of the 1970s when the proportion of the
national import bill made up of oil was pushed to 37 per cent. It must
be remembered that two out of five Japanese regularly vote at
national elections for 'anti-business' or Marxist candidates – which is
precisely the same proportion of the voters which put a British
right-wing Conservative government into power in the 1980s with
huge absolute majorities in the parliament . . .

   Certainly change will come, and will steadily absorb some of the
most effective characteristics of Western organisation. But it will come

slowly. Boards and senior managements can still protect their individual positions. And the Bushido concepts of self-renunciation and obedience to superiors are still very strong.

Among the slowly developing conflicts, one ancient Japanese characteristic is likely to continue, and to prevail. In the days of the Samurai, each warrior strove to be his lord's *best* warrior. Each lord strove to be his Shogun's *best* lord. Today each Japanese producer naturally strives to be the world's *best* producer in that field. With such an objective, and such purposeful dedication to achieving it, many will continue to achieve it.

8   Types of director

Desperate courage makes one a majority.

ANDREW JACKSON

We two form a multitude.

OVID

Three men united against a town will bring it down.

ARAB PROVERB

Mix

The average US board is two-thirds non-executive, and three-quarters non-executive in larger corporations. A large UK company's board is one-third non-executive, with smaller companies having fewer, or no, non-executives. Industrial companies with none begin to wonder whether they should engage one or two. British building societies, in contrast, some of which handle many times larger amounts of money than industrial companies, have boards which are exclusively non-executive – and they are just beginning to wonder whether they should engage an executive director or two.

Within European countries using the two-tier system, some supervisory boards contain no executives, not even the chief executive. Some contain just the chief executive; some also contain the financial officer.

Japanese boards also defy logic (see Chapter 7). Before World War II they contained numerous non-executives; today they normally contain only a rigidly structured board hierarchy of executives. It might be tempting to argue that the success of Japanese industry results, therefore, from its control by self-perpetuating, self-protecting executive boards which operate without any effective form of internal, or external, monitoring. Such argument would miss completely the real lessons of Japanese success:

- their debt/equity ratios, commonly between 3 and 8, which can fuel a much faster growth rate than is achievable by a US or UK company working on around 1:
- their consistently lower bank rate, which makes a high debt/equity ratio a little less dangerous;
- their cooperation between industry, government and lenders, which determines which sectors will be enabled to grow, and which will be allowed to wither through the progressive withdrawal of funding;
- their goal-oriented participation through all levels of their companies;
- their methodical planning and intensive marketing.

Many of these characteristics are already helping Japanese-owned subsidiaries in the UK, Europe and the USA to develop more strongly than most of the native industry.

Boards are a response to their own environment, to the history which has described them, the forces which impel or impede them, and the cultures which encompass them. This is as true for the post-World War II Japanese board as it is for the galloping-egalitarian Swedish board. It is as true for the conservative, cautious, complacent and commonly just-too-slow-off-the-mark British board as it is for the often hyperactive American board. One of the first elements of good planning is to have a cold-blooded look at one's strengths and weaknesses, and to work out what to do about them – for example, how best to compose the board as a group which can overcome these assumed characteristics.

The board has to:

- analyse, evaluate, decide, plan, instruct, monitor, adapt, monitor . . . and so on round the cycle;
- hire and fire the top executives who implement board decisions, and who in many cases contribute to their making;

- measure resources, agree their deployment, and define the returns which they must generate;
- structure, organise, communicate, improve;
- look reality in the eye, however uncomfortable this may occasionally be.

It needs people who can contribute consistently to all or most of these processes; who can see the implications of board decisions in their effect on the business as a whole – on men, money, markets, methods, all in one.

It needs the chief executive, head of the chain of managerial control which runs unbroken from the boardroom through to the shopfloor itself. It needs the best-experienced finance director it can obtain for the money it can pay. It needs a business development director, by whatever title, who can interpret how the market might react to each decision on the agenda, and how the machinery of the company can handle each decision. It may or may not need other functional heads, dependent only on the nature of its business and how often they would actually contribute to decisions – not dependent on how well they have in the past carried out such decisions. Board membership is not a reward for good executive performance.

Beside this core of key executive directors, the board needs a number of part-time directors who do not work in the company, who do not covet anyone else's job, who are not going to play internal politics, who do not owe their careers to being on good terms with the chief executive. People who can sit alongside the employed executives, able to judge without fear or favour.

A good non-executive director needs to have intellect, integrity and courage. Of these qualities courage is the most important, for without it the other two characteristics are useless.

ANGUS MURRAY, MC, 1980

. . . personal courage . . . only a great director can find that resource and sustain it in face of indifference and sometimes scorn.

DANIEL T. CARROLL, 1981,
President and CEO, Hoover Universal Inc.

If the part-time director is to be able to meet the criterion of 'contribution' he or she almost certainly needs to have had board-room experience elsewhere. The non-executive role is very different from that of a good executive, different even from that of a good executive director. The non-executive has to know how to say what the executive director does not dare say, and that facility can only be learnt the hard way. (Which, as an aside, is why the writer prefers the description 'the uninhibited director', which is active and positive, rather than the terms non-executive, part-time, outside, independent or critical director, all of which are passive or negative. However, we'll continue to use non-executive here as it has widest currency.)

The board needs the key executives, whose whole careers depend on staying with the company long enough to make it a world beater, alongside the part-timers, who can join or leave in accordance only with the board's own requirements at any stage in the company's growth. It needs a mix of wise old men (not too old); aggressive young men; the cynical; the thoughtful; the men who feel it in their fingers. It needs those with the stomach to say what they believe is right, and to keep saying it until it is adopted or demonstrated to be wrong, or until the nuances of difference have become unimportant. And only such men.

The optimum proportion of professional or personal backgrounds and styles will change as the company changes, as its problems and opportunities vary. It should never be fixed for very long. Even setting useful guidelines on absolute size can be subject to sensible variations, though anything below five is going to be too small to contain sufficient variety of contribution, and anything above a dozen is going to contain too many non-combatants. Jung believed that group experiences take place on a lower level of consciousness than individual experiences (and that the ethical attitudes of groups are always 'doubtful'). The level of consciousness in a very large board can approach unconsciousness; there is no director in any large board who has not seen a few of his colleagues dozing off by item 3.

The guidelines on the balance between executives and non-executives are simpler; what does the board lack? For a start, every board without non-executives lacks objectivity. Non-executives must number at least two, even on the smallest boards. At times even the non-executive, if alone, can stray from objectivity, and 'desperate courage makes one a majority' can become quite exhausting. So one-third of the board is a workable minimum. If two-thirds of the board is non-executive there may not be room for the good executives, so this proportion represents a workable maximum for the largest boards. Between one-third and two-thirds thus constitutes a working range, with fewer non-executives on the smaller company boards, and more on the larger company holding boards.

It is not so much the numbers as the style. A dozen uninterested or complacent non-executives are not worth one with interest and courage. What matters when a board determines a strategy, describes an organisation, makes an investment, or selects a top executive, is that it has in one forum, around one table, sufficient width and depth of understanding, and caring, to be able to grapple competently with all the aspects of the decision concerned. It needs that the majority of those assembled can state opinions, without personal or specialist interest, which are directed wholly to the objective of corporate advantage. If this means, in any specific company, that the board must have a non-executive majority because the executives are professionally limited or personally timid, so be it. But if the chairman is democratic, the chief executive a true leader of men, and the executives all experienced and free-spoken, then a non-executive minority will suffice. This happy combination is seldom found.

The board has to breed a thoroughbred strategy, and it has to feed it and train it and whip it, and win races with it. The breeders and farriers and trainers and riders will be very different kinds of people, bound by the common objective of winning races. And bound by the understanding that they need each other, irrespective even of whether they like each other.

The chairman

I am not afraid of a knave.
I am not afraid of a rascal.
I am afraid of a strong man who is wrong, and whose wrong

thinking can be impressed upon other persons by his force of character and force of speech.

WOODROW WILSON

Democracy in its most literal sense has been common in darkest Africa since long before the Ancient Greeks invented the word. Down to the very smallest hamlet, decisions on daily matters are taken at meetings which all concerned are entitled to attend. Anyone with anything useful to say most certainly says it, and almost everyone else puts in a few words too. Meetings become very long, and would ramble about for ever without a firm hand to control them. So they have someone in charge. Everyone squats on the ground, except the man in charge. He has to be higher up, central and visible. He sits on a chair. It is often just a little three-legged stool. In parts of West Africa the Stool is a lot grander, and has become an object of veneration in itself. But the meaning is the same; the person in that chair is in charge of that meeting.

He is often the wisest, or the wiliest. Sometimes he is just the toughest. He knows his village and his tribe, and he normally has a fairly shrewd idea what is best for them. When he does not, they may starve. His role is to steer discussion, cut short the man who talks too much, and ensure that those he knows have something to say actually get a chance to say it. He summarises the discussion and delegates the actions – but he does not undertake the actions.

He has two other primary functions, one ceremonial and one strategic. In the former he gets carried about looking splendid to the public at large, and providing a focus for local unity. In the latter he leads the closed councils of the elders when matters of survival, such as war or migration, have to be decided on behalf of the clan or tribe as a whole. On these matters the elders make collective decisions. Again, he summarises these decisions and delegates the actions, but woe or remote accident betide him who rides roughshod over the elders.

The role of the chairman in business corporations has developed beyond such limitations, and has certainly extended beyond the original intentions of the Acts which establish such organisations. But the chairman is the chairman of the board. He is not chairman of the company. There is no such position as chairman of the company.

Under the articles he chairs the general meetings of members, or shareholders. The sample set of articles attached to the UK's Companies Act, known as Table A, and adopted in whole or in part by most companies, describes the role most clearly. If the chairman fails to arrive within fifteen minutes of the time appointed for the meeting to begin the directors may simply elect another chairman from among their number present. By another section in Table A, the directors elect a chairman for their own board meetings, and if he fails to arrive within *five minutes* of the time appointed they may also elect an alternative. *He has in theory no more intended permanence than that*.

The board is allowed to determine, by a specific decision, that the chairman hold that office for a defined maximum period, assuming that he normally manages to be punctual. But the board seldom does this. The convention has developed that the chairman is there for as long as he chooses. The convention has also developed that he can perform almost whatever roles he chooses. His roles in fact are:

- to preserve order, and conduct the meetings of the members or directors in a proper manner;
- to allow members in general meeting, or directors in a board meeting, to have reasonable opportunity to speak, though he himself decides when to curtail further discussion on any point;
- to ensure that decisions are fairly made, if necessary by counting hands or by poll;
- to decide on technicalities, such as the validity of proxies;
- to place a casting vote in the event of a tie;
- to adjourn the meeting if so requested, or agreed by a majority, or if the meeting becomes disorderly. But if he does this improperly, the members may elect another chairman to continue the business.

Practice has vested in chairmanship duties and powers far removed from this definition of the leadership of meetings.

It is natural, and beneficial to the maintenance of smoothly working routines in the boardroom, that the leader of the meetings should retain the chairmanship for as long as he performs the role better than others could do. It is also natural that the public company chairman, who is visible in the chair at meetings of the members, should become identified as the company's external spokesman, heading discussions with shareholders, the media, analysts and brokers. If he is as good at external PR as he is at conducting meetings, then he is clearly the best man for that role, too. But if he is not good at PR, the board should put the control of its external relations into another director's hands. It is allowed to do so.

But there the 'natural' extension of the chairman's role ceases. Any further extension must depend exclusively on whether or not the chairman could handle any other roles better than any other director.

The almost universal convention has developed that all the bucks stop at the chairman's desk. They do not in law. There is little sense that they should do so in practice. They stop at the board. The board may delegate most of the routine bucks to a chief executive, and remove him if he mishandles them. The chairman's role within the board is to ensure that the responsibilities for all the bucks are clearly defined, and equally clearly monitored. When the chairman is also the chief executive he may feel with a little more reason that he does have to handle all the bucks. One of the dangers in combining these two quite different positions is that the other directors may feel, also with reason, that they carry very little responsibility for anything. There are numerous other dangers. The role of wisely steering a diverse boardroom towards productive decisions is fundamentally different in character and content from the role of productively implementing those decisions. Yet 50 to 80 per cent of the largest British and American corporations combine the two roles; the proportion is highest in the very largest organisations, and the proportion is increasing. It can be most difficult to understand why the institutions and the individual directors allow this to happen, as it can severely inhibit their ability to influence or control. Are they *really* so careless of their responsibilities?

The chairman leads the board. The chief executive leads the management. The board holds the chief executive responsible for management's performance. It would be naïve to expect that a chairman who is also the chief executive will force his board to review the performance of management ruthlessly and fire him if that performance is not good. The man is also human. When both roles are vested in one person, no pensionable career executive director is going to challenge the quality of his bosses' work in open forum. A team of non-executives might. But it is a hundred times harder to challenge the performance of a combined chairman/chief executive than it is to request a review of the performance of two separate people. It is that much harder to demonstrate to the satisfaction of all, particularly to the combined chairman/chief executive, which part of the combined roles is being performed badly. Every reader who has tried it will know that it cannot be done. The situation should not need to arise. The directors should not let it. The directors, and they alone, elect the chairman. And they alone elect the chief executive. They are responsible. The directors should be aware that any strong man will naturally seek to enhance the extent and categories of his power; that is a characteristic of powerful men. The role of the board is to define and delimit power, and to channel it productively.

Prior to World War II, ICI was dominated by one man. The experience was so traumatic to the board that it later resolved to ensure that this could never happen again, and the board recorded a decision that would prevent any future chairman from also being the chief executive. In the 1980s, after the company had declined in comparative performance through many years, the board appointed a new chairman to help beef it up, and he was given wider, though precisely defined, powers than had been delegated to his predecessors. He became 'chairman and principal executive officer', but he was: '*categorically not chief executive, a concept which offended against ICI's carefully nurtured collectivism*'; the role of PEO was a: '*typical ICI compromise*' (Foster, 1987). In practice, because of the size and complexity of the company it was still run much in the same way it had been, but with a chairman of the board particularly well suited to the needs of the company at that time in its development.

Some of the larger US and Japanese corporations avoid the problem by substituting for the chief executive position a three-man president's office which operates as a single entity. While the original motivation in forming the grouping may have been that three heads acting in unison can manage complex situations more effectively than one alone, it has not escaped them that this also prevents autocracy, the accrued power and roles of this office not being readily re-absorbable, later, by a single dominant chairman.

In cold logic, the only environment where the combination of the roles of chairman and chief executive can make productive sense is the small, privately owned company with up to about 100 employees, where the chairman probably also types the envelopes during a crisis. Certainly once over about 100 employees – the boundary depending entirely on the nature and complexity of the businesses concerned – a separate chairman will invariably improve the objectivity of the board, and improve its control of management performance.

The board may delegate specific duties to any of the directors, including the chairman. But it has to formally define and record these, so that there is no misunderstanding. If it does not, who can chastise the chairman for doing everything, even for doing most of it badly?

His functions besides leading the board and the general meetings, could possibly be agreed to include heading and organising the following:

- external relations with shareholders and media;
- external relations with the lenders. Certainly. The banks usually have a bigger stake than any single shareholder. But the chairman would be wise always to cooperate here with the finance director who will not wish to be excluded – add the chief executive and one of the non-executives if things are tough and the bank has to be convinced that the board is sound;
- external relations with analysts and brokers. Probably. But the finance director might be better at this;
- external relations with governments and civil servants. Possibly. But if any one director has close working relations with any one ministry, delegate that one to him, not to the chairman. Irving Shapiro, chairman and chief executive of EI du Pont de Nemours, the world's largest chemical company, stated that he spent 4/5 of his time in liaison with Congress policy-makers and Washington bureaucrats and only 1/5 in managing the business. (Which suggests, as an aside, that it might have been better to have had a separate chief executive who spent 5/5 of his time managing the

business.) Japanese chairmen in larger corporations frequently spend virtually all of their time on such external relations, but are not involved in routine general management;

* external relations with industry bodies and trade associations. Just possibly. When these organisations are concerned with very broad economic policies, then the chairman can be a sensible choice, putting over the attitudes of the company, gleaning the attitudes of others, and reporting back to the board. But where these organisations are concerned with methods and mechanical questions then the chief executive, or maybe the technical director, personnel director or production director, could be a better choice. Even when those functions are not represented on the board, managers can always be co-opted individually to report to the board;

* external relations with customers and suppliers. Never, except coincidentally, or in a PR combination with another director more closely concerned;

* internal relations, such as that strange favourite of chairmen, the house magazine. Never, ever. He is not chairman of the company;

* other internal functions, such as planning. Seldom. The convention has also developed that the chairman is the head of planning, and of the definition of strategy. Not so. These are responsibilities of the board as a whole. Their complexity is one of the main reasons for needing a diverse board. The chairman may be a primary contributor, even the cleverest contributor, but he should not be in charge of defining strategy any more than he is in charge of defining tactics. Leave the coordination of these functions to the business development director. If the chairman is given control of any function which is largely performed outside the boardroom, albeit finally decided within the boardroom, he will inevitably encroach on executive territories and create confusion, tension and frustration among the executives. Employees lower down the chain will not sense any confusion; they will simply assume that he really is in charge of the lot – which he is not;

* balancing the board. Certainly, but not alone. Yet another convention has developed that the initiative for deciding when the board needs a face-lift lies exclusively with the chairman. This

leaves him, in most cases, to locate additional or replacement non-executives, and he can hardly be blamed for bringing in his own chums if no one else is making any suggestions. The captain of the team may be one of the selectors, but he is not the only selector. This may seem the rankest heresy to many a chairman, but just pause for a moment and consider the characteristics of power. The chairman was elected to the chair in the first place because, at that time at least, he was acknowledged by his colleagues as being the natural leader of the board. Power derives from position. It can be well used and increased, or it can be abused. The powerful chairman will often be satisfied with a pliant or servile board, which suits his own purposes, but which is quite useless, or is harmful, to the development of the company. He may not even recognise its destructive servility. Cognitive dissonance, or old-fashioned self-deception, is as common in the great as in the humble. Thus if any director senses that his board is inadequate, through age, complacency, incompetence, or conformity, it is his responsibility to seek to effect change through the board, without waiting for an initiative from the chairman. It may never come.

Few directors will take on such an uncomfortable task. To make it easier for them, establish six board routines:

1 All executive and non-executive candidates to be vetted by a board committee before presentation to the full board.
2 Each appointee to be given written terms of reference describing his expected contribution and time commitment.
3 Board composition and performance to have an annual spot on the agenda.
4 Each director, at least each non-executive, to be required to produce a concise report for that agenda item which describes how he sees the board's problems and needs – including how he views his own role.
5 The chairman to review the performance of each director in the boardroom with the individual concerned, and to expose a summary of his conclusions at the scheduled meeting.
6 The chairman to be elected, or re-elected, at the close of that meeting.

Some of the directors will not like this process, but anything distaste-ful becomes easier to swallow if turned into a habit. If they find they are 'busy men without time for reports and such like', then they are too busy to be of much use to the board. They are not there for the ride; they have to make the horse win races.

Mr Chairman, make your directors work, especially your non-executives. Give them reports to produce, reports to advise on, staff to evaluate, planning sessions to attend, customers to woo, ministers to hassle, diplomats to charm. Run your directors and your board, not the company. Make them speak. That is a start.

The chief executive

During the nineteenth century the boards of companies were normally composed entirely of part-time, or non-executive, directors. Detailed management and commercial questions had to be resolved by formal committees of the board, or by ad hoc decision by indi-vidual directors. This arrangement became both onerous and clumsy, and led to the concept of delegating daily management to one of the directors, who would become a full-time employee.

The articles of most companies now enable their boards to appoint one or more such managing directors, and to delegate to him or to them whatever functions the board chooses to define, for whatever period and remuneration. Being an employee under contract of employment to carry out these functions, the managing director is normally released by the articles from the requirement to retire by rotation and seek re-election to the board, which all the other directors have to do on average every three years. In law he can make decisions or enter into contracts on behalf of the company without reference to the board. He can similarly sign and seal documents together with the company secretary, who is usually his subordinate, without reference to the board, except in a very few companies which retain the older requirement that two directors must sign always.

It will therefore be clear that the board must not appoint a managing director without defining his limits of authority with considerable precision, or without describing in them the size and type of decision or contract which it requires him to bring to the board for prior agreement. The articles will normally refer to the title 'managing director' or 'president', though 'chief executive' is commonly used. The terms are not necessarily interchangeable. If the MD or the president are, by their contracts of appointment, responsible directly to the chairman, not to the board as a whole, then the chairman is in practice the chief executive – whatever it may say on their business cards.

Within the boardroom itself the chief executive is neither 'chief' nor 'executive'. He differs from the other directors by being the primary link through which instructions for action are passed, and through which results of these actions are reported. Which means he is different as a manager, not as a director. When the board judges the performance of the chief executive, and perhaps decides to remove him when that performance is consistently inadequate, it is judging his work as a manager, not as a director.

At the board meetings he may argue whatever case he feels appropriate in seeking to influence the board to make decisions which match his own judgement. That is the role of each director. If the decision, nonetheless, goes against his own judgement, he has to carry it out as best he and his troops can. That is the role of each manager. While his vote in the boardroom is just one, his arguments will always carry just a little more weight than those of other directors, and he will always receive a more patient hearing. This places a special onus on the chief executive to examine his personal desires or preferences quite clinically, to ensure they are always sharply differentiated in his mind from his judgement of what is really in the best interests of the company.

As an everyday example, the chief executive with a Brazilian wife would be wise to ask one of his executive colleagues to present the paper about the proposed acquisition in Brazil, even if that colleague is known to be luke-warm to the proposal. Similarly when the board of a manufacturing company is debating whether or not to diversify into distribution, and the chief executive has spent most of his working life in distribution. Everyone has preferences or prejudices which cloud judgement. In a strong chief executive such preferences can become dangerous because of his strength. (And it can be good negotiating tactics, and induce a more sympathetic hearing, if he appears ready to step down a notch and debate from the side, not from the 'top'.)

The chief executive may not be, and need not be, the cleverest or the most experienced of all the directors. He must, however, be the best leader of men, the best user of men, and a quick and sure judge of the judgements of his key subordinates.

The larger the company, the more easily it is seen that the primary role of the chief executive is selecting, positioning, judging, enthusing and using the best men available to him. While he needs to be numerate, and will drown in a welter of tabulations if he is not, he does not need to be a financial expert. But he needs to ensure that he employs a finance director who is. He must understand the realities of the market-place, but need not himself be an entrepreneurial innovator. He can employ other executives who are, and can give them free rein under a watchful eye.

And so with the other functions, or areas of expertise, which are important within his particular company. Each of the executive directors should be capable of sensible consideration for the role of chief executive; their specific backgrounds matter little. What matters is that the chief executive can extract from men that little bit more than they believe to be their maximum. His ability to control and influence his subordinates is closely related to his visible ability to be influenced by them in turn. He differs markedly from the chairman, who deals primarily with men of like standing, in that his daily contacts can be with sweepers, machine operators, sales managers and personnel directors. His facility for manipulating men is seen, becomes common knowledge, and usually determines the quality of his reputation within the company. Happy is the chief executive who has discovered that he gains, rather than loses, stature each time he tells a subordinate in the presence of others that the subordinate's idea is better than his own; successful is the chief executive who leads his subordinates round to believing that they thought of it in the first place, because then they will do it better for him.

The good user of men places himself below others.

LAOTSE

The chief executive who is slow to 'give away' some of his apparent authority is usually poor at appointing men who are good enough to assume some of that authority. He ends up by insisting he has to do everything himself, in an ever-tightening circle in which he is both the centre and the circumference. Indeed like that mythical bird.

The chief executive who begins without the slightest intention of spreading controlled authority will drive away good people, and thus weaken the machine on which the quality of his own performance depends.

The chief executive's best friend outside the boardroom can be the non-executive who can detect the effect the chief executive is having on his team, and can provide a diplomatic suggestion or two.

You can distinguish the chief executive who will succeed from the one who may drive you into trouble by determining whether he would rather have a heart-to-heart chat with a good independent non-executive, or go to the dentist.

Other executives

Within the single-tier board all directors are intended to operate as equals, without 'executive', 'non-executive' or other categories of differentiation. In the European two-tier system, directors in any one tier, either the 'upper' supervisory board or the management board, are also intended to operate equally, though limitations are sometimes imposed on worker or union directors in the supervisory board. The unitary board is free to choose whether and which employees additional to the chief executive would be useful within the boardroom, and can appoint them as directors, subject only to ratification in general meeting, which is normally readily given. Within the two-tier system, the supervisory board has similar freedom to appoint executive members to the management board.

Once within the boardroom, such employees are released from the daily hierarchy, and no stigma must attach to the executive director who disagrees openly with his line boss at the board table, assuming naturally that what he says is sensibly and soberly expressed.

There are few limitations regarding who may become a director, the law disqualifying only:

- undischarged bankrupts, unless authorised specifically by the court (they cannot be managers either);
- persons specifically prohibited by the court for a defined period, because of conviction for a variety of company or criminal offences;
- – in the UK also persons disqualified (for a minimum of two years) by the court as 'unfit', under the Insolvency Act, because of their performance in an insolvent company;
- the auditor of the Group or of any of its subsidiaries – he also may not be an employee;
- a clergyman;
- a person over 70 years old (unless in an independent private company, or public company, whose articles expressly provide that he can; or unless the general meeting of members agrees that he can);
- the company secretary from being the sole director of a private company.

The articles of association may disqualify whatever categories the shareholders wish to exclude, and may also restrict membership of the board as narrowly as shareholders choose. Once the articles are adopted it requires a large majority to alter them, so a company would be wise to leave its catchment as wide as possible and disqualify in the articles only persons of unsound mind, which, oddly, is a condition not specifically recorded in some Companies legislation. The writer would also personally prefer to restrict age to 65, to avoid the sad spectacle of once respected ex-captains of industry damaging their records by feeble or disinterested non-executive directorship. However, it is clear that there are active and very valuable exceptions.

The commonly required share qualification, which can usually be satisfied by the transfer of a single share, may seem more trouble than it is worth. But it can prove helpful to the director himself to have formal member status, for example if he later concludes that he should stimulate the shareholders to take a court action against the board. Law regarding who may take action against the board, for what, is involved and evolving. On balance, the share qualification is worth keeping because it provides shareholder's rights. Whether directors should hold *more* than the minimum share qualification is a moot point. As a personal opinion, the writer believes that non-executives should not, in order to preserve their comprehensive independence. But then he doesn't believe in share options for executives, either, because the short-term objective of raising the share price has now been given topmost priority over medium- and long-term corporate strength. From the evidence of the record, one does *not* necessarily follow the other.

Given that the company should keep the predetermined qualifications and disqualifications for board membership as few as possible, the board should consider appointing only those executives whose contribution can be expected to cover a wide range of boardroom topics, not just subjects within an executive's own specialist field. If the board concludes that a key executive is unlikely to be able to contribute freely on most agenda items, but that his specialist knowledge is needed from time to time in the boardroom, he can be co-opted ad hoc.

There are several categories of executives whose contribution is most likely to be needed frequently, and thus who are the more obvious contenders for a directorship.

The company secretary

His situation can be a little awkward when he is not a director. The law recognises him as an officer of the company; he attends all the board meetings, and drafts the minutes for the chairman. Some argue that his daily functions are so detailed and specific that in practical terms they exclude him from an active role in the broader strategic deliberations which characterise the agenda; others that, as he sits there all the time, and is privy, if not party, to every nuance, he might as well be a director. He is very much the keeper of the board's conscience, as well as being the keeper of its records, and he is the prime internal source of legal information affecting board decisions. Sometimes the question is solved by combining the roles of finance director and company secretary, though the functions of the two are quite different in character. Decision on this question, as indeed on the question of any appointment to the board, should be made on the principle that a man's personal qualities and personality are much more important than his specific background. If still in doubt, he is better in than out. One of the most effective directors whom the writer has met, with the knack of always putting his finger on the critical factor in any complex case, happened to be a company secretary. This knack would have been of equal value to the board if the man's daily role had been quite different.

The finance director

The board needs within it a well-trained and widely experienced accountant who is up to date in all the intricate details which fall under the finance function; a few large corporations still don't have one. Many of the other directors are ignorant of these intricacies, and often a little frightened of them. While it can be possible to obtain this type of expertise in the form of a specialist non-executive, it can only be of practical value to the board if it is being applied daily in all the corners of the company, thus ensuring that contribution in the boardroom combines theory with detailed knowledge of the actual situation of the businesses encompassed. Chapter 11 shows that the absence, or inadequacy, of board-level representation of the finance function is one of the characteristics of companies which collapse.

The business development director

He is called by a variety of titles, including marketing, planning or sales director, depending mainly on which part of the total function seems most important in the company concerned. Terminology has become confused. The word 'marketing' today has as many different definitions as the word 'socialism'. Sometimes the head of sales reports to the head of marketing. Sometimes vice-versa. Sometimes a board separates the roles, and contains several bodies individually representing sales, marketing and planning. The roles are, however, completely interrelated. It is most effective to arrange that the heads of each role report to a single business development director, who controls the total function. The roles have the common factor that they are all most directly concerned with the realities of the market-place, even planning. A plan has no reality unless it is directed at using the characteristics of the markets to achieve defined objectives; unless it is composed in relation to the competition in those markets. 'Sales' is in the middle of the markets; marketing and planning are one step removed, mapping out how and where sales should be hunting, and weighing alternative returns.

All the strategic, investment and organisational thinking carried out by a board must, if it is to have any value to the company, be directed to the task of making a defined number of sales, at defined prices, to a defined clientele, against a defined competition, at defined costs and to a defined time-scale. The board which is without an executive director experienced in these roles will therefore be depriving itself of the expertise on which the company's survival entirely depends. Only the holding boards of the largest Groups, which operate in practice through comprehensive divisional boards, might sensibly feel that they do not need to include this function within their boardrooms.

The personnel director

The great increase in the appointment of personnel directors to British boardrooms in the 1970s was the result of a welter of new employee-related legislation during that decade, coupled with the ever-present threat of industrial unrest. Subsequent high unemployment has cut down the unrest – but apart from such negative reasons, the person-nel director could be considered as providing useful counter-balance where the chief executive is by nature insensitive to people.

The production director, or related technical functions

While boards of engineering companies are heavy with engineers, they often omit the heads of the engineering functions themselves. The Japanese centre performance on product and productivity, and we can learn from that.

The criteria for appointing these, or any other, director to any level of board are whether they will add to the skill or style of the boardroom, and whether they will, professionally and personally, improve the company's performance by helping to improve the board's decision-making.

The criteria of the law regarding the performance of all directors are in addition that:

- they must act in 'good faith' in the interests of the company. This involves a duty to act honestly as well as with 'due diligence'. Diligence includes assiduity as well as 'skill and care'. Skill and care, in turn, require levels of performance which can be expected of a 'reasonable director' with his particular knowledge or experience;
- they must act with 'proper purpose' in ensuring that what they are doing is relevant to the company's business, and is bona fide in the interests of the company, and not for any collateral purpose.

Standards of 'skill and care' were low in the nineteenth century, when directors were non-executive and were apparently not expected to know much about business. Court precedents in the USA, and the UK's Insolvency Act 1985, have stiffened these standards to the point at which even battle-hardened non-executive veterans in the USA, and potential company doctors in the UK, now often hesitate to join the board of a company which is known, or suspected, to be in difficulty. It can certainly be concluded that, in the event of action against directors for specific failures to perform, rather than for generalised mismanagement, the standards of skill expected from a research director, FIEEE, or a production director, FIProdE, in matters related to their specialised fields of expertise could be set high.

Which is something boards should keep in mind when measuring executives for directorships.

Associates and alternates

The extent of a director's present liabilities, and the certainty that these will become more apparent with time, bring into question the wisdom of the concepts of the associate and alternate director. Both categories can be created by the articles.

The associate director, sometimes called assistant, regional or special director, or a similarly qualified title, is not a member of the board. He has been given the title of 'director' to enhance his internal or external status. The danger can arise that external third parties believe, and are entitled to believe, that such a person really is a board director, and is therefore empowered to undertake commitments which are not in fact within his defined responsibilities. He could also be viewed as a *de facto* director in the eyes of the law; someone not appointed to the board but 'occupying the position of director', and thus bearing all the responsibilities, and liabilities, of a properly appointed member of the board. The device of giving a faithful servant who is close to retirement, or who is not quite suited to board membership, an associate directorship could be more safely replaced by some tangible, and less risky, form of thanks.

The alternate director is appointed by an existing director to represent him during periods of absence. For the length of such periods the alternate is a *de jure* director, with full directorial responsibilities. The device is most commonly used when one director's absence from a particular meeting, for whatever reason, may swing a crucial vote, or when that director is permanently overseas, or travels so often that he cannot attend most board meetings. If the debate he will miss is so critical, he can always find a suitable 'proxy', or can tell the chairman in advance how he would place his particular vote. Few boards will discount his opinion on a technicality if he troubles to make it clear in advance. If he is so frequently overseas, or is permanently based in Australia – and there are examples of the latter case in major corporations – the board almost certainly does not need him at all. Or else it needs someone like him who can perform the particular role properly and fully.

The responsibilities of directorship are not to be switched on and off like a ceiling fan.

The old retainer

Employees below board level are normally required by their terms of employment and the interlinked company pension scheme to cease working at somewhere between 60 and 65 years – in Japan at 55. Pressures to streamline overheads through early retirements are relentlessly pushing down the average. But board directors, like judges, can go on for ever, if the articles are so kindly couched; the same is true in Japan. Very old directors are therefore still common in the USA, UK and Japan.

One might have expected American boards to contain a smaller proportion of retired men. They are much readier than the British to fire an inadequate executive, and one could have concluded that they would also be more ready to prune away branches which have done their fruiting. The anomaly is easily explained. Executives are appointed to perform. Non-executives, often, are not. They may be appointed by a dominant chairman/CEO precisely because they will not. Naturally there are some older men who remain more fruitful and energetic than some of their younger colleagues. But it would be over-polite to suggest that they are common.

If the old retainer still has some wisdom or specific knowledge to contribute after the close of his executive career, better to use him ad hoc, or as a consultant – a common practice in Japan. The American Can Corporation today keeps *all* directors who have reached mandatory retirement age on an annual retainer of US$15,000 for life, on top of all their pensions, on the condition that they 'remain available for consultation'. That may be overdoing it, but in the consulting role these men can certainly be bolder and blunter, without any need to preserve the niceties of the old hierarchy. A retired executive is seldom truly independent as a non-executive. He can seldom freely interface with his successor, or with his former line boss. Do not keep him in a seat which another could fill more actively more often, just because he occasionally has something useful to say, or because you know his pension alone is not enough to maintain his life-style. Similarly, do not take onto the board a near-retirement executive from an acquisition you are making, either because you feel rather sorry for him, or because he'll be a grateful and obedient make-weight. Chances are that you might be making the acquisition of his Group, or of some remnant of it, because the executives of that organisation had not performed very well. Most of all, do not agree to the appointment of some aged ex-captain of industry because his still-remembered name will decorate the letterhead, or because having him aboard a much smaller organisation than his previous empire will bolster the chairman's ego. His wisdom and his acuity may still be intact, as the chat over drinks after the board meeting may disclose, but he will seldom have the stomach for the in-meeting toughness and blunt honesty which so many boards require.

> *Dismiss the old horse in good time, lest he fail in the lists and the spectators laugh.*
>
> HORACE

You know you cannot decently shout at him when he nods off.

The family

A heavy proportion of family representation on the board and in the management is natural with an embryonic or still young organisation, where directorship goes together with shareholding and the first stages of capital risk. But when the company reaches a size of about 100 employees – or higher or lower, depending on the nature and complexity of the business – it begins to need a good measure of professional management expertise and experienced business judgement sitting alongside the entrepreneurial flair of its original driving force, which is usually just one person, and rarely more than two in tandem.

Close relatives may or may not have the expertise and judgement. Statistically speaking, they are unlikely to be the best-equipped people available to fit into slots on the board. Continuity and the thickness of blood may add something to commitment, but it is a lot harder to fire cousin Charles if he is incompetent.

The maintenance of control by one family is, surprisingly, also seen in some large, publicly quoted enterprises which have the ability to choose their chairman, chief executive or other directors from the whole international pool of talent in commerce and industry. By the time that a company has 'gone public' and reached such size, the statistical probability that the younger members of the family are the best available people for these positions is clearly very small. True, they just may be, and with such large public corporations there are also large public shareholders who have enough weight to initiate change if performance is poor. At least if they trouble to. But such shareholders seldom (and to the writer's immediate recollection, never), query why corporations which have long been listed on the Stock Exchange still have as their chairman or chief executive a descendant of the founding family, which today holds only a tiny fraction of the shares. Nor do the directors. While it could be a little embarrassing for them to raise such a question with their colleagues, their embarrassment could be all the greater if the company settles into mediocrity, or worse. It happens. One listed company led in this manner received an approach regarding a take-over from what the rather smug scion of the founding stock called '*a cheeky upstart outfit with no credibility*'. The upstart quietly withdrew and bided its time. The listed company, already stagnant, began to run into all sorts of problems; within two or three years it had become just another of the many subsidiaries within the upstart outfit. (See Appendix I, UK, re incidence of family directors in large companies.)

With the majority of private companies, where the main shareholders are within the boardroom, any external pressure for improvement in performance, which so commonly equates with pressure for improvement in the board's composition, must come from the lenders. Their 'pressure', however, is normally confined to a comment or two to the chairman, passingly made and seldom pursued. The standpoint of most of those lenders which concentrate on supporting smaller companies has been confirmed to be that: 'we provide advice, and if the shareholders don't take it and go bust, that is their prerogative. It's their money'. But it is not, and it is not, respectively.

It is not the prerogative of shareholder directors or family directors to let the company steadily decline through prolonged indifference, or through the incompetence of cousin Charles or grandson George, or through the now legally outdated belief that if you own most of the shares in a company you can do with it what you will. You cannot. On top of which, the lenders, creditors and taxmen have a larger stake risked than any of the shareholders. It would greatly help performance in the small company sector if the lending bankers made a routine of repeating this to the shareholding board of the family-oriented company, which on the one hand enjoys limited liability on its investment, and on the other hand employs real people.

The maverick

In Texas in the middle of the nineteenth century a certain Samuel A. Maverick was found to be accidentally in the possession of a number of unbranded cattle. The term 'maverick' came to be used in the cattle districts for any calf or yearling without an owner's brand. And in time it came into general usage as a description for someone who has no master, or who behaves as though he has none.

In the USA the maverick may be viewed with caution, but also with a measure of respect. In a land where rugged individualism is believed to create strength and wealth from nothing at all, the man who vigorously differs is something of a folk hero. Assuming, of course, that he is also a performer, not just an eccentric. The American grows up in an environment where it is normal to form rapidly a large number of loose attachments, to join a large number of social or commercial groupings, and to dissolve such allegiances equally rapidly, without any stigma attaching to his doing so.

The UK environment is quite different. Team spirit is the cornerstone of cooperation, which is largely geared to cooperating with those who play in the same kind of team, or at least to the same rules. The British form fewer attachments, more slowly and more deeply. They join fewer groupings, and consider membership a bond. Within such groupings the maverick has little room for manoeuvre, if indeed he ever gets in.

The American executive who falls out with his company, with either his line boss or his board as a whole, will readily find alternative employment if he can show that personality or policy were the genuine reasons for his departure, rather than any failure in his own professional performance.

In the UK, such a man is 'dead'. This characteristic flaw in UK corporate judgement has been confirmed by psychologists and recruitment specialists who work on both sides of the Atlantic. Quite apart from the damage which it may have on potentially useful men, it can also harm the company in two ways. First, it can deny to the company or its board the very style of input which it most needs to avoid seizing up. It institutionalises similarity and conformity, and it minimises innovation and change. Secondly, it means that the thousands of *in situ* executives who recognise this corporate characteristic will strenuously avoid any behaviour which smacks of the maverick, irrespective of whether or not their own wits tell them that the moment is ripe for a measure of expressed dissent or purposeful abrasion. They will let the fertile moment pass, and the corporation will not benefit, or learn, or change. It will freeze into conformity, which outwardly is the twin of complacency. In the absence of an element of irreverence, all groupings, including the board, will sink into passive submissiveness.

The maverick does not conform. He is idealistic, as well as individualistic. He is confident, which adds to the discomfort he can cause in environments which are inherently fearful, and which will become more fearful as the external environment becomes more demanding. He is loyal to the objectives of the corporation, but is insubordinate, aggressive and impatient when it takes its eyes off those objectives.

He can be a bit of a corporate pain. Pain stimulates.

The court jester

The role of the court jester, or Fool, has been traced in England to well before the conquest of 1066. He was chosen for his quick intelligence and acute perception of human characteristics, and was licensed to speak to or about his superiors with a unique freedom. This freedom was not absolute, and the risk he could still run in playing his role led him often to use riddles rather than cutting comment.

The role was not solely negative, or simply to make fun of the foibles of established pomposity. He was to act as an uninhibited sounding board for his king, who was otherwise surrounded by subordinates and sycophants. He clothed himself in a coat of 'motley', composed of patches of past garments. His weapon, apart from his wit, was the 'bauble', a stick with an inflated balloon-like bladder at one end. With this he would strike his victim of the moment. But without hurting. Sometimes he overplayed his hand and suffered dismissal or the stocks. Seldom worse, because his activities were accepted by all as being of positive intent.

Charles I was the last British monarch to have a court jester. But instead of a wise Fool, he engaged Muckle John, a simpleton, thus downgrading and effectively eliminating the role in England. We all know what happened to Charles I.

The same downgrading of the role of the Fool had occurred in the period when the power of republican Rome gave way to the weakness and degeneration of imperial Rome. Progressively the canny adviser gave way to the imbecile, and his whole purpose was perverted. In France also, from the fifteenth to the early seventeenth century, the role of the Fool became wholly negative. Societies of Fools were made up from groups of priests who satirised their leading contemporaries by dressing up in learned gowns at the annual Festival of Fools, and then derobing to expose the motley beneath. There was an annual secular equivalent which centred on having a good laugh at the affairs of the appointed Lord of Misrule. Rather like the board having a collective chuckle at the developing idiosyncrasies of the chairman or chief executive, without doing anything positively helpful about them.

Any person in a position of eminence will develop idiosyncrasies. They come with eminence, and are exaggerated by it. Which is why mediaeval kings and Roman emperors did what the Fool indicated to keep them in check.

The Fool was naturally a godsend to the writers of his day. Shakespeare used him three times to memorable effect. Feste in *Twelfth Night* simply highlighted the follies of men. Touchstone in *As You Like It* satirised the behaviour patterns of society. But in *King Lear* the Fool moves steadily downwards through the play from the role of desperately helpful adviser to but a painful chorus of the king's deepening personal tragedy. *King Lear* was written in 1606 when there was a mood of general despondency throughout England. Elizabeth I had died in 1603. Public finance had fallen rapidly into chaos after her death. A flush of indiscriminate knighthoods and related preferences had been carelessly granted by the new king. The

Gunpowder Plot of 1605 had failed to blow up all the decision-makers. Since 1604 the country had been in the grip of a general depression.

A disquieting but familiar scenario, in which the Fool moves from the simplicity of truth and common sense to ultimate despair. He had tried to help his king by advising what could be done more wisely. His king did not want advice, lost his daughters and his sanity. And his Fool. Perhaps Shakespeare also intended that there should be a moral in all this.

Non-executives

There are experienced men who believe that the non-executive director (or 'part-time' or 'outside' director) is quite useless. There are others who believe, equally strongly, that a wider or more active use of non-executives is the single most important change which boards in commerce or industry can make to improve the overall standards of performance of their companies. Both beliefs can be supported by real-life examples. The non-executive has often been proved to have been unable to prevent corporate collapse. Companies large and small, publicly visible or hidden away, have fumbled along for years, or else died noisily, while carrying boards resplendent with some of the most prominent names in the corporate world as their non-executives. Their stories are being repeated in other boardrooms, right now.

The non-executive can also prove harmful. When fundamentally ignorant of the detailed situation of the company on whose board he sits, he can do little more than judge superficially on any question of critical conflict, and then place his vote on the criterion of where the centre of gravity appears to lie. Or on some more honourable criterion which may be equally wrong.

It is not that the concept of non-executive directorship is faulty. Or even that the individual quality of the people who play the role is open to doubt. It usually is not. The inadequate performance of non-executives results from one or more of the following reasons:

- the selection of the people most suitable to specific boards at specific stages in their development is misjudged, the process of recruitment used being less rigorous than that applied to the engagement of a clerk – selection is suited to the purpose of the dominant director;
- criteria for contribution are not established in advance of appointment, and contribution itself is not monitored thereafter;
- the number, and particularly the variety, of non-executives on the board are insufficient; but primarily because
- very, very few non-executives have spared, or even been able to spare, enough time to their non-executive roles to get to know their companies well enough to be able to contribute anything of the remotest value to the companies' prosperity.

The American and British non-executive today provides on average just over one day per month to his company. It has been known for many years that this rate of contribution is far too low. The British Institute of Management, among many others, has reported that:

> *A non-executive director rarely gave more than two days a month to his company and half the companies with non-executive directors expected them to give only one day or less. Given that it will probably be at least a year, and probably two, before a non-executive director has a sufficient grasp of his company's affairs to make a real contribution, and that even then he will only see board papers, attend on average monthly meetings and make occasional visits to the company's establishments, his influence must necessarily be limited.*
>
> BRITISH INSTITUTE OF MANAGEMENT, 1972

It has been separately confirmed by practising non-executives that, at this rate of contribution, it does indeed take well over a year to be able to add anything useful to a boardroom's deliberations. When we take into account that the appointment of the non-executive is made against an observed need in the boardroom, often quite urgent, it is proper to ask:

From what other adviser, consultant or profession would the board, or its management, accept, and pay for, such a long period of non-contribution?

Within larger companies the managers are accustomed to sitting alongside non-executive co-directors, and are well aware that most of these are in no position to be able to query or threaten entrenched positions.

Within the predominantly or exclusively executive boards of small or medium-sized companies, which have the greatest need for active non-executive contribution, there is commonly great resistance to the appointment of non-executives. Not always – the high-flyers with their eye on the top of the ladder will sometimes welcome such colleagues as an aid to their own exposure. But, coupled with an element of concern about the probing of executive performance which the non-executive is supposed to introduce, there is the strikingly widespread belief that, on the hard evidence, the non-executive is not able to 'add anything'.

The only valid reason for introducing non-executives to a board is that they can 'add' by doing what the executives cannot, or can add to what the executives alone can only partly achieve. This includes:

- providing objective evaluation of the businesses of the company;
- providing unprejudiced evaluation of the real performance of the chief executive and other key managers, both within the board and down-line. This can be the most important role where the chief executive dominates his colleagues for either the right or the wrong reasons, and is a role which no executive director can be expected to carry out with 'true' judgement;
- providing independent opinion on questions of strategy, investment, divestment, structure, internal relationships, limits of authority, budgets . . . these opinions being uninhibited by considerations of career, status or personal empire, and thus often likely to differ greatly from prevailing executive opinions;
- providing experience of the external environment – markets, methods, competitive practices, governments – which can pro-

vide either new knowledge or a new standpoint from which to view the same knowledge;

- providing, especially to the small or medium-sized company, new expertise in professional or management techniques, in technical or financial disciplines, or in the evaluation of business performance or business alternatives;
- providing a pool from which the chairman or his successor can be appointed, and providing when necessary a check on the chairman himself. They recognise when the emperor has no clothes, and can tell him. It helps no one if he catches pneumonia, and the executives will certainly not comment.

They can also be used by the board in:

- providing additional or better links with external organisations, as well as internally; creating confidence among investors and lenders; carrying out whatever monitoring or support exercises the board may choose to delegate to them.

Even in the very largest organisations, where the team of top executives may well know as much about the external environment as the company can need to know, and where they can provide all the necessary expertise, professionalism, and clear-headed analyses, there will still be a great deal of executive in-fighting which needs independent refereeing. There will also be a marked short-fall of independent objectivity among the full-timers.

Harry Roff, who founded and led MSL, the world's largest executive recruitment company, has stated that *'less than one in four executive directors have this capacity for critical objectivity – largely because of the pressure and influences of their executive duties'*. The extent of these pressures and influences was measured some years ago in a Swedish study, which demonstrated that the maximum time that an executive is left on his own during a normal business day is 14 minutes. The maximum time without interruption was found to be 9 minutes. Which illustrates neatly the natural difficulty faced by an executive in switching from the exercise of his practical daily role to the cerebral objectivity of the boardroom, and back again.

It also forces the question of how many full-time executives can sensibly be considered as potential non-executives for other company boards. How many can make the switch? How many (of those whose companies will release them) can release themselves? The full-time executive who is able to spare the time from his daily role; who is allowed to spare that time, without spasmodic hindrance by his employing company; who is already well experienced in working at board level, and who is freely able, by competence and character, to impart of this experience to another company in another environment, can be a valuable non-executive. But if he 'is not' any one of the above, then he would serve all parties best, including himself, by confining himself to his executive role.

The pool of full-time executives is the most obvious source of potential non-executives. There are other pools, both existing and developing, which will be considered in the following sections. The board which is searching for non-executives should dip into all the pools. It should balance its mix of non-executives as carefully as it balances the total number of outsiders against the total of in-house executive directors.

With board size ranging from five to twelve, and with the proportion of outsiders ranging from one-third to two-thirds, then boards are looking for between two and eight non-executives apiece. Consider a hypothetical, middle-of-the-range board of a medium-sized company, with a total of eight directors, half non-executive, and with the four in-house directors including the chief executive, the finance director, the business development director and the engineering director. It has a non-executive chairman, who used to be a chief executive in another company, and who is now chairman or non-executive in a handful of separate companies. It has three other non-executives.

There is not much point if all three are full-time executives elsewhere, with similar backgrounds to the chairman, and to the company's own chief executive. Five similar backgrounds, plus three executives, does not bring in the variety, or create the productive mix, which was considered in the book's early chapters. Having, say, four working chief executives on one board can be counter-productive. Their daily work is giving orders and taking specific and individual decisions, neither of which they can do in the boardroom. They either bring their power drive with them, in which case the boardroom becomes a shambles, or, *more frequently*, they sit quieter than all the others, being 'out of context'.

Appointing a Chief Executive from outside as a non-executive can bring problems into the boardroom, particularly if it is a new experience for that individual.

G.H.G. HARRIS,
CANNY BOWEN & ASSOCIATES

If this were not the prevailing situation, then there would be a lot less complaint about board performance in the USA, where corporations trawl deeply in the pool of full-time executives and chief executives to obtain their non-executives. Unfortunately the UK continues to follow blindly that unthinking example.

In the hypothetical board which has been considered, two of the outsiders might usefully be full-time executives in other companies, from two separate disciplines – for example a finance director and a marketing director. They should be directors elsewhere, not just executives. Directorship is far removed from managing. The other two should be quite different. Compounding a fertile mix of non-executives is just as important as balancing the team of in-house managers who are selected for the board. They can be chosen from the catchments of consultants, academics and professional directors, which are the widest and deepest of all catchments in the variety of backgrounds, styles and skills which they can provide. But these two, also, must have demonstrated successful board-level experience.

Directorship is work for teachers, not for trainees.

Not . . .

The dos and don'ts for composing the non-executive team apply as well, and with as many sound exceptions, to all levels of board, except the holding boards of the very largest corporations. These differ by being remote from detailed company management, which they leave to their divisional boards. How they compose themselves may reasonably vary from these guidelines. How their divisional boards compose themselves may not.

The board may sensibly consider whom it will as a potential non-executive director, but:

Not the company's banker or merchant banker, per se. If there is one on the board who bubbles over the brim with good ideas about the new venture in Venezuela, or even about the management succession in Manchester, and who by nature defers to no one, terrific. But if he is there because the board needs advice on funding, or seeks goodwill in the City, then the company would benefit by engaging a more skilful finance director instead. Any ad hoc requirement for very special forms of financial expertise can be hired by the day. The proportion of US boards with such non-executives is steadily decreasing.

Not lawyers who provide services to the company, or brokers. The proportion of US boards with this category of non-executive is also decreasing. Question is, are they also business strategists, or management experts?

Not representatives of connected businesses, such as suppliers, customers, distributors. The board cannot sensibly open to them its management accounts, competitive trading problems and price build-ups, let alone its deeper long-term thinking, which may involve dropping those suppliers or distributors.

Not retired executives from the company, or from other companies, unless they retired young in order to play this kind of role.

Not retired civil servants or diplomats, unless they have spent some part of their careers at senior levels in commerce and industry and really understand what it is all about. Their experience of chairing or sitting on committees bears no relationship to chairing or sitting on a company board. They are not going to start learning new tricks at 65. The board which appoints them for the assumed asset of the contacts they made during their careers seldom uses, or needs, those very specific contacts (and they may also have retired by now).

Not retired generals and admirals. If they are still close to the men who purchase the company's missiles and electronic systems, it can engage them ad hoc, also. On commission perhaps. Either they are going commercial wholeheartedly, or they are not, but do not put them on a board where only one item in ten could have their remotest interest.

Not politicians, unless they too have business experience and are there as businessmen. If you believe you need a politician on the board in order to get a good hearing in a relevant government department then you really have problems. The question is, again, are they also business strategists or management experts? Many make-weight politicians or ex-politicians, without significant relevant experience or understanding, are only on a board to further the chairman's own political ambitions, or his breathless chase for a spot in the Honours List. Others, like the excellent ex-minister with forty-seven separate directorships in the UK today, are carrying their continued service to their country beyond laudable limits.

Not people with a 'name', just for the name. The London *Times* newspaper recently carried an advertisement seeking 'a Titled Person' with 'membership of a good club' for a board directorship. A few days later the same columns carried an ad placed by 'a nobleman of eminent international family' who was seeking just such a position . . . they deserved each other. If the non-executive is there just to decorate the letterhead or dignify the lunch table, forget it. No one who matters is taken in by this any more.

Not a woman just because she is female; or a coloured man just because he is coloured; or a local councillor on the assumption that he has some useful local knowledge, or can given the company an acceptable face in the local community.

Not any other of the curious appointments which some American companies are making to their boards in the belief that this enables

them to take into account the special interests which these
appointments represent. One of the large American banks has had a
succession of 'student' directors. They must have some hilarious
discussions. The board is charged with preserving the interests of the
company as an entity, not the interests of minorities within the
community, or even of the community at large. There are plenty of
other laws which look after such interests.

Not anyone who cannot devote to the company an absolute minimum
average of two days per month, or who cannot increase this significantly in some months when there is a crisis.

Not anyone who holds more than five or six other directorships,
though loosening the limitation a little for the senior executive of
another Group who sits on the boards of a number of its subsidiaries
as a normal part of his executive job. The arithmetic is simple enough.
Allowing for holidays, weekends, administration, personal administration and the odd bout of flu, most people can only work
productively for about 200 days in a year, executives included. If a
director is devoting a minimum of two days per month, or twenty-
four days per annum, to each directorship, then seven of these will
consume 168 days. The incidence of board meetings, committee
meetings and planning sessions will always be such that the logistics
prevent him from working productively without breaks in his programme. He has less than three days per month for unavoidable gaps;
just about enough for those sudden crises. Throw in weekends, forget
about holidays, never mind the family, and still the most he could
add is a sortie or two to the Middle East, where they work Sundays.
The non-executive cannot do much useful work when there's no one
else around. The law in France and Germany limits the number of
supervisory board directorships one person can hold to eight and ten,
respectively, and there are proposals that the numbers should be
further reduced. In America and Britain there are thousands of
directors with dozens of directorships apiece who must worry from
time to time that some of their companies might ask to see them
again.

Not the acquiescent status symbol. In the words of Bruce Henderson (1980), Chairman of Boston Consulting Group, one of the cleverest of the consulting houses: '*Most chief executives want little from board members except public support, private philosophy, and no arguments and no initiatives. For these reasons their normal preference is for high status friends with high visibility and high responsibility which precludes much time spent or much interest in board membership or responsibility*'.

Not ever the acquiescent chum who has not been vetted by a committee of the board to discover his potential contribution, who is clearly there to keep the chairman or chief executive more comfortably *in situ*, and who demonstrates few relevant qualities other than dogged loyalty to his sponsor, and a friendly mien. Let the puppets hang in the strings already attached.

But maybe . . .
Maybe the technical specialist, but only if the company is so fundamentally technology-based that most items on the agenda need his presence; only if he and the technical director can keep from each other's throats; and only if it really is not possible to hire him as a technical consultant instead.

Maybe a major shareholder or his nominee. The shareholding director, or nominee, has to keep at the front of his mind, always, that he is there to look after the interests of the company, not just those of himself or of his nominator. Even when it comes to voting on dividends. The majority can always vote him down, at least in a public company where that director represents a minority, and has just one vote, anyway. Not so easy in a private company, where a large minority shareholder may come from another family, or from a feuding wing of the same family, and may introduce stresses into the boardroom which have nothing whatever to do with the business in hand. Worse where the shareholder director controls a majority of the shares, and consistently forgets that voting in the boardroom is by number of hands, not by number of shares. Worst of all where the dominant shareholder director controls only a minority, but where there is no counter-balancing minority, so that he can in practice run the show as though it was all his own. This occurs quite frequently in companies converted to 'public' status within the preceding decade or two, where the media, and almost everyone else, continue to call it 'his' company.

Given these common disadvantages, there is still much value to be gained by an institutional shareholder requesting a board to appoint its nominee when the institution concludes that the board concerned is weak, or too in-bred. Company performance would be greatly improved if major institutions would only bother to do this more often – if they would just take that little bit more interest. The effort demanded from the institution is minimal. It has only to select the kind of man who would be most helpful to the board concerned. After his appointment the man is 'the company's man', not in any way 'the institution's man'. He is on the board to help the company, and thus the shareholders in total. If the institution has its own 'pool' of potential candidates, it can offer the board two or three alternatives from which to make its selection. If the institution does not have such a pool, it can ask the board to advertise. It can trigger action.

Maybe the nominee of the main lender – particularly in a small or private company, which should be maintaining a close relationship with its bankers. The bank can suggest two or three names from its pool, or ask that the board advertise, or point the board in the direction of those organisations which assist in the recruitment of non-executives. Again, very little effort is demanded of the lender, beyond an active interest. Within the European two-tier system, the 'upper' supervisory board frequently carries representatives from the company's main bankers.

Maybe business-oriented academics, if they have already demonstrated their value as directors on other boards. Half of the major US corporations have one. If the academic has not, yet, operated on a company board, but some of the directors know his style and believe it would fit, he can be tried out within the company on a 'consultancy' exercise. This will illustrate whether he can grip the realities as well as the theories. It will indicate whether he can develop the working respect of the senior executives, and prove to that critical gathering that he can contribute something of value. The board can find that a lively, business-oriented academic can be more quick thinking than most of the directors; can conceive more realistic alternatives to evaluate than anyone else; knows a lot more techniques to consider and questions to properly ask; sees at least the theoretical errors in cases proposed; speaks without prompting, and usually coherently. Directors are expected to 'ask searching questions'. It is a fact that most of them never do. The academic non-executive will. It is part of his everyday life to do so.

Maybe the business or management consultant, but again only if he already has years of executive or non-executive directorship experience. The consultant whose career has been entirely within consulting houses may find it difficult to switch from giving advice into decision making or decision implementing. The argument most frequently raised against appointing consultants as non-executives is that they, too, are suppliers of services, who might either 'push' their services or inhibit the company from engaging alternative consultants for specific assignments. This argument misses the point that when engaged as a non-executive the consultant joins the board as a director, not as a seller of specific services. The fact that he is a consultant by background simply defines the nature of his experience, and the likely style of his approach to the company's situation – the two criteria on which any potential director should be judged.

The consultant who has already gained extensive management and directorship experience can be a most productive non-executive because:

- he has worked in a much wider variety of commercial and industrial environments than most executives cover during their careers;
- he is clinical in his approach to problems or opportunities;
- he may have experience of a wider range of functions than most executives;
- he has no inhibitions in telling home truths to top managements;
- he is likely to be the first, not the last, to suggest that some other consultant be brought in to handle a project which he and the

executives conclude they cannot handle together. Which, as an aside, is a good argument for the one-man-band consultant, rather than one from a traditional consulting house which has mouths to feed.

All non-executives are like consultants when performing parts of their roles, so the management or business consultant with board-room experience is a natural candidate for a non-executive direc-torship – most particularly in the small or medium-sized company, where he can fill gaps in professional or managerial knowledge without crossing chains of command.

Robert E. Kelly, Professor at Portland State University, has written of the advantages of the 'internal consultant', who is quicker and cheaper than external consultants, as well as being personally account-able for his recommendations. When such an internal consultant also holds a seat in the boardroom his work in trouble-shooting, teaching, evaluating and implementing will be conducted under the additional pressure of legal responsibility. The proportion of US and UK boards containing this kind of contributor, whether as a full-time executive director or as an 'active' non-executive, is immeasurably small, des-pite the fact that this category is potentially much more productive than any other at board-level.

Maybe the full-time executive director, chairman or chief executive from another company. But only if he can, is willing to, and does, consistently meet the primary criterion for every non-executive – a minimum average commitment to the company of two days per month. It consumes one day per month to prepare properly for a board meeting, by studying the papers, and then to attend it. It consumes another one day per month, at least, to get around the company and really understand its strengths, weaknesses, fantasies, foibles, and high-flyers – including those who are still flying low down.

However great a person's experience and demonstrated com-petence, if he does not spend enough time to get to know the company of which he is a non-executive, he will not be able to transfer that experience and competence to the solution of that company's problems and opportunities. His judgement can be brought to bear only on the papers tabled before him, which tell only a small part of the story. To take an everyday example, it does not help if the non-executive with vast experience of production companies in the Far East votes 'go' on the new factory for Taiwan if the division or subsidiary handling Taiwan is about to blow up from overwork, or alternatively has too little skill at the top of it to be able to control the project, or if the Group chief executive supports the project while everyone in the division down to the tea-ladies is against it – but he knows nothing of all that because he has not been able to talk with the division lately. It does not help if the non-executive who has bought and sold more companies than most managers have had pay-slips votes 'no go' on an acquisition without which the division's product range will remain so incomplete that it will lose most of its markets in one year flat, and the humblest sales manager knows this – but he does not know this because he only read the relevant board paper concerned on the train that morning. It does not help if the non-executive votes for a new chief executive who is supported by the two or three other directors whom he does know quite well, but is strongly opposed by the several executive directors whom he has never troubled to speak with (and by the tea-ladies and sales managers). It has not helped in those corporations which have gone under, or in countless others which manage to float along while the international competition goes sailing swiftly by.

The non-executive cannot be held culpable for poor managerial performance, but he can be held culpable for not having challenged and checked it. That is his function. It is most difficult to understand why so many men, who have achieved high reputations for their executive performance, have been so careless in their standards of non-executive performance.

The NYSE requires that there be two outside directors in any company which seeks a listing. In the 1970s, and again in the 1980s after the gap of a difficult decade, there have been flurries of activity to promote the introduction of a similar requirement in London. The reports which had triggered this promotional activity, the organisations behind it, and the several recruitment specialists pursuing it, all concentrated their attention almost exclusively on the recruitment of new non-executives from the catchment of full-time executives in other companies. They can learn from the experience of Dr A.J.F. O'Reilly, one-time Irish football idol, chairman and chief executive of the H. J. Heinz Corporation, and a non-executive director in Allegheny International when the spotlight began to shine on some darker aspects of that board's performance. In his own words, the limits to the power of the non-executive had been: *'limits of time and information'*.

But there should be no limits to the power of any one director compared with those of any other director, executive or non-executive. The law recognises no differences between the directors, and the courts will not be impressed by any one director's plea that he didn't have the 'time' to perform his role responsibly, or that he didn't have the information which he knew he needed to perform the role effectively. If the board has appointed, or has maintained *in situ* any one director who is known, or who is later shown to have had too little time, or if it is seen to have provided any one director with too little information, then the board as a whole, and particularly the chairman of the board, should be removed by the institutional shareholders without delay or sympathy.

Maybe the hybrid or professional director.

The hybrid director
The first two hybrid directors to receive widespread publicity in Europe were appointed by BOC International. Primarily non-executives, they were delegated a number of defined functional roles which were intended to consume about a quarter of their time.

At first sight the concept of the hybrid director could seem to run counter to the conventional wisdom that the non-executive should maintain a strict separation from the management, at least in larger Groups. At second sight, it is only sensible that a board should delegate described part-time functions to those directors best equipped to play them, particularly if the directors concerned would not be able to play them full time, or if the roles themselves do not justify engaging a full-time employee of the same calibre. Looked at another way, if certain non-executives have expertise which can be used to supplement the skills of the executives, why not make use of it any way you can? There is no restriction on how the directors can be deployed, either in law or in sense.

While the first well-publicised example of the hybrid concept was in a major international Group, the largest area of potential application is naturally within smaller and medium-sized companies. The smaller the company, the less distinct the borderline between board policy and the executive management. The more management detail comes up to the board, the more the board itself operates as the top rung of the management ladder, and the more there is to gain by charging experienced non-executives to move into the organisation for a spell to provide real assistance; for example in:

- helping to introduce new systems;
- describing new organisational structures;
- defining new review-and-report formats;
- building a planning mechanism;
- evaluating or even implementing a specific market assault;
- taking charge, in crisis, of a small new operation, or a set of territories.

This kind of contribution can be as productive to the company on a four – six days per month basis as if the men were full time. The 'pulse' of work triggered in the short period can require a further three weeks or so to progress and be developed by the management. After which the hybrid comes back in for another 'pulse' of input; withdraws; returns; and so on until the task is completed.

The difference between this role and the work of a wholly external consultant is that the director concerned is part of the board itself. He thus carries a significant additional level of enforced responsibility. Furthermore, he starts by knowing the company, and has no unproductive learning period. Among the thousands of companies which could profit greatly from engaging this kind of contribution, there are very few indeed in the USA, UK or Europe which do so. Take encouragement from New Zealand. A study of NZ boards for the Singapore Management Review (Chandler/Henshall, 1985) found that local directors are becoming more active under pressure of legislation. Companies are making greater use of functional committees of the board, and in parallel with this trend is the greater use of independent, or non-executive directors who are delegated defined spheres of responsibility – that is, who are 'hybrid' directors.

The professional director

The management writer, Peter Drucker, and Bruce Henderson of the Boston Consulting Group, have both argued the problem of composing an effective boardroom through to the conclusion that the potentially most useful member of the board is the professional director, who sits on a maximum of five or six boards and commits all his time and experience to this handful of roles.

> . . . the effective board member has to be a 'professional director'. Indeed board membership should be recognised as a full-time profession for a really first-rate man.
>
> PETER F. DRUCKER, 1974

The limitation on the total number of directorships is critical. It is to be hoped that the era of the man who sits on a dozen or more boards is coming to a close. The catchment area for people who play the professional director role, or who could and would play it responsibly, is currently limited only by the market's own limited awareness of this kind of potential non-executive contribution, or by its reluctance to engage it. Those who play the role share the common characteristic that they retain enough flexibility to switch into, and out of, a deeper commitment to any one of their companies, in step with how the companies' separate requirements shift in emphasis. They can slip into or out of a chairmanship, a temporary chief executive slot, or a part-time functional role to fill a gap or unravel a tangle.

None is the 'gifted amateur' of the folk-lore which surrounds the concept of the professional director. The amateur, by definition, does it for fun. The professional director lives by it. Which, for a start, strengthens his commitment and the force of his contribution.

Consider the arithmetic, and evaluate the potential contribution of the professional director against other forms of outside support. As a guideline:

- take the salary of the highest paid director. You want someone who is at least as experienced as that man;
- multiply it by two. (The multiplier needed for gross cost budgeting is around 2.5 in many financial companies.) Remember that the director who is not employed 'full-time' elsewhere has no company-funded pension scheme, cars, holidays, bonuses, share options or other perquisites;
- divide by 200, there being only 200 productive days in a year. This gives the per diem;
- multiply the figure obtained by the number of days per annum which it has been agreed he will contribute to the company, which gives the annual fee.

If the chief executive is the highest paid director on a salary of $100,000, costing his company $200,000 gross, then the professional director receives a per diem of $1,000. If the start-point in your arithmetic is a salary of $1 million, and if the end-point for a 2-day-per-month professional director of $240,000 per annum looks too high, then go back to the start-point and query whether *that* is too high. You cannot blame the end-point by claiming that what you really want, part-time, is someone who is 'cheaper', or less worthy or less capable – can you?

When a large corporation with a highly paid chief executive engages a professional or hybrid director for, say, four or five days per month for a lengthy period, then it may sensibly arrive at a lower rate than derived from this guideline. But keep in mind when doing the sums that geography, logistics and conflicting board timetables will always leave the man with considerable unfilled, and therefore unremunerated gaps which he must absorb. He is making his services available to you at times and timings chosen to suit your company, not his own preferred programme, and 'availability' must have a price.

By comparison, external professionals such as accountants, merchant or investment bankers, or management consultants are charging clients at considerably higher rates today, and they continue to rise. The reader should make updating checks from time to time in his own country. In the mid-1980s in the UK a range of £70 – 150 *per hour* (translated directly but not comparatively into $120 – 250 per hour) commonly applies, while partners in accounting firms, bank directors and the haute consulting houses are already charging a great deal more. Thus with a professional or hybrid director the company can have 'on tap' a man who has wider experience than alternative external professionals; who carries director level responsibility and legal commitment; who can be turned on and off at about the same gross cost per day as a senior executive; without the complications of executive service contracts or clauses in the Employment Acts.

The concept of the professional director runs counter to the thinking of virtually all the organisations currently concerned with locating non-executives for companies which want them. One of them has put this succinctly by saying that the non-executive needs also to have 'an executive power base'. Why a non-executive should need a 'power base' is far from clear. Anyone playing the professional director role, sensibly, will have had one or several such power bases during his executive career.

The *Harvard Business Review* of May – June 1976 published an article by Joseph W. Barr, himself a professional director on several boards, which summarised a survey of opinion from 160 large companies on the question of using 'professional directors' instead of the existing categories. The survey found that there was much support for the concept. Those objections which were raised by some respondents could be grouped into the following:

1 A dislike of the term 'professional director'.
2 A belief that the chief executive officer of another company could still contribute, despite the time problem.
3 A concern that the professional director might blur the lines between management and the supervision of management by not being able to keep his hands off day-to-day operations.
4 That the professional director would want his own staff.

5 That the extra remuneration paid to the professional director might impair his independence.
6 That 'We wish we didn't have any outsider directors, especially no professional directors'.

The last comment says it all. But taking the objections one by one:

1 The term used naturally matters little, and most alternatives would raise equal objections.
2 All the accumulated evidence is to the contrary. There is also concern about the high proportion of interlocking directorships which result when company A lends its chief executive to company B as a non-executive and receives back the chief executive of company B as a non-executive on its own board. There have been anti-trust suits regarding such interlocking arrangements, and the boards of financial institutions have come under particular scrutiny in the USA.
3 The role of the non-executive can be defined to include as little or as much involvement with management as the board sees fit. The outsider who cannot keep his hands off day-to-day operations when told to do so can be removed.
4 The professional director would make use of the company's existing staff, for the provision of existing data, for secretarial services when necessary, or for any other ad hoc requirement. There is no reason why he should need to add to the company's numbers in any way.
5 The professional director who operates on a small number of boards would not be dependent on any one of them.
6 Few executives like to have non-executives sniffing around, if they have anything which they do not want to be seen, or which embarrasses them. The executive who is working well, has ideas to contribute, and is looking for a way up the corporate ladder will be only too glad to expose his activities and suggestions to an independent outsider who is willing and able to bring them to the board's attention.

Late in 1979, when there was much Press commentary on the role of the non-executive in the UK, Kenneth Fleet, of *Financial Weekly*, castigated the recruitment of non-executives from the ranks of '*generals, admirals, corporate has-beens, "professional" non-executives, thrusters, amateurs and cranks*' on the basis that '*however clever such men may be, they can contribute very little of real value because their time and interests are too divided* '. The same commentary supported the recruitment of non-executives from the ranks of full-time executives, and only from such ranks, and rounded off the article with further castigation of the professional director with 'six, ten or twenty' different directorships. This neatly illustrates the confusion on the role of the non-executive which continues to delay their fuller and more responsible deployment through companies of all shapes and sizes which need them.

First, there is a whole world of difference between six directorships and twenty. Six can be the ideal number. Twenty can be a bad joke. Second, the full-time executive has *less* time available than the professional director, not more. Third, the full-time executive's interests are *more* divided, not less, than those of the professional director, who does not have a one-company career to protect it; is not interrupted every nine minutes; sits on fewer boards than the senior executive director in a Group.

Every one of the scores of intelligent or well-intentioned US and UK commentaries on the past failures of the non-executive which have appeared in print in the last decade (Mr Fleet's article included) has focused on the problem of the time needed by the non-executive to play his role well and responsibly. Is the company worth at least two days a month, or not?

Fees for non-executives

Calculation of a realistic fee rate for non-executives who are employed full-time elsewhere can be based on 'net' rather than gross cost comparisons. Use the same arithmetic as above for professional or hybrid directors but omit the step 'multiply by two'. This matches, perchance precisely, with current American proposals that a 2-day-per-month non-executive should receive 10 per cent of the 20-day-per-month chairman's fees, or 10 per cent of the full-time chief executive's salary in corporations where the chairman is part-time.

The Korn/Ferry studies (see Appendix I) show that American non-executives receive a much lower rate, but are on the whole satisfied with prevailing levels. This is not surprising when most of the non-executives are employed, and paid, 'full-time' elsewhere; their non-executive positions are 'incidentals', and indeed may be viewed by some as a welcome break to the daily management routine.

Smaller companies, with less well-salaried chief executives, may have to adjust the arithmetic upwards a little to attract a useful calibre of non-executive. It is hoped that the guideline will help stiffen their resolve to settle for nothing less than the required calibre and the required level of commitment. Anything less on either count can mean money down the drain.

Fee rates in practice still vary greatly, from a few hundred pounds per annum to several thousand dollars per day, dependent, presumably, on whether the director and the board concerned view the role as a 'decoration' or as a solemn duty. The non-executive will normally give in return what the role is visibly worth. Hence the prevalence of cronies and dilettantes. It is conventional wisdom that the non-executive should be financially independent, and thus able to wield his ultimate weapon, resignation, without fear of damaging his personal situation. The rather puritanical implication has been that the fees are not important to him. Certainly the non-executive must not be so dependent on any one company's fees that he dares not resign from its board when the company is behaving in a way which he cannot accept and cannot amend. But if an employee is motivated by the level of remuneration for his efforts, why not also the non-executive? Any director will inevitably, if subconsciously, gear the depth of his involvement to the value which he can see the company places on his services.

Actions for non-executives

A prospective non-executive should:

1 Determine if the company is recruiting seriously and methodically. If it has advertised, if he first meets a committee of three – four board members, and if the committee can succinctly describe

the company's situation, and what it requires from the new non-executive, then it probably is. If it has not advertised, if he meets only one director, and if he has difficulty in unearthing details of the company's situation, or why it is looking for a non-executive, then it certainly is not. If it cannot recruit well, then it probably cannot do a lot of other things very well either.

2 Query the committee of directors regarding the company:

> its shareholders, and the relations between them, if a private company;
> its business, markets and competition;
> its key problems and opportunities, both current and anticipated;
> its performance and financial situation, as evidenced by current and recent past accounts presented by the committee.

3 Determine the composition of the board and senior management, and the structure of the company as a whole:

> Who does what, how well?
> Is the chairman also chief executive, and does he intend to remain so?
> Does the chief executive appear to lead or dominate?
> Does the finance director have at his fingertips all the opinions and data which he seeks? Particularly a sound cash flow forecast? If not, it could be that the data presented are misleading, or wrong.

> Are there other non-executives, and if not, are there plans to recruit others? Of what kind, and when? If the concept of a non-executive is new to that boardroom it can be good policy to engage just one to begin with, but on the understanding that, once the credibility of the concept has been established in the company, there will be others. One man alone can find it difficult to force through effective change. He risks getting classified as a 'boat rocker' if it is always just him who says that change, of whatever kind, is needed, and this can delay or destroy the executives' acceptance of the value of non-executive contribution.

4 Meet all the directors and, if reasonably possible, a number of the senior managers just below the board. Speak freely with them; seek to elicit gently what concerns them most about the company, and about his possible appointment to its board.

5 Determine whether he can fit in. The term 'chemistry' is often used. In fact chemistry is all about the production of new chemicals, which implies change to the original mix, not a comfortable maintenance of the status quo. As long as the 'chemistry' will not lead to constant explosions, it should be judged solely on the likely changes it will induce, not on miscibility.

6 Ensure that what he is expected to contribute is understood and accepted by the board as a whole.

7 If all parties still remain interested, but if the prospective non-executive is not happy with the accuracy or reality of the performance data presented to him, he should consider asking for a meeting with the company's auditors or bankers. At this stage, any such discussions must be handled with utmost diplomacy, but if he cannot exercise diplomacy outside the boardroom then he is not going to be very effective inside it either.

8 Agree on the content and extent of information which will be provided to him as a routine, and that he will obtain a comprehensive initial induction into the company on appointment.

9 Agree a minimum and maximum length of appointment, normally at least two years and at most five years. The company should have changed so much in five years that it then needs a quite different mix in the boardroom. He may still be useful after that period, but the question should be formally reviewed, not neglected by default.

10 Agree a time commitment and a fee rate. If the board wants less than an average of two days per month, it does not want enough. If he cannot give at least two days per month, he cannot give enough.

Once he has joined the board, he should:

11 Ensure he receives the agreed induction. Otherwise everyone else will forget about it.

12 Ensure he receives the agreed information in the agreed format, and to a regular timetable.

13 Ensure that he maintains contact with all the directors, and with other key executives below the board. He must temper his comments and thinking in the boardroom with his direct knowledge of the people involved.

14 Ensure he has an annual review of his role and performance with the chairman.

15 Ask for items to be placed on the agenda if he feels key issues are being overlooked, or deliberately suppressed, never simply accepting what is put before him.

16 Ensure that board reviews of performance go beyond just expressing satisfaction or concern; that they lead to minuted decisions regarding future action by the management.

17 Ensure that the board looks forward as well as backwards; not just forwards through the budgeted year, but into the longer-term plan period also.

18 Participate to an agreed extent in the planning process. This may mean attending some long weekend sessions with senior executives – which can be one of the very best ways of getting to know the company's businesses, staff, strengths and weaknesses.

19 Accept specifically delegated projects where he is the best placed to carry them out. Besides thus helping the company, he may develop a better 'feel' for the company's real situation in its external environment through such projects. Often the company's true competitive position is quite different from what the executives believe, and from what is consequently reported in the boardroom.

20 Accept directorships in divisional or subsidiary boards if he can be of assistance to those companies also, and if he feels he can thereby improve the quality of the linkages through the company from top to bottom.

21 Ensure he gives the time agreed, and more if the company runs into problems. In practice he can perform about seven such roles as a professional director, or one, only, if employed full-time elsewhere.

22 Speak out if the board is observed to be failing:

> to define policies and objectives, or maintain planning and budgeting routines;

to deploy and measure returns on resources;
to properly define management's authority, or monitor its performance;
to maintain, and use critically, a sound financial reporting system;
to maintain effective communication and participation, company wide;
to monitor its own performance as a board, or
to keep within both the letter and the spirit of all the laws.

Describe how to improve the board's performance, and if judged necessary, have this minuted. Ensure that corrective action is actually carried out.

23 Remember always that the board has to act for the benefit of the company as a whole, and that the directors are the agents of the company, not of the shareholders or of any other specific interests, least of all their own.

24 Remember in crisis that his weapons include talking with the company's auditors and bankers and, in the final extreme, with the shareholders. In private companies the main shareholders may be within the board, so threatened approach to the auditors or bankers may stimulate a more responsible reaction.

25 Remember that, while resignation is his last weapon, it can often harm the company rather than help it, particularly if a well-publicised resignation is not accompanied by a clear statement of the reasons why he felt compelled to resign. Further, that resignation may remove from the board the only person who is able to help it at all.

If the prospective director is being invited to join the board of a company in crisis he will need to deepen some of these initial investigations:

- to ensure he has adequate liability or indemnity insurance;
- to look more closely at his prospective co-directors to determine their probable competence and current mental composure;

- to look more closely at the accounts to ensure that the company is still solvent, can continue to trade, and has at least a reasonable chance of trading out of trouble;
- to ensure also that payments to government departments are all up-to-date. He would be wise to obtain a *written* confirmation of this from the MD, finance director or company secretary.

CAVEAT DIRECTOR.

Taboos

For many years the boards of large American corporations have contained two non-executives for every executive director. Yet most remain just as inflexible about the terms and taboos for the non-executive as any conservative British board. Most have demanded adherence to the same old rituals that the non-executive:

- must not get involved in the detailed management of the corporation, and therefore must not be 'burdened' with too much information;
- must not get involved in any way at all with down-line managers, and, absolutely certainly:
- must not be involved, even remotely, with the control, hiring or firing of senior managers.

A thesis of this volume, in contrast, is that all directors, particularly the independent non-executives:

- *must* get to know the reality behind the bald figures in the boardroom papers, which means absorbing more rather than less information. Not just in order to be able to help make sensible board decisions, but in order to be able to prove to the court that he really did make an effort to know what was going on;
- *must* get to know the key senior managers; the reliability of their judgements, and hence of their proposals which are brought through into board papers; their capability and capacity; their optimism, or alternatively their concerns about the condition of

the company. The latter is important where there are doubts about the chief executive, and can be difficult for the non-executive to handle without giving the chief executive's subordinates the feeling that he is going behind their boss's back. *But how else can the non-executive form a responsible judgement in such circumstances if the only information he receives is from that chief executive?* While it can be difficult to handle, a non-executive should have become well experienced through his career in detecting and learning from a manager's nuances of expression without volunteering or exposing his own opinions. *That* is one of the everyday techniques in managing men. And the non-executive:

- *must* insist on knowing about the comings and goings of key men, their reasons for resigning or for being dismissed, and what kinds and styles of replacement are being sought.

A hybrid director was engaged by a major corporation to assist with the evaluation and organisation of some subsidiaries. The key men in the units concerned were found to be bursting with questions about 'what was going on up there', and with good reason. When the questions were duly reported, in bowdlerised form, the holding board concluded formally that it really was not a good idea to have any of its number talking to down-line men . . . so it cancelled the messenger service because it didn't like the message, and it learnt nothing from the contents of the message. Take a second opinion:

Daniel T. Carroll, President and CEO of Hoover Universal Inc., wrote in the *Harvard Business Review* (Carroll, 1981) about challenges and responses for directors. They:

- need wider information, not just financial summaries;
- must carry out more pre-meeting preparation, must 'work at it';
- should undertake specific training where there are gaps in their experience or understanding;
- must get to know the '*lower organisational echelons*'; and
- must get involved in their hiring and firing.

Further, that the board collectively:

- should regularly review individual performance and attendance;
- should adapt its composition as the corporation and its requirements change;
- should maintain the highest ethical standards; and
- should actually allow the individual director to make a contribution.

The value of Carroll's comments, which parallel many of this volume's proposals in both detail and spirit, is that they are made by a practising, full-time executive director – not by an academic, management writer, professional part-timer, management consultant . . . or by any of the other categories whose contribution and comments the more fearful executive or non-executive directors will commonly seek to brush aside.

> *Taboos are primitive protective mechanisms designed specifically to prevent the tribesfolk from asking questions.*

Employee representation or participation

Those who argue for the appointment of union directors or worker directors to controlling boards do so on the basis that without such specialist directors there is a continuing risk that the board may ride roughshod over the interests of the employees – not on the basis that their presence will improve competitive business decision making.

Those who argue against, do so on one or more of the bases that:

- established trade unions are already well placed to root out both collective or individual abuses and to exact remedies where the company has been at fault. Further, that this wholly proper position of power is already itself too often improperly abused;
- the great majority of trade unions themselves do not want to see the introduction of employee directors, preferring to manoeuvre or do battle, as they judge fit, outside the boardroom;
- employee representation has not helped to build better businesses where it has been applied, and is already creating divisive tensions

where it has been over-applied. Witness the saga in 1980 of Mannesmann and the Free Democrats versus the Union I. G. Metall and the Social Democrats in West Germany, a country whose government consists of a coalition between the same Free Democrats and Social Democrats; a country where disruptive industrial action had rarely been taken for any reason, and seldom before 1980 for purely political reasons.

- the 'them' who want it, as opposed to the 'us' who do not, still cannot make up their own minds as to whether such directors should be employees or union officials. Or from which union. (British Steel has to grapple with twenty-eight unions.) And that half the workforce are not members of any one of those unions;
- all the executive directors are employees, too, and even that tiny fraction which might ride roughshod over the workforce, given the chance, has learned the hard way that it will not be given the chance.

In view of the distance between the two arguments, various alternatives have been suggested to seek to bridge the gap. The Industrial Society in the UK, whose own constitution embodies a cooperation between unions and industrial managements, has long promoted the concept that the annual report of a company should name two of the directors as representing the employees, and should record that both of them have the employees' confidence. This implies that steps would need to be taken to confirm, internally, that such confidence in the two directors does in fact exist. This process could be hedged about with all kinds of opportunity for sabotage, character assassination, filibustering, or just plain stubbornness, and the exercise might not be able to be conducted without internal harm. The Japanese solution noted in Chapter 7 makes good sense.

The concept of worker directors and union directors has been tried in the UK. The Post Office experimented with seven such directors on its board for two years, and gave it up. No one has been reported to date as having said that the experiment achieved anything that could not have been achieved by appointing any group of seven sensible people. On the contrary, some of the Post Office directors have gone on record as saying that the presence of identifiably separate interests on the board had clogged up the proceedings.

Stripped to its bones of political or emotive irrelevancies, the concept of employee-representing directors can be seen to be fundamentally absurd. In all human relationships, just as in all animal relationships, there are territorial boundaries. When animals cross boundaries, they fight. Humans have developed two options: to cross a boundary and make war, or to cross a boundary in order to cooperate. But this does not eliminate the fact that the interest groups still exist, behind their boundaries.

The overriding responsibility and objective of the board, also in law, is the interest of the company as a whole. Interest groups have, by definition, another overriding objective. That is why the boundaries of any interest group can come up to, but not into, the boundaries of the boardroom. That is why there should be no specialist interests represented on any board.

In the Peoples' Republic of China, the first capitalist venture since the communist revolution was the formation of a joint-stock company in the Jindi Peoples' Commune in Shandong Province. The company is run by the stockholders' representatives. There are no employee representatives; no union directors, no worker directors.

In little of the debate on this debilitating subject has it been highlighted that in West Germany, on whose laws the original proposals for union directors and worker directors were modelled, the law also requires that: collective agreements are binding on all parties; unions and their officials enjoy no legal immunities; unions must be independent of political parties; and closed shops are illegal.

In none of the debates has it been suggested, even with tongue in cheek, that union or worker representation on boards should be matched by directors and managers having seats at all the most important union meetings, and that directors and managers should be empowered, by law, to influence union policy making. That concept is equally absurd. But not more so.

Participation

Employees do not want directorships. They want: to be informed; to be able to have their grievances readily reviewed; to be well rewarded; to be involved when they feel they can sensibly contribute.

A routine for 'participation' throughout the company will increase employee satisfaction, and thus improve employee morale, co-operation and productivity. Participation includes communication and consultation.

Communication covers details of people and organisation; progress made by the company; policy made by the board. It is to enable innovative comment, or complaint, to pass smoothly and certainly upwards, and facts and judgements to pass clearly downwards.

Consultation covers problems or projects. It is intended to eliminate misunderstanding; to achieve an acceptance of changes proposed; to obtain the contribution of employees, where they have one to make; thereby to achieve improved performance. Employees must know they are genuinely involved, that they are an integral part of the company and are viewed as such by the board, and that their prosperity depends on the prosperity of the whole. Without involvement there can be no real commitment. Without commitment there can be little chance of adequate performance.

> *If he works for you, you work for him.*
>
> JAPANESE PROVERB

Each company has a unique structure or character. Each needs to adapt its participation mechanism to that structure and character. One firm guideline is that the groupings formed for communication and consultation should parallel the structure of the company. There should be a 'works council', by any better name, at holding board level, outside of that board but containing some of its directors; one in each division; one in each subsidiary. The councils should be identified with the business units with which the members themselves identify. Composition of the councils must be decided by each level, with the board keeping an eye over the whole to see that they do this with sense and sensitivity. About half line and functional management, about half employees, including, where relevant, the union representative – though this is one forum which the union representative must not be allowed to dominate. Each council should contain one representative of management who is able to take on-the-spot decisions on straightforward questions, which almost inevitably means the unit's chief executive.

Boards may consider aiding participation by:

(a) schemes for profit sharing among all or some of the employees, and/or
(b) schemes for allocating shares among employees.

The problem with (a) is that motivation becomes too remote when the scheme is extended beyond top managers and directors. The return to other employees is best left in the form of fatter wage packets. The problem with (b) is that most employees work in subsidiaries, or private independent companies which have restrictions on share transfer. The individual performance of a subsidiary may differ greatly from the performance of the parent, whose shares are allocated, and again the motivation and interest become too remote. Boards which, nonetheless, decide to extend one or both types of scheme down to the shopfloor can create dissent, rather than satisfaction, if the weightings from top to bottom are inadequately balanced. Too many schemes look like cream for the top and crumbs for the bottom. Better to 'weight' the arithmetic towards the bottom; the men at the top will still gain more in absolute terms, but less pro rata to salary. Question is, *which levels of the company most need external motivation to perform?*

Resolve to introduce such mechanisms can be stiffened by the knowledge that participation in Europe works well between unions, employees and managements, at operational levels. They all tend to ignore the existence of the more political supervisory board level. Employees are interested in their persons, not in politics, and they will help establish businesslike schemes, given the chance. So give them the chance. Let the board, at all levels, work out the schemes and the council compositions together with the employees.

Do not forget the representation of the 'middle level'. Detailed creativity in a company, as contrasted with broader strategic innovation, emanates largely from the specialist or middle-manager level, which is sandwiched, and squeezed, between the shopfloor and the boardroom. The Japanese have long recognised this in their painfully slow, but thoroughly effective, 'ringi' system of consultation.

The only effective participation scheme is one which covers all levels equally, as a glove covers all the fingers.

9   External responsibilities

The law at large

There are detailed statutes affecting almost every aspect of a company's daily operations; there's the Corporation Act covering the administration of the company; and there's the criminal law.

When the Russian government became suspicious about the Uzbekistan Republic's massive overfulfilment of the planned target for cotton production, for which large bonuses and a bagful of medals had already been disbursed, it used one of its spy satellites to measure the size of harvest which could be achieved against the figures actually presented to it. Soon afterwards the Uzbek minister concerned was executed by firing squad, fourteen of his assistants were sent to the salt mines, and 2,600 others are still being 'investigated'. Yet:

. . . many of the people who swindled the backers of Lloyd's insurance market out of hundreds of millions of pounds have gone untouched and untroubled by the law (Economist, 1987).

Perhaps the most striking shared characteristic of East and West in the 1980s has been the rise in frequency of exposed criminality in men holding positions of control or influence. The Hungarian government had to establish a new Economic Police Force to handle the surge of *'speculation, corruption and other crimes'* which followed its latest reforms to introduce Western-style incentives. So also in China. So also in almost every Western country from Australia in the south to Sweden in the north, where the Fermenta AB abuses appear to have occurred despite the presence of a most distinguished board of directors. In the USA, John Shad, Chairman of the SEC and the 'man at the forefront of the campaign to clean up Wall Street', funded an ethics and business leadership programme at Harvard Business School, stating that:

'I've been disturbed most recently with the numbers of graduates of leading business and law schools who have become convicted felons. . . It's the cream of the crop, that's what's so distressing' (Oram, 1987).

It's no longer just a problem of insider dealing and other crimes by individuals, though Oscar Wilde reminded us in *An Ideal Husband* that:

'Private information is practically the source of every large modern fortune . . . and public scandal invariably the result.' Today major firms and corporations are also involved; one of the largest US stockbrokers was found guilty of defrauding small banks of $10,000,000,000; General Electric pleaded guilty to defrauding the US Air Force by filing 108 fake invoices. Pained protestation that 'only a tiny fraction are involved' is no longer credible.

Morality affects performance. When a respected City commentator (Harris, 1987) wrote about *'the combination of greed and incompetence now coming to light'* he wrote about a *combination*. We are suffering the results of having replaced the concept of excellent reward by a common assumption of the right to receive excessive reward, by whatever route. When some of the directors and friends of Guinness received fees for their support the figures concerned were in the millions, not in the thousands or tens of thousands. We have taken our eye off the ball.

The company and the employees

'The company as an entity comes first, the shareholders and employees come equal second.' No law ever said it precisely like that, though the UK's 1980 Companies Act, now replaced, came close. Japanese Companies legislation, like most US state legislation, places no *direct* responsibility on the board to look after the interests of the employees; it doesn't need to. There are numerous myths about Japanese management, including the belief that the employee has lifetime job security. This happy situation applies to only 20 per cent or so of the workforce, mainly those employed within larger international organisations. Corporate insolvencies or major redundancy programmes are also quite common. But overall unemployment remains low, largely because the Japanese train and develop their workforce as rigorously as they research and develop their products. America and Britain have become rather cavalier about both; results are seen in the comparative levels of loyalty and determination which are returned.

In Britain, the situation is made worse by the low level of initial trainability of much of the workforce which results, not from any lower capability, but from too limited schooling. Only 30 per cent of British children continue their education beyond the age of 16 years. In France, the figure is 70–80 per cent; in Germany, Japan and the USA it is 90 per cent. Couple this fact with the British companies' continued reduction in training overheads in order to report higher profits, and the size of the problem becomes quite desperate. Don't be taken in by claims that British companies are now 'leaner and fitter'; it isn't just fat, but also brain and muscle which they are wasting away.

The shareholders

The employee, and the director, shareholder, banker or accountant – even the attorney – can be excused any confusion he may feel about what is, precisely, the board's prime responsibility. The laws themselves are sometimes confused. They do state that the board is primarily responsible to the company as a whole, which means to the company as a separate legal entity with a life and being all of its own. But it is not surprising if the directors, and others, equate 'the company' with 'the company's shareholders' because other parts of the same laws also do just that. The American Bar Association wrote that:

> *The fundamental responsibility of the individual corporate director is to represent the interests of the shareholders as a group, as the owners of the enterprise, in directing the business and affairs of the corporation within the law.*

ABA, 1978

The definition, unfortunately because authoritatively, moves the practical interpretation of corporate law a shade away from its origins.

The shareholders do not own the company or the assets. They own shares, which gives them certain rights. The company only belongs to them, in a formal sense, at a time of dissolution, and even then they come last in the list of interested parties. The realities, quite apart from the legalities, are that, in all but the smallest private companies, the shareholders

- are numerous;
- can include little old ladies and mighty institutions;
- can have quite different prime interests, such as short-term dividends versus long-term capital gains; and
- can therefore be collectively served only by a board which focuses its attention exclusively on the survival and prosperity of the company.

In large public Groups, where the majority of the shares are owned by a variety of institutional investors, the objectives and interests of one institution, in any one year, can differ from those of another – or from its own interests in any other year. One may have bought in at £1 per share, and be satisfied by a quite different level of return than another institution which purchased at £2.

Even in the small or new private company, where the members may have staked their last penny on that investment, the board can only protect their combined interests by first ensuring the survival and prosperity of the company as a whole.

The only time when the board must specifically focus on the shareholders' interests is when the company is subject to a takeover bid. Here, ownership of shares may change hands at a collectively determined price. Here, the existing owners of the shares must be given clear details of all the options open to them at a point of discontinuity in the company's history. They may make different judgements on what to do with their shares, dependent, perhaps, on the different prices at which they bought into the company – so even then the board can only place them 'equal first'.

The board owes the shareholders very few other specific duties:

- to register share transfers;

- to present the annual general meeting with a balance sheet and profit and loss account, together with the directors' and chairman's reports;
- to call general meetings, whether annual or extraordinary, within the required timetables; and
- to ensure that minorities are treated equally, and without 'unreasonable prejudice'.

The shareholders can decide to treat their shares like lottery tickets, or to keep close to the workings of the company. As a group, they slowly choose to become more active. The directors may find they face action from the shareholders for resisting a take-over bid which could have increased the value of their shares; for making a bad acquisition which does not produce the anticipated returns, and most acquisitions do not; for investing too much in research and development for nebulous new products; for doing too little research and development and falling behind the market . . .

The quiescence of many a board may simply reflect the acquiescence of the average shareholder to its level of performance. One of the large institutional shareholders stated recently the opinion, in mid-recession to boot, that of the several hundred companies in which it invested, less than two dozen caused it concern. The Governor of the Bank of England stated in 1978:

> *Institutional shareholders should take trouble to ensure that directors of companies in which they have important investments are doing a good job. If they are doubtful or uneasy, they should ask for explanations and expect to receive them . . . if in the end they are dissatisfied, they should, individually or collectively, take steps to change the composition of the board.*
>
> GORDON RICHARDSON MBE

While the shareholder cannot alter a decision made by the board (such as buying a property, or fixing a maximum level of dividend), and cannot view the minutes of the board meetings, he does have in his hands the one power which most directly affects the performance of any company, of any shape or size – the power '*to change the composition of the board'*. In this, the general meeting of the shareholders is the company's 'supreme authority', a description frequently met in books on corporation law in many countries – yet the general meeting itself is most commonly an empty routine, empty of content, empty, often, of shareholders.

The directors can pay too much attention to the shareholders, to the exclusion of the continuing interests of the corporation – for example maintaining dividends by increasing borrowings (Lawson, 1980). Meanwhile, the shareholders can pay too little attention to the activities of the directors and managements of the companies in which they invest their own or, more frequently, other people's money. Few consider that *visiting* the companies in which they invest has any practical value (Lee/Tweedie, 1981). They rely primarily – often exclusively – on printed material sent to them, such as commentary in the Press, stockbrokers' reports, and the company's own annual and half-yearly statements. But these are limited and incestuous sources. Financial Press comment is often just an uncritical rewrite, or verbatim reprint, of a company's own hand-outs. Company reports can be a fairy-tale, particularly interim half-yearly unaudited statements which parade a motley of set routines for 'explaining' why the half-year's figures never add up to half-a-year, and shouldn't be taken as an indication of anything at all. Communication between the directors and the institutional shareholders, who hold on average 70 per cent of the company's shares, is too often conducted like a game of charades.

The shareholders have the power to change the composition of the board. It can therefore be argued that the shareholders' responsibilities to the company are at least as real, and as great, as the directors' responsibilities to the shareholders.

Creditors and lenders

The trade creditor is the least protected component in the trading process. When a company is liquidated, he comes second from last in the queue, followed only by the limited liability shareholders, and preceded by: receivership fees; fixed charges (which means 'bankers'); preferential creditors, such as taxes and wages; floating charges, where they are permitted (which also means 'bankers').

In the run-up to collapse and liquidation he has access to registered accounts; he has access via bankers and credit reference organisations to the same basic categories of information on the company's financial situation as available to shareholders, but it is always older and thinner. He does not have the shareholder's ability to question the board on the anticipated future financial situation, or to pressure the board to carry out improvements. He has to judge the limit to which he will risk supplying the company with goods or services not paid for in cash, and there is no limitation to his risk beyond that individual judgement. In times of recession he will commonly extend the size of his collected risks to the point of insomnia, just to keep his works in motion. And at precisely the same times the abuse of the trade creditor by his customers is similarly extended.

The prime responsibility of the company to the creditor is to pay his invoices to time. Unreasonable extension of the payment period constitutes a breach of contract. The smaller supplier can seldom afford to sue a larger customer, and thus often submits to mistreatment when he is himself at his weakest. When a company breaches an external responsibility by failing to pay its creditors to time, it is also causing itself internal harm. When a company begins to rely on breaking the rules, it begins to lose track of, and control of, its real situation.

The writer was once involved in assisting a company fast approaching collapse. One of the first actions was, naturally, to phase the debtors and tighten the chase for cash. Another action was to compile an accurate record of its overdue creditors. By the time the company was able to do this, it had gone bust. The board had run away from their business responsibilities. Their business had run away from them.

Yet in times of trouble the board will normally acquiesce in the stretching of payment periods. This can be the worst of decisions, or of matters left undecided. It can increase the company's problems rather than alleviate them. Elastic payment periods get noticed; creditors ring around; rumours begin; customers hear them, and business falls away – just when it is most needed. The 'old faithful' repeat orders are withheld; the faithful old supplier says 'enough'; alternative suppliers hesitate.

The board would be wise to insist, in good times and bad, that the same firmness is applied to meeting creditors' invoices as is applied, or should be applied daily, to the collection of debtors due. And it should not differentiate between categories of creditor. If the company can survive only by a methodical breach of supply contracts, then it not only does not deserve to survive, but it assuredly will not survive for long.

The lenders, primarily the commercial banks, are always in a stronger position. Their charges on the company's assets can greatly exceed in value the total amount which has been lent. In practice it is often the bank's decision about the *overdraft*, not the board's decision about the *business*, which determines at which point the company becomes technically insolvent.

Sometimes the decision is clear cut. The company, on all the evidence carefully and responsibly collected, has no chance, or almost no chance, of ever trading out of trouble; the excess of liabilities over assets will continue to grow. Sometimes it is a question of how long the bank will 'stick with it'; it does, after all, receive interest on the overdraft. The bank cannot be blamed for basing at least part of its decision on how close the 'distressed sale' value of the assets lies to the total amount which would have to be lent. It can, on the other hand, quite often be blamed for watching the company's situation slip steadily over a long period of time, without pressing the board to make changes. The bank knows, better than anyone, that the process of receivership can drain large sums away from what would otherwise be available to other creditors:

- receivership fees are steep;
- distressed sales can bring below-book prices;
- 'going concern' parts of the company lose customers, and their own potential sale price reduces;
- some debtors begin to find good reasons why they should not pay.

The board has a responsibility to its bankers to ensure that the financial or other information which it provides when requesting loan or overdraft facilities is as accurate as the board can make it. But this also places a responsibility on the bankers. When a board requests extended facilities because of trading or other difficulties, the bank quite properly requires that it subsequently receive regular data from the company in balance sheet and profit and loss formats, together with cash flow forecasts. It may request to receive these monthly. This puts into the bank's hands fresher and fuller data than are available to shareholders. While a director can quite properly tell an individual *shareholder* that he cannot make available more information than is generally available to all the shareholders, woe betide the director of a company in difficulty who refuses such access to the bankers. The shareholders may have the power to hire-and-fire the directors, but the bankers have the power to call in the overdraft and sink the company. In periods of difficulty the bank inevitably becomes close to the board. It can sense the board's weaknesses. At least it should be able to, if the bank manager is competent. It can recommend changes. It can press for changes, particularly to the composition of the board.

Given the bank's singular ability to protect its own position, and given the extent of the information it can properly require, it can be argued that from the first moment that trouble is detected the bank's responsibility to the interests of the company, which include the interests of the employees and of the other creditors, is as real as the board's responsibility to the bank.

The customer

Consumerism remains more restrained in the UK and Europe than in the US, and still shows none of the wilder American extremes. There is little sign of any enthusiasm for putting consumer representatives onto boards. The unexciting experience of nationalised industry boards, which experimented with such representatives, suggests that others will not be in a hurry to try the same.

A consumer has the natural objective of obtaining as much as possible for as little as possible, with the tightest strings attaching. Boards, in contrast, have to be free to make up their own minds how to obtain a sufficient number of customers, at a sufficient price, to a sufficient but not triple-plated specification, at acceptable cost. (All, coincidentally, the most confidential of competitive business data.) The role of lobbying for improved service, specification or price is thus best placed outside the board, in a separate consumers' consultative committee if the board finds this helpful – and then only in the case of nationalised industries or other corporations which luxuriate in monopoly or near-monopoly situations where normal market pressures do not automatically apply. For the rest, there are today adequate external pressures on companies in the USA, UK and Europe from numerous national and supra-national bodies. Indeed they are too numerous and often either tread on each other's toes or avoid taking any significant steps which might cause such conflict.

When researching for this book the author contacted ten of these official and semi-official bodies in order to determine how many EEC Directives on consumer matters had been issued at the time of drafting. Not one could answer the question, or refer the author to any other organisation which might be able to. The EEC Consumer Action Programmes are broadly sensible and useful; many of the organisations which monitor the programmes are less so. Their inadequacies can disguise the quality of the practical work which is being done.

It is difficult for a consumer goods company manager to argue against the value of careful controls on electrical and mechanical safety, health hazards, food additives, labelling, the commonisation of standards, and on after-sales service. Resistance on the question of what it costs the manufacturer to take account of new rules have more validity in the USA than in Europe and the UK.

In the USA, where consumerism began and where it has become unreasonably noisy, a strong backlash to the consumer movement is growing, based largely on the question of resulting cost and price increases. Four factors affect this question more heavily in the US than they are ever likely to do in Europe and the UK:

- the frequency of 'class' actions, a phenomenon almost unknown in Europe and the UK;
- the frequent assessment and exaggeration of damages by a US jury, rather than by a judge, as in the UK;

- the relating of damages to be paid to the subjective extent of the 'misdeed' by the company, not to any objective assessment of the harm actually incurred;
- the fact that US lawyers commonly work on a 'contingency fee' basis, taking as much as 30 per cent of a successful settlement. Some such settlements, in the millions of dollars, seem in European eyes to be out of touch with reality.

Loudest complaints from manufacturers in Europe and the UK relate to the cost of product liability legislation, which is less onerous, and subject to lower court awards, than in the USA. As leading insurers calculate that even a doubling of a company's product liability insurance would raise cost from about 0.01 per cent of turnover to only 0.02 per cent, the complaints are exaggerated. Further, such costs are shared equally by all manufacturers in the same business and can be passed on equally, without the slightest chance of the consumer noticing. There would be no shift in competitive advantage or disadvantage, which is what the board has to worry about when composing its marketing strategies.

A company goes out of business if customers stop buying its products, even if it loses only a quarter or a third of its customers. They may choose to stop buying for a range of reasons, from danger, to price, service, fashion or nationalism. The board's responsibility is to the company, to ensure that the products are such that the customer goes on buying them. It has few direct responsibilities to the customer, beyond using its best endeavours to ensure that the products are safe, and properly described and advertised. With industrial goods there is little problem – description of goods, performance and specification are laid down in a detailed contract. With consumer goods the borderline between commercial sense in satisfying the customer and legal responsibility in protecting the customer is getting blurred.

If directors were doing their jobs properly, consumer organisations would not exist. Tough, but it is true.

                                        MISS EIRLYS ROBERTS, CBE, 1980

The consumer movement grew up because companies were not exercising enough 'commercial sense'. The movement now has a momentum of its own, and legal requirements will go beyond 'commercial sense', seen from a company's viewpoint. But legislation is necessary. Voluntary codes seldom work to the benefit of the consumer.

While industry as a whole characteristically abhors legislation of any kind, the producer *can* be aided by a clear statement of responsibilities which affect all producers in the field, equally.

And in the long run, what is good for the consumer will be good for the most effective of the competing producers.

Competition or 'a conspiracy against the public'

Both the USA and the UK enacted legislation in 1976 against restrictive trade practices. Aimed at preventing collusive price-fixing and related abuses, there were significant differences in approach.

In the early 1970s a number of cases were brought against contracting companies in the mechanical and electrical services fields for their collusive tendering in the 1960s, a process whereby the bidders for a contract came together covertly to decide which of them would win the particular tender at what price – the others then agreeing to increase their own bids well above that figure.

Similar collusion had been detected in the fields of ready-mixed concrete, road surfacing materials, and telephone cables – also companies selling mainly to public authorities which had major construction projects to complete. The net result was that the public authorities, which in the final analysis means the general public, ended up paying inflated prices to these subcontractors.

The same practice was unearthed in the fields of copying equipment, gas boilers, polyesters and bread. In the USA it was the folding box corporations which made the news. Tips of very large icebergs, submerged masses of managements which have concluded that they cannot keep their corporations above water by skill alone.

There is nothing new about the practice. Adam Smith wrote in *The Wealth of Nations* in 1776:

*People of the same trade seldom meet together, even for mer-
riment or diversion, but the conversation ends in a conspiracy
against the public, or in some contrivance to raise prices.*

But it is against the existing civil law, hence the court actions. It is
against the public interest. And it is commercially inept. When the
companies were instructed by the courts to desist, they found that
after a number of years of surviving on artificial prices they were no
longer able to build up a commercially competitive tender. It was all a
bit like the situation of the ageing Afghans who purchased hormones
from the pharmaceuticals company in which the writer first cut his
commercial teeth. True, these artificial aids kept them in the conditions to which they were accustomed for as long as the aids were
available. But once deprived of them, the gentlemen discovered that
they had chemically emasculated themselves, irreversibly.

Many of the largest UK contractors involved in these practices
began to run into losses when the practices were brought to the
attention of the courts. Uncertainty led to price-cutting, which led
them into deeper losses.

Yet although the practice was illegal, against the public interest
and demonstrably destructive in the longer term, the new Restrictive
Trade Practices Act of 1976, which was introduced to protect the
customer and the community, did not make the practice a criminal
offence (except where the colluding parties had already been ordered
by the court to desist).

It is a criminal offence in Canada, Australia, West Germany and
the USA, and is prohibited with greater or lesser severity in most other
parts of Europe. In the USA twenty years ago General Electric was
convicted of price-fixing. It was fined half a million dollars and had to
pay massive civil damages. Several of its executives were sent to
prison. In West Germany in 1975 fines totalling £10 million were
imposed on a large number of construction companies, and on nearly
500 individual managers who had been involved in the practice. Yet
the practice continues. In 1986 fifteen chemicals companies, including Shell, Hoechst, ICI and BASF, were fined by the European
Commission for running an illegal price cartel for polypropylene,
used in a very wide range of household products. Given the size and

standing of the companies concerned, and the volumes of the product sold, the fines totalling 57 million European Currency Units (ecus), or $64 million, were disproportionately small. When a few months later the European Commission fined fifteen steel-makers for acting in concert, the penalties were even lower – 50,000 ecus, or $57,000 apiece. The Commission has power to fine a company up to 10 per cent of its turnover, potentially $1.5 billion in the case of ICI, or more than a whole year's profits: '*That would deter – and deterrence is needed*' (Economist, 1987).

The EEC has introduced a variety of regulations which are intended to keep free enterprise 'free' by outlawing any practice which restricts, prevents or distorts competition. Member countries also have local legislation. The UK's Competition Act 1980 avoids the pitfalls of the USA's anti-trust laws, under which each potential breach is battled through the courts at huge cost to both corporations and taxpayers. On the other hand, it brings sharply to mind that the political tone of governments and trade ministers can change with time, or their actions vary according to the external pressures of the moment. The UK government of the early 1980s, for example, refused to allow the constable of the Act, the Director-General of the Office of Fair Trading, to force the London Stock Exchange to remove some of the restrictive practices within that body's operations – this official retreat being made despite the many separate scandals which had disgraced the self-regulating Lloyds of London insurance market, the self-regulating commodity broking community and the self-regulating Stock Exchange itself.

It set a poor example to corporate executives, and would serve to 'relax' the pressure on those still actively fuelling apparent corporate performance by restrictive practices such as price-fixing.

Of the many forms of corrupt practice, this one is significantly different. Unlike old-fashioned bribery of officials, it excludes the customer. That is why, in the end, it will rebound against the executives concerned with more than old-fashioned righteousness.

The community

The CBI stated, in 1973, that '*a company, like a natural person, must be recognised as having functions, duties and moral obligations that go beyond the pursuit of profit and the specific requirements of legislation'*. But the company is not like a natural person. It is created, described and confined by specific legislation. It is created for a specific purpose. In the words of the US Supreme Court (Trustees of Dartmouth College v. Woodward), it is:

> *an artificial being, invisible, intangible, and existing only in contemplation of law. Being the mere creature of law, it possesses only those properties which the charter of its creation confers upon it.*

The company's relationship with its environment in achieving that purpose is similarly defined by legislation, such as the Acts concerning health and safety, pollution, taxation and employment, which are intended to ensure that it does not abuse its community, in the widest sense of the word. Each nation's Companies Act also defines a range of limitations on corporate behaviour which have the same objective.

The company must comply with all laws which affect all similar companies. It should not fancy out ways of being more good. It should not seek to develop the qualities of a natural person, such as goodness and charity.

Companies are not created to be charitable to their external community. They are created to do business, and through that process to create wealth for

- their own internal community of employees;
- the public-representing institutions, and individuals, which own shares in them;
- the taxman, and through him the community at large. He has the largest stake of all.

The board has quite enough to do attending to those responsibilities. It is the role of governments to attend to the community.

10 Internal responsibilities

Electing the chairman

The CBI recommended in 1973 that chairmen of public companies should be appointed and reappointed on a year-by-year basis, since which time the recommendation has received no further comment, perhaps because it smacks of the rankest heresy, or produces visions of corporate anarchy. Yet in view of the near-hypnotic hold which a dominant chairman can exert over his co-directors, to the detriment of their contribution, and thus to the detriment of the board's performance, there is huge merit in the CBI's recommendation. Also within private companies.

Because he is the one director who remains years after the scheduled retiring age; because in current practice he controls entry to the board; because the media come to identify him as 'the company' and the company as 'him'; because of the very fact that he has been there longer than the rest – the chairman is usually seen as something akin to the Rock of Gibraltar. His developing eccentricities become very visible alongside the strenuous efforts of his co-directors to avoid all signs of eccentricity. He is called 'Chairman' outside the board by those who will call even the fiercest chief executive 'Adrian' or 'Charles'. And he is the one director who all the other directors will agree is pushing through what none of them want, but they let him push it through anyway. He has become institutionalised. His continuance in office through the thick and the thin, without murmur from the directors, represents one of the least understood, and least actioned, of all the board's responsibilities. True, he is often the wisest, or once may have been. But not always, and not forever.

The long dominance of a board by a powerful chairman can generate harmful side effects. One-man bands can become bullies. The chief executive, and other executive directors, can lose heart.

169

They will move, if they are good, or sink into submissive obedience if not so good. Ever since Man came down from the trees, stopped chewing greenery and became a hunter, the leader has needed the active cooperation of his group in order to catch their quarry – not passive submission. If the brilliance for which the chairman was elected in the first place begins to fade, or be overridden by egocentric objectives, the mechanism of board control will rust and seize fast.

Too often the chairman is elected to that role after a period as chief executive, as though this is a natural progression. It is not. The two roles are fundamentally different, and in most cases require quite different personalities and styles. A newly elected chairman who is about to relinquish the chief executiveship will seldom promote an equally tough man to succeed him to it. He will seldom lead his board in critical review of the plans and mechanics which he devised when he was himself chief executive. And he will seldom be able to keep his fingers out of the managerial pie, which has to date been his whole life.

One of the non-executives should be better for the chairmanship, if he has already absorbed himself into the culture of the organisation by chairing a divisional board or two. Selecting the right man is not difficult if the non-executives have had close relations with the company, and have been judged in these relationships by the other directors. Those who only managed to turn up for the monthly meetings disqualify themselves for lack of interest.

The difficulty is not in finding the replacement, whether from within or without. The difficulty is in understanding that the board really does have both the right and the responsibility to replace an unsuitable chairman, and then in making its intentions clear to the incumbent. If the board adopts a twelve-monthly re-election routine, this becomes, with a little preliminary lobbying, a great deal easier.

If the foreman fails to orchestrate his little unit productively, he loses his job. If the sales manager consistently mishandles his sales force, he loses his. If the head of engineering cannot maintain a team which delivers the goods in reliable format, he too is replaced. It should not be different with the chairman of the board.

The chairman manages the board. The board, through its chief executive, manages the management. The management manages the company's budgeted businesses. If the chairman manages the board badly, or not at all, or with objectives which are privately oriented, then the whole chain of innovation, development and control will certainly fail.

Choosing the chief executive

One-third of our Managing Directors are pretty good; one-third are middling; and one-third are so appallingly bad that I do not know how they survive.

LORD WILFRED BROWN, 1980

The board's most important single decision is its choice of a chief executive. The vote on this appointment commits the company to a style and standard of operational management which it may live with for many years. It is the most difficult of all decisions to change in the face of later evidence that it was wrong. It is a single vote about a single person, which shackles many directors with bonds which are real, though wholly unrealistic. Bonds where logic is allowed to be overridden blindly by primaeval loyalty. It can be most difficult, but most necessary, to remember that loyalty must be to the strength and survival of the company, not to a very special kind of colleague. It is the one appointment where the board should prefer to recruit an outsider if there are any significant doubts about an internal candidate – the exact opposite of normal good practice in preferring existing staff for all other positions.

In the USA around two-thirds of chief executive officers are promoted from within. The pattern of their executive background, prior to moving into general management, differs markedly from the pattern in the UK. More than two in five come from the marketing function, which is three times as many as in the UK; only one in five come from the finance function, with a similar proportion from manufacturing/engineering.

In the UK there is an inbuilt assumption that an engineering company can only be headed by an engineer, despite the fact that it can be apparent to the board that the company's situation requires quite different characteristics. Electing a chief executive means matching an individual to a very specific situation. All executive directors are potential candidates, or should be able to be. All are aware that an incautious word about their future superior can blight their careers. Few therefore contribute actively to this decision, and most judge where to place their vote according to where the centre of gravity seems to lie – which in practice means where the chairman has made clear he intends to place his vote. Most executives who throw caution to the winds and say precisely what they believe to be true about an inadequate internal candidate who has the vote of the chairman (and thus almost certainly has the votes of the one-day-per-month non-executives) do so only in the prior knowledge that they plan to be working elsewhere in the very near future. Yet saying what they believe to be true may indeed be saying the truth, and it is their duty to say it. Executive directorship can demand a distressing level of personal courage.

The chairman is normally the prime mover in recommending, and where necessary in bludgeoning through, the election of his own preferred candidate to be the chief executive who will manage the managers. It can usefully be argued that the chairman's role is to steer the board, not the management, and that he should therefore be the least forceful of all in this process. This is true particularly if the chairman is also the outgoing chief executive, and is recommending his own replacement. The probability that he will recommend someone whom he can continue to 'line manage' from the chair is high. Or, if forced to accept the need to recruit from outside, the chance that he will reject the first round or two of candidates presented is also demonstrably high, on the natural human basis that 'no one can follow me'. But the chief executive must not be, or be open to the charge of being, the 'chairman's man', his shadow, his younger self, his vicarious power.

Many of the currently prevailing style of one-day-per-month non-executives have the experience, and even the impartiality, to be able to match candidates to the job, but have so little specific knowledge of the people and businesses in the company on whose board they sit that they can give little more to this critical decision than the least courageous of the executives. The harmfulness of casual non-executives is most clearly seen when there is disagreement among the executives about succession. By simple ignorance of their company, or by a lack of practising interest in it, they come to form that very centre of gravity into which the unthinking votes are thrown, thus dispiriting the executives whom they are intended to stimulate.

Where candidature for the position of chief executive is not clear cut, or where there is a strong measure of executive disagreement, boards frequently choose to postpone the final decision by adopting the interim mechanism of appointing two or more joint managing directors. For any company, other than the very largest, to do this must be wrong. One person must carry the ultimate managerial responsibility; one person must take the most difficult operational decisions. Only one American President can press the button which fires the nuclear missiles. What if there were two? When the joint French and British administrations in the New Hebrides decided to stop playing that charade, out came the bows and arrows.

One bad general does better than two good ones.
NAPOLEON

The placing of multiple chief executives on a holding board can only make sense if the corporation's businesses really can be divided into a number of divisions which have absolutely no operational overlaps. But then the joint chiefs will need to form a caucus which works out its own preliminary assessments on investment priorities, as best it can, before investment proposals come to the board for decision. And somebody has to head that caucus and speak for it. A natural leader will almost always emerge.

Worst of all compromises is when a chairman who combines the position of chief executive comes close to retirement, but cannot safely slip the chief executive role because of the level of board disagreement about his nominated successor. This is one of the most common reasons for introducing the joint managing directors mechanism. It is also one of the most dangerous. Directors will find that, come the appointed day for the chairman to slip his joint managing directorship, they 'really cannot go back on it now', and they will inevitably pass the mantle of chief executive to the man about whom so many doubts were expressed not so long before.

If there are any doubts about the qualities or style of an internal candidate for the role of chief executive, then he must be rejected. There must be no doubts about the chief executive, and least of all in the boardroom itself. History will certainly place its own verdict on his subsequent performance into the public record.

Recruiting executives

One-third of the short-listed top managers whom I vet are found not suitable for the position concerned; usually because they are not clever enough, or not tough enough to stand up to the pressures.

DOUGLAS MACKENZIE DAVEY, 1980
Industrial Psychologist

Appointments to the board must be judged on two criteria: whether the candidate's skills will add significantly to the sum of the existing directors' capabilities, and whether his personality will enable him to contribute actively and consistently to the bulk of the board's decisions. When recruiting externally, many boards will carefully judge the candidate against the first criterion, but few will measure him against the second.

Recruitment of senior staff is the most difficult of all management functions. The chances of error are multiplied tenfold when the appointment also involves a seat in the boardroom. There are some helpful personality-analysing techniques which can be employed, ranging from interview by psychologists, to gobbledegook question-and-answer papers which produce miraculously accurate descriptions, to handwriting analysis, or graphology, now almost a science. The Germans frequently use it when making senior appointments; the French and Israelis always use it. The writer has used it with dramatically accurate results. Such techniques are never 100 per cent foolproof, but added to the judgement of the recruiting panel they can powerfully reinforce subjective conclusions, or open new lines of enquiry, which may unearth characteristics which would be harmful in the position concerned. Yet few US and UK companies insist these aids be used. Most recruitment consultants eschew them. And some candidates refuse to be tested by them – often with good reason.

It is surprising that prevailing practice for recruiting senior executives in the USA and UK boils down to the board selecting someone from a handful of possibles presented to it by an executive search consultant, or 'head-hunter'. Surprising, because one would not expect the board to be satisfied by applying its judgement to such a small catchment only, which has been compiled at the judgement of an outside organisation, or individual, who does not carry the board's responsibilities. Certainly the process of recruiting senior people is so often fraught with internal politics, power chasing, and plain ignorance of what the board really needs, that each senior appointment should only be made with the help of a truly professional recruitment consultant, who provides both an unprejudiced evaluation of the type of person needed and an unprejudiced evaluation of the candidates located.

Large companies should in theory have space for the permanent placing of such expertise within their own personnel department, but few, in practice, will permit their personnel staff to speak freely about the most senior of the existing executives. This naturally prevents any useful internal review of how possible candidates might work alongside the *in situ* men, who will be keen to safeguard their own positions at all times. Thus most personnel departments today are concerned only with applying simple legal routines, and are not enabled or requested to make any strategic contribution to their company's future.

And thus companies make themselves dependent on external professional recruitment consultants. Some of the head-hunters can be called professional. Few are psychologists; almost as few have worked in senior management; very few have *themselves* sweated in the boardroom hot-house in the kind of industrial and commercial companies which they serve. Most can offer their clients little more judgement than conclusions and recommendations based on the apparent message from references, notoriously unreliable, and the apparent nature of a career history and 'track record'.

Time and again someone who has made an appalling blunder in one company is head-hunted smartly out to an equivalent role in another company, carrying no doubt the glad references of colleagues who are only too happy to see him go. Only space and the laws of libel prevent this from being illustrated, but the reader must know his own examples. Too often the references and the record are deceptive. Too often the head-hunter, without the aid of the personality-analysing techniques which he does not routinely use, is no more able to spot an alcoholic or a schizophrenic than any other layman. And these categories do get appointed to boards. If the writer has seen examples, so too, he would wager, has the reader.

The secretive short-listing of a few men by a head-hunter allows the lazier company clients to 'assume' that a thorough vetting has been completed, and they can decide to 'skip over' any further professional evaluation, such as aptitude testing, personality analysis or psychological review. Such companies fail to recognise that the head-hunting process can only, in some cases, tell them something about a man's *past* in *another* environment, but nothing of value about his *present* characteristics, or his suitability for the *future* environment in which the vacancy is situated. These two factors, alone, can explain many of the 'inexplicable' cases where a senior man, who is known by his colleagues to be a 'walking disaster', is head-hunted away to an even higher-paid role where he can do even greater damage. It happens every day. The reader who cares to confirm this can do so, with a little patience spread over a few months, but without probing any deeper than into the kind of newspaper or journal in which corporate results and corporate appointments are regularly reported.

When the British Civil Service recruits senior administrative personnel it subjects candidates to a range of tests which enable the selection of persons with a specific set of aptitudes and backgrounds. In this function it acts with more professionalism than most large companies – though it can separately be questioned whether it is recruiting the most *effective* kinds of aptitude and background, given the unsatisfactory results of so many of its recent endeavours, such as the Zimbabwe and Falklands Islands negotiations, or the many sex-and-spy scandals which periodically produce a few pages of public outrage. Aptitude can also be confused with attitude; the strangest feature of the recruitment by the British Civil Service of the traitor Kim Philby, who defected to Russia after causing great damage to his country, was not that he passed the aptitude tests but that he was allowed to pass them at a second attempt, having been rejected the first time for his political views . . .

Seldom do head-hunters relate their own conclusions about a candidate to a judgement on how he will be able to cooperate with his proposed new co-directors; often as not they only meet one or two of those directors. Seldom do they analyse the business situation into which the successful candidate will be slotted; few are equipped by managerial experience to do so. Yet the use of head-hunters for the recruitment of senior staff in the USA and UK is today routine, and really senior posts are no longer advertised, as they were only a decade or so ago. The performance of boards has not improved. For the first time since the Industrial Revolution began, in Britain, the import of manufactured goods into Britain exceeds exports of manufactured goods from that country. While the mushroom growth of the head-hunting process may not be, for certain, the main cause of decline, it is clear that it has not helped in any way, apart from making life easier and cosier for managements, who are not paid to seek ease and cosiness. Despite this dismal example, many Continental European managements are increasing their use of covert head-hunting – and, as an aside, their two-tier board system has not helped them to remain wiser. Even in Denmark, where the law restricts the keeping of personal files, and thus in theory frowns on the head-hunting process – even there boards are being seduced into the easy option of using head-hunting instead of the more onerous but more productive process of advertising recruitment and its related, open, competitive selection procedures.

The recruitment of senior staff is such an important board responsibility that the directors most closely concerned could benefit by stepping back a pace, pausing, and giving a little logical consideration to how they go about it. The process of head-hunting grew up in the USA where there was no nationally distributed newspaper which would be read regularly by the nationwide catchment of potential top-level executives. Recruitment advertising could therefore be rather hit-and-miss, and a 'search' for likely candidates could make sense. But so could geographically localised advertising; the executive dug into sunny California might be reluctant to move to New Jersey. It is a big country, and Americans are becoming less mobile, not more so. Many of the US 'searches' are geographically confined. Thus even in the USA there is only limited justification for the occasional use of head-hunting as opposed to open alternatives. In the 'home' of free enterprise and equal, open opportunity, should not recruitment, the most important managerial function, be free and open? Should not all have free, equal, open opportunity to apply for management positions and directorships? Or should directors remain able to make *their* part of the nation less free, less open, less equal, less competitive and better protected?

Covert head-hunting continues in the Continental European countries which have forbidden it by law. Some directors are stimulated by working through this limited, secretive process, even if it means being party to a breach of their local legislation – and to a breach of their responsibility to their company to recruit the best staff possible from the widest potential catchment. In some European countries all vacant positions must, by law, be openly advertised, either in the company's name or through a professional, such as a lawyer, accountant or consultant.

The primary arguments used in favour of head-hunting are that: top executives do not read the jobs ads; and the best people are working successfully, do not want to move, and have to be drawn out to better things (i.e. better for them) by covert, rather than overt, means.

The largest recruitment consultancy in the world, which carries out both head-hunting and recruitment advertising, has put into print that the first argument, in their unrivalled experience, is simply '*not true*'. A director of the Price Waterhouse executive recruitment service, another leading consultancy, reconfirmed this conclusion in 1987. Witness also the extent to which the head-hunters themselves use advertising when recruiting head-hunters. Or the way in which they obtain coverage in the 'Jobs Column' of the *Financial Times*, which is quite simply free advertising.

The second argument must raise a chuckle. If a man really does not want to move, he will not. Or should not. The implication that someone else, who may never have been a director or senior manager, knows what is better for his career than he does himself only raises doubts about his judgement. The second argument is also a fiction. When seeking to defend covert recruitment, the managing director of one of the best-reputed head-hunters stated that: *'the day an American executive arrives in his new job he completes his c.v. and sends it out to headhunters to let them know where he is'* (Shellard, 1986). Which demolishes, comprehensively, the grounds on which this disturbing secretive practice has been promoted to companies. All manner of nonsense has been written into recruitment fiction and management mythology to enable head-hunters and their clients to maintain a too-easy relationship. For example:

- *'The only suitable men are working in the same kind of job in the same industry.'* This simplifies the search and reduces its cost to the head-hunter. More critically, it prevents cross-fertilisation and thus prevents any of the benefits of hybrid vigour.
- *'They must not be unemployed, self-employed, or merger casualties who deserved it anyway.'* The real reason is that the head-hunter's research office can't trace such men in its routine directories of companies in specific industries, plus that the head-hunter doesn't want the hassle of describing backgrounds which do not fit into a routine pattern.

  This particular piece of nonsense, more common in the UK than in the USA, is damaging to companies. Many studies, for example by the Cranfield Management School with the help of a redundancy counsellor (Dixon, 1987), have demonstrated that while unemployed executives tend to be less conformist and less politically shrewd in the corporate jungle (which some readers may rate as 'plus' points), they are on balance *'more energetic, imaginative and creative'*, or have just been unlucky numbers in the take-over game.
- *'They must be under 40 years, or 45 years, or . . .'* Why? The average 'upper quartile' chief executive (i.e. the man holding the

most onerous role) in Switzerland is 57; in France is 59; in Holland is 58; in UK is 58; in USA is 57.

Why do senior men swallow this kind of nonsense?

- *'He must have an in-depth knowledge of the plastic hydraulic widget market in Belgium.'* In fact the client company is stuffed full of men with precisely that kind of expertise and really needs new approaches, new backgrounds, new experience, the freshness of new comparisons rather than the weary staleness of repetition.
- *'We don't want any white knights in shining armour.'* This really means that we don't want anyone who will query what we are doing and how and why, either because 'we' are not doing very well, or because we are keeping alive by illegal price-fixing.

Directors, working through head-hunters as middlemen who take a written or implied brief, can filter away potential candidates who are more capable than they are before the shortlist gets anywhere near the board committee – if there is one. (See Clough, 1981, below.)

- *'It's the chemistry which matters.'* Just a variation of the above.

And the universal:

- *'Big men need big, big motivating.'* Which means big, big pay and perquisites, even though psychologists have long since confirmed that the highest-flyers, the best performers, are not motivated primarily by money. Certainly the highest-flyers look for good rewards, but as long as these are provided within fair limits they are more strongly motivated by a combination of occasional recognition of their achievements, plus an unending challenge. In contrast, the head-hunters make *their* income by taking 25 – 35 per cent of the first-year salary of a new man they have introduced to a client company – so they want to 'talk up' salary levels just as high as they can. Of course, all the head-hunters deny hotly that this happens; the reader may reach his own conclusions about the 'probabilities'. It is no coincidence that the rate of increase in the pay and perquisites of senior employees in the USA and the UK during the last decade or so has become a matter of shame. Recruitment and remuneration has entered a Looking Glass world. When the chairman/chief executive of

Beecham was abruptly fired, a replacement was sought by head-hunting, without advertising. The conclusion was reached that there was *no one suitable in all Britain*, and a new man was brought in from the USA. The salary of the outgoing man had been high by prevailing UK yardsticks; the salary of the replacement was *three-and-a-half times higher*. It should not be necessary to spell out the useful lessons which can be learned from this extraordinary case.

The search process is far from mysterious. It is simple. That is why so many ill-equipped organisations have set up as head-hunters, to the detriment of that very much smaller number of firms which do employ skilled recruitment consultants and which can occasionally help companies. Truth also is that the recruitment consultants make a bigger fee, for far less work, by head-hunting instead of by taking a percentage on advertisements plus a lump-sum. *Their* words, not the writer's.

The head-hunter's work is easiest, and his income flows most readily, if his clients select new staff by 'satisficing' rather than by optimising. Recruitment by covert means would scarcely exist if companies sought the optimum recruits by alerting the widest range of potential candidates by overt methods – 'scarcely' rather than 'not at all' because in about one case in a hundred the covert approach might be excused. However, companies often use covert head-hunting for reasons which cannot be excused. At the beginning of a 'hunt' the client may give the head-hunter a listed specification of the type of man wanted, which can, and often does, include criteria which are quite unconnected with the demands of the position concerned, or are foolish, or are illegal. The client records his prejudices, conscious or subconscious; the head-hunter usually accepts the brief without batting an eyelid. Head-hunting is a service business and services follow their markets. Any supplier of services knows that if he presses a client to take a more responsible line on some matter he risks losing that client to another similar supplier – there are plenty of them. That is why merchant bankers, as well as head-hunters, do not make any significant effort to change the way in which their paying clients operate or behave, a fundamental failing which the merchant bankers, if not yet the head-hunters, have often admitted. •

Left to his own devices (and a surprising proportion of senior recruitment is done by single directors operating without checks), a man will tend to recruit someone who is 'pliant', someone who is weaker, someone who will not outshine him or his own record within the organisation. Even when recruitment is conducted by a committee, the group of selectors will often move from the optimum candidate to the one *most readily acceptable* (see Chapter 4 on groupthink). The group will only move in small and limited steps from a detailed specification, which leads them to 'more of the same'. Acceptability means conformity; conformity can result from mediocrity. Such channelled selection fertilises the ground in which groupthink can flourish. The group begins to take progressively worse decisions; its comparative performance declines. There will be all sorts of public and private explanations for the decline: the company should be centralised, or decentralised, or the internal culture (whatever that means) needs a new look. But the reasons are always simpler. No products, however good, no staff, however dedicated, can overcome the harmful effects of an incompetent, or limited, or self-interested board.

It is helpful to note the comments of one of the more professional head-hunters writing in the *Director* magazine of the Institute of Directors:

> *As executive search consultants we have seen many a competent new chairman completely out-voted by his own board members when he proposed a desperately needed outside general manager, a modern marketing director, or a capable production director to replace incumbents . . . Similarly, we have often seen situations where an incompetent but dictatorial chairman could repulse constructive and necessary action proposed by executive directors below him, at the expense of the best interests of the company's shareholders . . . These situations are damaging to the company, disastrous for British industry, and wasteful of talent . . . In actual cases my company has seen mediocre directors prevent the hiring of a capable specialist because he might prove a threat to the entrenched directors. Similarly, such unqualified directors, by acting together, may make life impossible for capable technicians and trouble-shooters.*
>
> W.S. CLOUGH, 1981

As the Age of Communication overlaps with the Age of Information we find that the most important of all managerial functions, the recruitment of the leaders, is being performed with less communication and less and less information. Potential candidates for a vacancy are not able to become aware that the vacancy exists because it is not 'communicated'; potential employers limit their 'information' on what is available to them to the two–four persons who are presented to them. The 'knack', if it may be called that, in the head-hunting business is to present the client with names which will be readily acceptable. This means putting forward only those names which will not ruffle feathers and which will not require any tedious explaining. It is not the head-hunter's responsibility to improve the quality of the client company's management.

If companies took the trouble to try recruiting by advertising and by head-hunting simultaneously, they would get some surprises. Time and again old-fashioned advertising has been demonstrated to bring in more suitable staff. Maybe not always, but certainly often enough to suggest that the board which does not advertise has absolutely no reason for confidence, ever, that recruiting without advertising has located the best men it could appoint to conduct the affairs of its company. The board is responsible for the quality of the men who conduct the affairs of its company. There is something faintly ridiculous about a board delegating the largest part of its single largest responsibility to outsiders. Something more than ridiculous about a board working on the assumption that these outsiders – any outsiders, however competent – can really locate all the relevant good men without advertising. When operating for client companies the writer has seen it demonstrated, often, that they cannot. When operating for himself in advertising for recruits for an independent directors' cooperative venture, the writer received some hundreds of replies from men of high calibre and wide experience. In pursuing the applications of the several score most qualified men it became clear that almost every one had suffered a career 'hiccup', then another in rapid succession – and had then moved into the scratchy field of 'consultancy' as the only remaining relevant source of work. In almost every such case it was strikingly clear that:

- those highly qualified and widely experienced individuals, being unemployed or self-employed, were out of the head-hunters' areas of hunt. From being readily marketable by the head-hunters they had, in practical terms, become invisible and unmarketable.
- the individuals concerned had all had sensible and successful career patterns – but in almost every case they had at one point been moved off course by the seduction of a head-hunter's introduction to another company.
- they had then moved into a position inadequately described or understood.

If the selection process is secret you will only find out if the job is wrong for you when it is too late.

HERRIOT, 1986

This led to another rapid move, and then another . . . until their orderly, sensible career patterns were dishevelled to the point at which no head-hunter would bother to explain the dishevelment to any future client, irrespective of the patent qualities of the men concerned.

Good men have their careers disrupted and destroyed; good men are then deprived of the chance to apply for positions which would enable them to restart those careers. Companies end with a less effective management mix than they could obtain in an open market. The only reason why those who despise the head-hunting process do not speak out against it is their fear that doing so will get them 'struck off' the head-hunters' good books, on which future careers today depend totally.

But don't blame the head-hunters for making a living however they can. Blame the company directors and government ministers who employ them and escape from their most important managerial responsibility, the selection of senior staff. Blame the company directors and ministers who still shield themselves behind this, the flimsiest of all the management deceptions.

For effective and responsible recruiting:

1 Establish a committee of the board comprising, for example, the chairman, the chief executive, one more executive and one more

non-executive. When recruiting executives for posts below board-level drop a non-executive or two, but include a non-board executive. Charge the committee with vetting the draft job specification drawn up by the chief executive, and perhaps helping to improve it.

2 Select an experienced recruitment consultant, if there isn't already a suitable judge within the personnel department. If necessary talk to several and vet them as rigorously as you will vet the candidates. Involve the selected consultant from the outset, including in finalising the job specification. Let him know whatever he wants to know about the job, the company, the board. The better he is, the more he is likely to ask.

3 Advertise widely, either in the company's name, or in the name of a professional firm, dependent on the circumstances of the vacancy.

4 Only head-hunt, also, if the job specification is highly unusual; for example, if a very specialised technical background is essential. Only head-hunt, also, if the process is still legal. And in such very rare cases, which most directors would never meet in their careers, vet the head-hunter, too, as rigorously as you intend to vet the candidates.

5 Ensure that all the replies are seen by the committee and consultant. The time-wasters and the unqualified may number 180 out of 200, but they are quickly put aside. The consultant can do an initial separation for the committee into bundles of 'yes', 'no' and 'maybe'.

6 Compile a long list of possibles and probables. Reduce to about a dozen by discussion between the committee and the consultant.

Do not reject men who are older than the age considered ideal. (They are probably not as old as your chairman.) Age discrimination is already illegal in the US, Canada, France and elsewhere, and such legislation must become more widespread.

Do not reject men who are redundant, self-employed or unemployed just because they are one of these things. If they look interesting on paper, but you are worried why they are not in employment, ask them why they are not. They may have a better reason for having left their last job than many a senior executive has for staying in his.

7 Interview the dozen or so, with committee and consultant all present.

8 If the head-hunt has produced a couple of heads, include them and treat them just the same as the others. They are no different, whatever the head-hunter may say, or they would not be talking to you. If a head-hunted candidate emphasises how difficult it will be to winkle him out of the marvellous job he is doing elsewhere, drop him. If he does not want you as much as you want a good man, he is not your man. If he has to be seduced by paying him more than other good men, he is not worth the extra. The concept that the only person worth having is someone who really does not want to move is a myth. It is also a nonsense; that must be self-evident.

9 Whittle down to three or four. Put these through professional psychological testing. If any object, let them drop out. People should want to know their true personality characteristics; this is part of honing their own effectiveness. Remember that straight head-hunting, or recruitment without personality testing, will at best tell you 'what a person has done', not always whether he has really done it well, and never, repeat never, what he really can do and achieve. Every job is different; what he has done in one may bear little relation to what he can do in another job, or another environment. Further, the record of 'what he has done' is often nebulous, or is just a record of what others have done for him, or is intentionally misleading.

10 Whittle down to two or three; and present these to the full board. The board has time; it is not going to be doing anything more important on that day. And it takes a lot more time to clear up the shambles after the subsequent removal of an unsuitable recruit.

11 Collectively agree on the best candidate. Ask the remuneration committee to settle his pay and perquisites package; they can do it straight away as they are sitting at the same table and can go next door for five minutes.

12 Tell the selected candidate. Take up references if you have to, for example if technical competence needs a level of confirmation which could not be achieved in interview. Remember that no one will give bad references, even if deserved, and few will give

accurate references, so you are left to rely on the board's subjective judgement, plus the psychologist's objective judgement. The psychologist, and very often the skilled graphologist, should at least be able to determine if the man concerned is a conman or a liar. The writer has seen both categories exposed by such analyses, and later confirmed by hard facts.

13 Call him in to fix final details, including his initial induction. In his first two or three weeks he can ask all the silly questions he likes without damaging his standing. During that period his colleagues will enjoy supplying him with any relevant information. After that he is on his own.

If, on the other hand, the board has decided to promote an internal candidate, it should still use the opportunity to induce the person concerned to be put through the same aptitude and personality tests as would be used for an external candidate for the board. A manager should welcome (fear a little, but welcome) being put through them at this most critical point in his whole career path. Some multinationals, such as ITT, always put internally promoted executives through psychological analysis before their promotion is confirmed.

Character, mental condition, and thus aptitude to handle a board position, often change measurably around the same time as a person reaches board-level, because most of the stresses and changes in his life, including domestically, occur at around this time. The board has to determine whether the candidate can handle the change from being a manager only, to being a manager part of the time and a director the other part; whether he can handle a situation at the board where he has to disagree with his superior, the chief executive, and press an opposing case. A good chief executive is aware that he is no graven image, and he grows and flourishes under stimulus. The key to balancing the board is to ensure that the mix of directors does provide a constant stimulus to both thinking and performance. Executives appointed to the board need to be measured against this requirement.

When a director fails, because he has slowly declined in one way or another, or because his job has evolved beyond his capabilities, or because he was badly recruited in the first place, the board has to stiffen its resolve and remove him, sideways or out. The problem in

carrying inert ballast or dangerous cargo is not that it costs a few
thousands to have it on board. It costs that much to decorate the romp
room each year. The problem is that the non-contributor deadens. He
pulls down the level of your game. He fills a seat which someone else
could use more profitably.

> *The real trouble lies in the self-perpetuation of the mediocre; of*
> *managers who are never brilliant and never atrocious, but whose*
> *use of the assets is less effective than the dumbest shareholder*
> *could manage for himself.*
>
> ROBERT HELLER, 1985

The removal of inadequate directors is today most commonly
accompanied by the payment of a large golden handshake, often
beyond contract limits. This gives huge offence to the 'lesser' employees who cannot protect their own hides at the company's expense in
this way. It is slowly beginning to give a hint of offence to some of the
major institutional investors who have let this practice develop in both
the USA and the UK from about 1970 – before which it had never
occurred. It is in reality no more than a form of self-protection by the
executive directors (now described by the chairman of the board of
one large institution as *'the shareholder's worst enemy'*) and a form of
buying-out by the non-executives for having failed to ensure that the
recruitment had been done responsibly in the first place.

Pay, perquisites and pay-offs

The late Supreme Court judge, William Douglas, concluded that
corporate directors had become *'financial gigolos'*.

In the 1960s American corporate performance was good by any
yardstick, and total executive remuneration was also good, both in
amount and how it was constructed. No senior executives grumbled,
and many lived the life of Riley.

> *The watershed year was 1973, when the head of GM was paid over*
> *$1 million.*
>
> THACKRAY, 1983

In that year the oil price was quadrupled, which triggered a pandemic of greed, first in the Middle East, then almost everywhere else. Almost. Again the exception is Japan.

In the 1970s a study (Albrecht/Jhin, 1978) was made of the remuneration of 148 highly paid chief executives in the USA which sought to relate it to the turnover or assets or performance of their corporations: *'we started on the assumption that there must be some relationship between what a chief executive does and his salary – but we didn't find any relationship whatsoever'*. Later studies (Monks, 1984 and 1986) found the same lack of correlation between pay and performance.

By the 1980s:

> *In most large corporations the board of directors has also given up its real prerogatives on determining the pay of top management. Outside compensation consulting firms are routinely called in . . . Healthy stock options are handed out almost traditionally. They are geared not to the performance of the company, as they once were but to the Standard & Poor's or the Dow Jones Index. When the stock market goes up, everyone cashes in; when it goes down, the board issues new options at lower prices.*
>
> GENEEN, 1985

In the mid-1980s the highest paid American industrial executive earned $11 million in salary and bonuses plus a further $9.5 million in stock options. The third highest earned $8.4 million while his corporation made losses of, coincidentally, $8.4 million. On Wall Street, meanwhile, the investment bankers were earning *five or six times as much* as the highest paid industrial executives by the relatively simple work of advising such industrial executives on acquisitions. Top American salaries rose on average 18 per cent in 1986, when inflation was 2 per cent, when the American trade deficit was $190 billion, and when comparative corporate performance was declining. In the UK, when the nation's highest paid executive received a pay increase which was huge by local standards, his board described their performance as *'passable, but not terribly exceptional '*. When his income rose another 40 per cent the following year the analysts were describing his company's performance as '*D for Disappointing*' (Questor, 1984). In 1986 the chairman of BP received a 15 per cent pay increase as profits fell by 70 per cent, from £3.6 billion to less than £1 billion . . .

The reader can doubtless think of numerous similar anomalies in his own country. The writer has a sackful of examples, even the strangest of which must reluctantly be excluded because the absolute figures can be misleading; while a salary of $1 million is now quite common in the USA, one of £100,000 is still considered high in the UK. It is not, always, the quality of the individual executives receiving such payments which needs questioning, but the amount, locally considered, which they obtain compared against the real contribution which they, *personally*, have made to corporate performance – also the amount, locally considered, against local conditions of all kinds. In Japanese corporations, with relatively few exceptions: '*There is probably only a five times differential* (in salaries) *from top to bottom*' (Spencer Stuart, 1986).

This range illustrates Japanese recognition that a corporation is very largely dependent on the innovation and performance of lower and middle levels. The accepted routine is that the directors' pay increases are linked to the employees' increases; say 3 per cent for one, so 3 per cent for the other. In contrast, real income differentials in the USA and the UK are commonly twenty times, and frequently forty or more. This at a time when '*hourly workers find it hard to make ends meet*' in the USA (Scotese, 1985), and when 43 per cent of employees in the UK are calculated by the EEC to be earning below the 'decency' threshold. The numbers living in poverty in the UK (using the official definition of poverty) rose from 6 million in 1979 to 9 million in 1983, when the government understandably stopped issuing the figures. Responsible estimates at time of writing, in 1987, range from 12 to 16 million, in a population of 56 million. Nonetheless, in 1986 topmost salaries in the UK rose by 45 per cent, and in some sectors of the City by 150 per cent, while tax advantages for those with the highest incomes continued to improve and diversify.

Quite apart from the developing risk of an eventual new storming of the Bastille, the inflationary 'pull' from the top will certainly continue to make US and UK costs increasingly uncompetitive. Performance is never improved by throwing more money at well-paid men and hoping they will try harder. The concept is childish.

The anomalies are greater when considering perquisites rather than pay. Incentive schemes and salary supplements, such as stock options, cars, top hat pensions, houses, company apartments and so on and on are most heavily concentrated at top levels. When Sir William Duncan was appointed chairman of the still halting Rolls-Royce company his package was like thousands of others today; high basic salary, and properly so, and a performance bonus. But did Sir William need an incentive to stimulate him to do his job better? Wasn't he going to do his job as well as he could, anyway? Once upon a time, about a decade and a half ago, senior men were employed at senior salaries because they were expected by others, *and by themselves*, to produce good performance – that was the norm for senior men, not something which required prompting or seduction.

Large or super-large bonuses and related ancillaries can be double-edged. They may be appropriate for a new recruit who has to turn round a dying machine tool company, and who knows he will, for sure, end up paying heavy alimony as a result; they are not so appropriate for established men working in established companies in the booming retail chain business. They can also be of negative value. The writer has experienced cases where bonus schemes for some subsidiary company executives were so high that the parent Groups were effectively prevented from planning or implementing the kinds of new developments which a changing market-place demanded – the executives concerned wouldn't cooperate because the proposed changes might, just might, trim their bonuses for a year or two. The companies had to stand still, while their competition walked or ran past. Paul Thorne, a senior psychologist with RHR, concludes that we have probably already gone over the top: '*more likely, incentives will create more birds of passage, more inflation, more resentment from those who have not, and yet more obsession with money issues*' (Thorne, 1987). They can also have a directly opposite, and equally damaging effect to that of creating birds of passage, because: '*The guy who sticks with you only because you have him locked in financially is worse than nothing. He is a liability*' (Tarrant, 1985).

And the anomalies become greater still when considering pay-offs: several million pounds to the man brought in to try to turn round the Crocker National Bank when he was asked to go; several million dollars, and several hundred thousand dollars per annum for life to the deposed head of CBS. The sums involved have become unreal, and:

> *the golden parachute phenomenon may have done more to discredit CEOs among the general public than such widely publicized instances of white-collar crime as fraud and embezzlement – and rightly so.*
>
> SCOTESE, 1985

When the Morgan Grenfell merchant bank required the resignation of one of their take-over experts for breaking the bank's rules during the Guinness affair they negotiated a compensation package: '. . . *he resigned* (sic) *and is therefore entitled to compensation under our guide-lines*'. Corporations can consider aligning their own guidelines and practices with the law: '*You are not automatically entitled in law to payment for the full unexpired term of an employment contract*' (Sylvester, 1986). They have known this for years in Scandinavia and other parts of Europe, where it has been tested in the courts. In the USA and UK, in contrast, the limits of compensation for termination of contract appear to be defined by how much can be slipped past the shareholders and media without *active* disagreement.

The reader will know of the placebo effect, whereby neutral substances dressed up as pills can make a patient feel better. There is also the pricing effect, whereby the higher the charge for the treatment, the better the patient will feel. It can be seen in all parts of the market, from the psychiatrist's couch to the African bush. Many of the villagers at the writer's first post in Africa preferred to queue at the private doctor's surgery for an injection of water which cost them a lot (and which the doctor admitted was only water), rather than go to a nearby government hospital where treatment was free. 'I am paying a lot more, so I must be getting better treatment' is just a variant of 'We are paying him a lot more, so he must be better'. The headhunters – Western style, not African style – have not been slow to induce supine clients to raise the proposed remuneration for the head they have hunted, on which they obtain a percentage; why not, it's the client company which is responsible for the decision on what it will pay. Naturally the client directors most readily conclude that everyone else is getting expensive these days, so they have another look at their own salaries. Up, up go the pay, perquisites and eventual pay-offs.

It's time for boards to strip away the deception that big men only perform when given big, big incentives, and reach through to the quite contrary reality that: if men are overpaid when they are under-performing, and if they are given big presents when they are asked to leave, *then there can be no incentive to perform*.

Appointing non-executives

Prevailing practice is that the chairman decides when the board needs a non-executive; talks with his business contacts for suggested names to supplement his own catchment; selects the man he judges suitable; presents him to the full board, or to a committee of the board, for approval on the nod.

Because most other directors are passive throughout this process, it cannot be surprising that the average non-executive is viewed as 'the chairman's man' from the first day he walks into the boardroom, whether or not he was originally selected to be just that. He becomes identified with his sponsor, and he remains in unison with him through the thick and the thin. His value to the board is small, or negative.

The tacit assumption is that the chairman, as the leader of the board, carries the sole responsibility for ensuring that the composition of the board is soundly balanced. Naturally this is a responsibility of the chairman, but it is not his alone. Indeed, where the chairman is by character autocratic, it will inevitably be the other directors who sense most keenly the need to introduce an element of counter-balance. Left to his own devices, an autocrat is someone who collects a '*team of people whose advice he does not intend to take*' (Argenti, 1983).

Any single director who believes that his boardroom needs a little more independent objectivity, or any other category of part-time participation, should marshal his facts, lobby his co-directors mercilessly, and insist that the matter be itemised on the next agenda. If voted down, but still aware that the need remains, he should return to the fray after the passage of a few more months have helped to demonstrate, more strongly, the case which he is seeking to make. It is a nerve-wracking exercise, which few directors will care to undertake more than once. It can be made a great deal less awkward if the board has an annual spot on the agenda to review board composition, to review the performance and contribution of the existing non-executives, and thus to collectively decide, as a routine, whether changes need to be made.

The appointment of a new non-executive should be as methodically conducted as the appointment of a new executive. The board should:

1 Establish a committee of the board, consisting of the chairman, two other non-executives, if there are any, and one executive. The total should be three or four. Whether or not to include the chief executive is a moot point; should he be a primary judge of someone whose primary role will be to judge him in the future?
2 Provide the committee with a broad statement of the observed needs of the board in terms of background and style of candidate required, seen against the main strategic problems and opportunities facing the company, and against the existing backgrounds and styles already represented on the board.
3 Require the committee to refine these terms of reference to a format which can be advertised, while still keeping the catchment area broad. The board will always be looking for widely based business experience and an unprejudiced, lively judgement, not for specialists.

The value of the directors to the shareholders lies not so much in their technical or professional qualifications as in their personal qualities, amongst them the wise and practical judgement they can bring to the attitudes of the company.

CBI, 1973

4 Empower the committee to select a recruitment consultant well experienced in the field of non-executives. Be prepared to pay him a fee which reflects the amount of work which he will be expected to do. Use his judgement to check that the brief produced by the committee does match observed needs. He will need to meet most of the directors, to determine their personalities and styles.

Note: this particular recommendation is a counsel of perfection. There are very few recruitment consultants who have significant experience in this field and a non-board-level personnel director is no substitute. The head-hunters are used to finding executives who will slot in without ripples, whereas a non-executive should be expected to make ripples. It could be better counsel to suggest that the reader forgets about the consultant, tucks this present book under his arm, and moves on to 5, below.

5 Empower the committee to advertise, whether in the company's name or in the name of a professional firm. There is a wider range of first-rate talent available than is known to any of the best recruitment consultants. Advertising will produce a much wider spread of alternatives than will result from a simple head-hunt, or from a file search in the offices of the consultant, or from the existing contacts of the directors.

6 Leave the committee and the consultant to trim the alternatives to two or three, who are then presented to the full board.

7 Concentrate on the candidates with the most varied background and most flexible approach. If the board is looking for just one non-executive, and particularly if he is the first non-executive to be appointed to that board, do not go for the narrower background, even if it seems more directly relevant to the most burning problems of the moment; this may delimit too tightly the board's subsequent vision of what the non-executive contribution, in general, can produce over the years.

8 Double-check in full board that the selected candidate really does meet the original specification within reasonable limits, and that both he and all the board members fully understand what, and how much, he is intended to contribute, including in terms of time and geography. If he will be unable to visit the units in Aberdeen or Abu Dhabi, then he probably is not going to be able

to do much else, either. Candidates also need the chance to de-select themselves. It is today becoming quite common in the USA for prospective non-executives to turn down an offer of a directorship because they themselves conclude that they will not be able to give the time required.

9 Settle remuneration. Keep in mind that: '*most board fees are too high for the work done to earn them, and too low for the work that should be done*' (Geneen, 1985).

10 Post-decision, establish an initial programme of induction, so that the new non-executive can be a useful contributor within weeks, not months. Agree his routine information requirements, and how they will be met. Establish dates for future meetings, including boards, committees, planning sessions. Introduce him briefly, but rapidly, to all senior managers. Give him: current accounts; brief company history and recent past accounts; budgets, plans, investment appraisals, study reports; structure diagrams with names and brief backgrounds; trade literature; copies of recent minutes.

11 Annually review his, and every other director's, performance, if necessary amending the agreed roles of the non-executive, or changing him.

The annual performance review should be as cold-blooded as the initial selection process. The person appointed may have lost interest halfway through the year, and this will have shown. Most boards still monitor the performance of their non-executives less rigorously than they monitor a junior clerk.

People and organisation

The board's management-related responsibilities concern people, planning and performance. The three are intermeshed; there can be no effective management of performance without adequate consideration of the placing and relationships of key people, and there can be no realistic planning without a close knowledge of both the aspirations and limitations of those people.

Chapter 8 considered the need for a company-wide mechanism for participation and communication which parallels the company's control structure. Communication is more than informing; it requires the two-way exchange of understanding. When the communication channels do not parallel the control structure, confusion can arise, or can be made to arise by those who feed on confusion, either on the staff or outside it. Decisions demanding action must be able to pass as smoothly downwards and outwards as any simple piece of information which requires no action.

The best control structure, and related communication system, is always first defined in theory, and then adapted in practice to fit the characteristics of the key people who will carry out those decisions. Whichever aspect of board responsibility we look at, we return to the fundamental responsibility of knowing and understanding the key people, outside the boardroom, on whom corporate performance will always depend.

Sometimes the structure itself can inhibit the best of people. One large international Group has for years operated a corporate 'matrix' structure of vertical design-and-production units, and a superimposed horizontal series of international marketing units. At each intersection between the vertical and horizontal sits a territorial market, with a described range of products to be promoted for sale within it. The head of the horizontal marketing line believes he is responsible for all local decisions, be they pricing, licensing, distribution or whatever. The head of the vertical line believes precisely the same. Sometimes success is achieved at one 'intersection' by the tougher minded of the two simply refusing to cooperate with anyone else, excluding anyone else from knowledge of what he intended to do in that market, and doing it. He succeeds by breaking all the corporate rules. The markets are as bewildered by all this as the managers, but they cannot do anything about it. The board can. It does not. The corporation's comparative performance continues to decline.

The chief executive is naturally the prime mover in evaluating and proposing an optimum organisational structure for the company. His opinion weighs heavier than that of the other directors, not only because he should be the best informed, but because he is charged with operational responsibility, and must be given his head as far as the board judges possible. But the board must consciously judge.

The chief executive might, for example, prefer to differentiate and separate the subsidiaries when some of his co-directors might conclude that the merging of several of them would be more effective. He might choose to divide and rule because that makes his life simpler – a valid enough reason if it does not reduce corporate potential. He might be wrong for good or bad reasons. He will always judge from a personal viewpoint; the board must always judge from a corporate viewpoint. The viewpoints may, or may not, coincide.

A new chief executive from outside the company will, almost invariably, seek to introduce organisational structures close to his immediate past experience. All organisms seek the minimum of simultaneous change, and the new chief executive may want to carry his environment with him, like the hermit crab which always chooses the empty shells of exactly the same species of snail as it grows from one size to a larger.

Or there may be other constraints. The chief executive's organisational proposals may turn out to mirror his own personality problems or neurotic tendencies (Kets de Vries/Miller, 1984). Two experts have identified five types of 'corporate neuroses' which they link to five personality problems in chief executives, and which can lead to corporate failure. Briefly, these are:

Paranoid Power is concentrated in a few hands, managers are mistrustful of each other. Risk is avoided, strategies are variable. Accounting controls and cost and profit centres abound.

Compulsive Ritual rules. Every step is overplanned, with a welter of operating instructions and detailed policies. Change and new ideas are avoided.

Histrionic Impulsive, hyperactive, dangerously uninhibited. Action – lots of it – by hunch and gamble, without relevant facts. Power is concentrated in one man who takes risks – lots of them – and for whom diversification, into anything, is the guiding strategy.

Depressive Passive and purposeless corporations, often in mature industries. Boredom and past practice prevail. 'There is no alternative', and so change is resisted.

Schizoid Apathetic executives discourage consultation and fear involvement. Gossip and infighting, with everyone protecting his own corner. Small changes occasionally made, usually unsuccessfully, for limited rather than corporate interests.

If the reader recognises a few of these characteristics in his own organisation, or in client companies, and if he is feeling strong enough, then he should read the article 'On the Prevalence of Madness in Businessmen' (Thorne, 1986). Inadequate competence, perceived in himself by a director, will lead to stress, which can lead to misjudgement, and then to mental unbalance. Anyone working alongside such a director, as a manager, non-executive, chairman or consultant, as the writer has done at different times, will tend to avoid thinking first of unbalance as a possible cause of corporate problems – that would feel too much like seeking an easy option, or disloyalty, depending on one's own role with the corporation at the time. But the evidence will accumulate to the point at which it cannot be ignored or rationalised away. For this reason, among others, the practice of dominant control of organisations is dangerous – yet it is being applied or assumed with increasing frequency in American and British corporations today.

The board can avoid being caught out by top people's personality problems, or 'by market changes which require organisational changes, or by growing pains, if it gives an annual spot on the agenda to review the structure, which could slot in neatly with the planning programme.

Planning

> *A man who does not think and plan long ahead will find trouble right by his door.*
>
> CONFUCIUS

The shareholders, bankers, accountants and employees will all readily agree that some of the board's most important functions are to establish corporate policies, set objectives and devise strategies. Yet surveys, old and new, demonstrate clearly that most boards still do not get involved directly with any of these functions (Henke, 1986). They leave it to the CEO. If he is 'paranoid', 'histrionic', 'schizoid' or of limited competence, his subordinates will never be quite sure what is going on, and the board will seldom be told. If 'compulsive', 'depressive' or of limited competence, then it is most likely that there is very little going on. When a number of successful subsidiary company presidents in a listed corporation with blotchy overall performance decided to query their CEO about the organisation's plans, they were shaken to be told that he had 'rubbished' the concept of planning many years ago. The corporation continued to drift, becoming sellers or 'distressed sellers' of a string of diverse units which it had failed to manage into health. There was indeed 'trouble right by his door'. The analysts, meanwhile, assumed that all the selling was part of an exquisitely planned strategy and marked up the stock; the financial advisers kept mum, because they earn best when a corporation buys and sells, for whatever reasons, good or bad. The board will get no nudging help from such outsiders, and precious little from its CEO if it does not purposefully decide and monitor what it wants him to do, including the production of operational plans for the subsidiaries and proposals, for board decision, for the development of the corporation as a whole.

Failing such purposeful deciding, the directors may find that they are not even consulted on major strategic questions; the chairman or chief executive has already determined from experience that the board is supine, will do as it's told without a murmur, and can be ignored or treated with contempt. In another listed corporation the CEO and an executive director (who doubled as company secretary, the role which is responsible for ensuring that board procedures are properly followed), negotiated the sale of a large part of the corporation's business for several months, without informing the board, let alone asking its opinion about what was in fact a complete reversal of the corporation's existing strategy. The board was only advised when the prospective buyer's final written offer had been received. The directors were far from happy, but by then, of course, it was far too late to go into reverse. No one was fired. So the process could be repeated; the board could continue to be ignored and treated with contempt – which by now it deserved. Consider, instead, the detailed actions required of a board which is responsibly involved in the management of its company.

In the 1960s the buzz word was 'marketing'. In the early 1970s it was replaced by 'business planning', or 'strategic' or 'corporate' planning, which are fundamentally the same, though some specialists insist on defining nuances of difference between them.

The real-life interface between marketing and planning became blurred. The essentially simple planning process developed a religion and jargon of its own. It became so complex and theory-ridden that many companies, especially the smaller ones which had most need of it, almost welcomed the dislocations of 1973–4 as demonstrating that the world in general, and their companies in particular, were quite clearly unplannable. Companies, large and small, trimmed back their planning department, where they had one, at just the time they had greatest need for it.

Any company which is working today without formalised planning routines is assuredly placing its survival at risk. Any company which is not budgeting and monitoring within a planned longer-term strategy is rudderless in a sea which will never be calm. The planning process is indeed essentially simple, but it involves a lot of work; it involves digging up previously unquestioned assumptions, and examining the corporate whole from its roots to its greenest shoots.

To the directors on the boards of major conglomerates, where the policies, objectives and strategies are almost exclusively financial, the following section may seem tedious, even irrelevant. But its contents, and the equally detailed parts of later sections, are real enough for their subsidiaries and for smaller independent groupings, to the managers of which they are addressed, in the hope that they can provide useful guidelines. The process begins with the board defining and communicating policies against which the company and its individual units can compile and evaluate their plans. Strikingly few boards have ever drawn up such a statement of policies, let alone amended them and communicated the amendments when the business environment changed, thereby demonstrating to their companies that they were alive to their situation.

The board's first attempt at defining its policies can be simple. It can refine them with time. No one down line will quibble about one or two points being left out, or being inadequately covered; they will welcome any guidance they can get as to how the board is thinking. The policies should include:

- its fundamental beliefs, if it truly has some. For example, the importance of individual contribution and reward, and of whole-hearted autonomy. Or alternatively, the belief that coordinated biggest is best, with strongly centralised control leading to collective performance and collective gain; or whatever else identifies a corporate ethic;

- what the company aims to achieve, in which businesses, where, how much – what the company is not, and will not do;

- its policy for business development, whether at home or overseas, by acquisition, diversification, organic growth;

- its criteria for such growth, and how proposals for investment and development will be handled;

- its criteria for the returns required for survival and growth; an ROC at X per cent above the rate of borrowing; a profit progression at Y per cent above the rate of inflation;

- its policy for the control and charging out of the cost of its 'centre', including interest (so that unit pricing can be realistic, and so that the centre itself can be seen to be exposed);

- its policy for employee remuneration – for example, middle of the top or middle quartile for the industry – and its routines for appraisal, induction, training, promotion and recruitment of employees; incentive schemes, if any;

- its management structure, with its advisory or executive committees and their functions and limitations; its parallel structure for participation and communication, the routing of suggestions and complaints, and how these will be handled;

- external relations, and how they will be handled, including customers, suppliers, government departments, trade associations, the media, as well as the competition;
- the planning and budgeting routines which flow from the above, and the monitoring and control machinery.

The board is responsible for compiling such policies, for defining the objectives which derive directly from them, and for describing the basic strategies by which the objectives will be achieved.

The policies are 'statements of intent', which provide guidelines for management. The objectives are 'desired performance results', which describe what the board wants the company to achieve, when. Most are quantified, and against a time-scale:

- a reduction in working capital by X per cent in Y years;
- an increase in ROC by W per cent in Z years;
- an increase in direct exports from M per cent to N per cent of turnover in P years;
- a reduction in staff turnover from R to S per cent per annum in T years – and so on through all the areas of board responsibility.

The strategies are the 'how'. While policies and objectives are exclusively board matters, the strategies are part board, part management responsibilities. They run through the whole of the plan period, which may be three, five or twenty years, depending on the level of board concerned, or the size of company.

The tactics are the 'immediate how', and are reflected in the detailed expenditures recorded in the one-year budget. They should always fall within the wider strategies, and represent step one in applying those strategies as the plan period opens.

When introducing formalised planning, the board will need to adopt a common approach for all units, so that it can rapidly make meaningful comparisons between units and coherently compose a corporate picture. It will find that managers who are not used to such disciplines will view the new forms and formats as 'more nonsense from Head Office', so the first round should be kept quite basic; it should ask only those questions which any manager, given a push, will agree he should be asking himself, and the answers to which will help him to produce better results in the future.

Always minimise the use of complex diagrams and avoid jargon. Organisation structures and communication channels must be simple. The evaluation of business probabilities may be difficult, but the processes of evaluation must be simple.

First planning formats should include:

1 A covering description on the way the formats are to be completed, with worked examples, if there can be any doubts. A statement of the number of years to be covered (three is quite enough at the first attempt) and the rate of inflation and bank interest to be used for each year. Both of these may turn out to be wrong, but the board will need data which has been compiled against the same yardsticks by all units.

2 A review of the main external factors which the unit believes will affect performance during the plan period, either positively or negatively, including critical factors which could kill or maim it.

3 An analysis of existing and planned markets and businesses which breaks the total business of the unit into a number of definably different activities. One of the objectives of the planning process is to isolate those activities which should be de-emphasised or closed, and those on which the unit should concentrate its time and resources. Each company, however small, has at least half-a-dozen definably different activities, whether defined by different types of customer, different ranges of products, different competitors, different methods of selling, or any one of a series of similar criteria.

4 A quantitative analysis of the performance, by sales, gross margin and net profit, of each of these definably different activities in the past year, the current year, and as anticipated in each year of the plan period. Every unit, be sure, will say that such analysis is quite impossible, because of shared overheads, overlapping markets, or absence of base data. They always do. Every unit, be equally sure, can be made to complete suitable analyses, and will get a surprise from doing so. The exercise always highlights that the unit is

bleeding from one or more places, unexpectedly. Or half expectedly; few managers will admit, without this kind of formal pressure, that an activity which they personally conceived and nurtured some years ago has by now failed. In every company which the writer has looked at, from the inside or from the outside, it has been possible to uncover, by analysis of this kind, one or more activities which were draining resources. There is no company which could not improve performance by such analysis, either by the board, or with a little external support. The simplest way to improve performance and generate more cash is to stop losing it. If the whole planning process ceased at this point, it would have achieved much.

5 An analysis of the main competitors in each of the defined activities, quantified as best possible by market shares. Record how the unit sees its own, and their, shares changing during the plan period.

6 A review of moves expected from the competition during the plan period, whether marketing moves, organisational moves (a merging of competitors, or their geographical extension) or the introduction of new products or services – and how the unit plans to respond. The primary element in a company's environment is its competition. Success is measured by how well you do in comparison with your competition. A major element of the company's planning is how it will meet and overcome such competition.

7 A cold-blooded review of the company's strengths and weaknesses, including external competitive and internal performance weaknesses; the moves it plans to make to capitalise on its strengths, and to eliminate its weaknesses, of both kinds. Unless required, formally, to think out and spell out these moves, it may do nothing at all, or do much less than the board judges necessary.

8 A quantified statement of the resources required to achieve its plan, including money and men. This may, for example, trigger a training programme.

9 A draft budget for each year of the plan, plus a forecast balance sheet for each year end, and cash generated or consumed. The formats may have to be tailored a little for different units at this

point, but not so much that the board cannot readily sum the
requirements, sum the returns, and compile a first view of the best
and worst corporate situation through the plan period.

All the unit plans come back to the board, via the planning
committee, for manipulation, and final approval. The first year of the
plan becomes the one-year budget, to which the units are required to
operate, and against which their success is monitored. The process is a
rolling cycle of policies, objectives, strategies, plans, operations,
monitoring – and consequent amending of any of the policies,
objectives, strategies, plans or operations which are found to be
imperfect.

The board initiates the cycle, and powers its continuous
momentum. The value of the process depends as much on the quality
of the monitoring as on the reality of the original policies and
objectives; these can always be amended in the light of experience.
Both the production of the plans and the monitoring of their suitability demand a great deal of the directors' time, both within and
outside the boardroom. Which is one reason for the recommendation
in Chapter 12 that the process be coordinated by a board committee.
But if reaching a final judgement on any one year's plans, and on the
one-year budget which flows from them, means that the whole board
has to lock itself away for a few days in a quiet country house, so be it.
The board has no greater managerial responsibility.

Performance

Recruiting, organising and planning are but preambles to the gritty
business of generating sufficient returns to be able to survive and
grow. The critical point in the closed loop of board control is receiving
the feedback and applying corrective actions; is monitoring the
performance or managing the managements.

The smaller the company, the more detailed the control information required. For even the largest, the minimum monthly information for making corrective judgements includes:

- a monthly comparison against budget of orders, sales, costs, overheads, gross and net margins, cash generated or consumed;
- a cumulative year-to-date comparison against budget of the same elements, with comparisons also against past performance, perhaps on a moving annual total basis. Order data should always include the gross margins calculated: *gross margin trends, past year/year-to-date/current month/margins on order book, can be one of the clearest and earliest signs of impending trouble*;
- the chief executive's running forecast of year-end results;
- a month-end balance and updated cash flow forecast.

Within subsidiaries or independent companies:

- a listing of phased, overdue debtors above an agreed figure, with comparison against previous month;
- similarly for creditors.

Plus at choice:

- trends in selected operating ratios, chosen in accordance with the characteristics of the trading units – for example, turnover or margins to working capital, stocks to turnover, or tenders submitted to tenders won. Trends in ratios can frequently highlight actions required more clearly than absolute data can achieve; they force more specific responses from the general managers concerned.

And for companies of all shapes and sizes:

- moves made by the competition during the month, and how the company has reacted. Success is always comparative; the marketplace makes it so.

When the monitoring routines are working like clockwork, then the managers will be providing the chief executive, and through him the monthly board, with predetermined conclusions about remedial action, not simply presenting a bundle of figures and waiting to be told what to do about them.

When the board maintains the machinery in good working order it 'monitors'; when it does not, it has to 'manage'.

The need for routine measurement against past performance and present budgets is today understood quite widely, in even the smallest companies, but how many of the largest have ever reviewed performance against 'what it could have been'? In booming markets, ranging today from chain retailing to electronic components, higher year-on-year targets and attendant bonuses are easy enough to set, and comparatively easy to achieve; perhaps the targets were set too low, and market share has been lost. Apparent performance improvements are commonly achieved by retreat from markets or loss of share. When the pressures of the late 1970s at last focused attention on the comparative productivity and near-death condition of the BL vehicles company, an intensive five-year programme was introduced, at the end of which everyone, almost, breathed a sigh of relief and said that it was all a great improvement.

Yet in that five year period:

- vehicle output had fallen from 785,000 to 525,000 per annum;
- share of the home market for cars had fallen from 28 to 18 per cent (in 1970 it had been close to 40 per cent);
- share of the home market for commercial vehicles had fallen from 20 to 13 per cent (in 1970 it had also been close to 40 per cent);
- survival continued to depend on an abnormally high level of margin applied on car sales in the UK, compared with in the European markets, which has never been adequately explained. Net results of plus-or-minus a few million pounds had meanwhile reached losses of £500 million per annum.

The directors can be too easily comforted by climbing part-way out of a deep hole into which they had earlier stumbled. When reported performance falls one year by, say, 25 per cent, it requires an increase of 33 per cent to get back to where you started. Down 50 per cent and

you have to climb 100 per cent; down 80 per cent and the improvement required becomes 400 per cent. It's a piece of arithmetic which
the analysts sometimes miss.

Performance reviews against the company's past, and against the
competition's present levels of achievement can include:

Selling and marketing   There are 90,000 Japanese salesmen working
in the USA, and just 5,000 American salesmen in Japan. Japanese
companies maintain 600 trading offices in the EEC, employing about
13,000 people; European companies have 100 similar offices in Japan
employing 850 (Nachiro, 1982). The Japanese have, to date, attacked
only a few international markets, but they have attacked them totally
in order to achieve market domination.

Planning   European executives on a management development programme in Geneva laughed at a Japanese executive when he described
his steel company's twenty-year planning (Franko, 1983).

Quality control   QC circles were in fact an American idea which the
Japanese absorbed, developed and made their own.

Productivity   Japanese-owned consumer electronics companies in
the UK achieve outputs which are 1½ times higher than local
US-owned companies, and twice UK company levels. Reject rates
were planned from start-up to be one-quarter of UK levels, and are
already down to one-eighth. But Japanese productivity is not universally high. It is far lower in many Japanese home-market businesses
than in equivalents in America and Europe – the lesson is that
Japanese productivity is high *where they need and plan it to be high*.

R & D   German companies invest twice as much in R & D as UK
companies, and Japanese companies invest four times as much.
Annual growth in R & D is around 6 per cent in leading European
countries, and below one per cent in the UK. The differentials
continue to widen; the situation is: *critical and very nearly irreversible*
(Porter, 1987). Annual domestic patent applications in Japan exceed
the total of domestic patent applications in the USA plus Germany
plus the UK by about 20 per cent.

Real growth   Concentration on winning market share has led to organic growth of Japanese corporations and to consequently greater returns to shareholders in the form of eventual capital gains. Japanese P/E ratios of 40–60 may look hysterically high to Americans and Europeans, but they are not 'calculated' on the basis of anticipated yield or dividend.

Financial executives play a relatively minor role in Japanese investment decisions (Abegglen/Stalk, 1986).

Meanwhile, at time of writing, nine out of the world's ten largest banks are Japanese; we can learn a great deal by comparing this proportion with the situation just five years ago, then ten years ago . . . and asking 'why?' and 'how?'

Manufacturing versus services   It is mentioned as an aside that Japan is the only major industrialised country where the share of services in the GDP is decreasing. In the USA 70 per cent of the workforce is employed in services, and the proportion is rising. In the UK it is 65 per cent, rising; in Germany 48 per cent, static; in Japan 50 per cent, falling.

The drift from manufacturing to services in the USA and UK is not simply a move away from 'old', 'heavy', 'smoke stack' industries such as steel, shipbuilding and machine tools; the USA and UK have also become net importers of high-technology manufactured products. The UK manufacturers have complained for decades that they would be able to compete lustily if only the £ sterling could be allowed to drop in value. It has in fact fallen steadily since 1966; from 1,000 yen to 225; from 11 Deutsche Marks to 2.9; from 12 Swiss Francs to 2.4 . . . In the only part of that period when the £ was rising in value, so was the UK's share in world exports of manufactured goods. When it began to fall again, the UK experienced its first ever deficit in trade in such goods . . . yet the manufacturers still complain that the £ is too high.

In contrast, through the same decades, the competing German and Japanese manufacturers have strengthened their real performance, and have consequently strengthened their market shares, their trade surpluses, and their currencies. If we run away from 'real' performance comparisons for long enough, it can become difficult to tell 'up' from 'down'. Within two weeks of each other in August – September 1986 the London *Times* newspaper carried two articles stating that '*Weak sterling* pulls reserves down' and '*Strong sterling*' pulls down a major company's reported profits.

We need to hold tight to reality, however uncomfortably it shakes corporate shibboleths. The decline of the US consumer electronics industry from the 1960s onwards, for example, had absolutely nothing whatsoever to do with the US dollar or other side issues. It resulted from management failures, producing lower real perform-ance than achieved by Japanese competitors, and it has been deduced that a similar decline is occurring in motor vehicles and other indus-tries in the USA today, for the same reasons, against the same competition (Abernathy, 1982).

Do the Japanese themselves agree? They tell us that:

> *Japanese success in the world market cannot be credited to them-selves alone. It owes much to the managerial negligence and administrative myopia of Western manufacturers and policy-makers . . . Too little R & D and too narrow horizons in time, space, product and market segments contribute to suicidal strategies.*

> OZAWA, 1983

11 Company collapse

Receivership is the ultimate sanction for bad management, which means for bad boards. Luck rarely comes into it. Analyses of collapsed companies by accounting firms which handle numerous insolvencies reveal a common pattern of weaknesses and mistakes, and misfortune is seldom a factor.

Certainly a recession adds stresses which are not in the board's power to control. Certainly the rate of corporate insolvency will grow apace. It will always exceed the published data, which does not include subsidiaries kept alive by internal funding long after they are dead, or bankrupt businesses interchanged between Groups, or such businesses which are quietly dissolved by their parent.

The detailed factors which lie behind company collapse, and to which boards must therefore apply priority attention, have been recorded by a major international accounting firm as follows.

Causes and symptoms in twenty company failures

Bad management	20
High gearing	11
No financial projections	9
Poor costing	8
Overtrading	7
Not reading economic signposts	6
Excessive overheads	6
Not selling production	6
Selling too cheap	5
Excessive research and development	5
Extravagance	4
Sales mix problems	4
Raw material shortage	3
Labour shortage	2

Overstocking	2
Engineering problems	2
Poor production planning	2
Fixed price contracts	1
Bad luck	1
Failure of bankers	1
Fraud	1

But these are just the symptoms. Behind them lie causes. In the words of the accounting firm:

> *It's odd how the public at large often see the collapse of a company as being a financial failure, but often this represents a misunderstanding of the position. True, collapse does not often occur until the company runs out of money, but the process of running out of money is often a mere symptom of the disease which has already taken hold.*

In their conclusions (which they advise are shared by all other major accounting firms and insolvency practitioners), the defects which place the business at risk are described as one or more of the following:

1 An autocratic chief executive who heeds no advice and flies the business 'by the seat of his pants'. He often collects people around him who do not argue with him because those that do argue do not stay.
2 Imbalanced skills. Perhaps too many engineers, as was commented on in the case of Rolls-Royce. Perhaps a failure of a growing business to recognise that people do not always grow with the job.
3 Overconfidence, manifesting itself in a failure to project forward the down side of projects or business decisions as well as the up side. Failure to appreciate the consequence for the business if the project goes wrong.
4 An absence of budget appraisal. No profit plan or cash flow plan prepared conscientiously and logically.

5 A failure to apply budgetary control. Budgets which go straight into the bottom drawer and are not used as a plan of action for developing and controlling the business, much as an engineer might use a blueprint.

6 A failure to use management information. Management refusing to believe the information which is produced, or ignoring it, or both. You will know the ploys used in meetings to discredit information when the message it conveys is unpalatable.

7 A lack of toughness in dealing with third parties. Often found in sales-oriented companies where people will concede any point in order to clinch a sale, and will then use the fear of upsetting the customer as a reason for not collecting the debt when due.

8 A failure to respond to change until it overwhelms them.

Also in their conclusion, these defects are characteristically followed by mistakes which expose the underlying defects, and which include:

1 The creation of contingent liabilities. Often companies, particularly companies within Groups, find themselves giving guarantees with potential liabilities substantially in excess of the company's ability to meet the claim under the guarantee without endangering their own solvency.

2 Incorrect gearing. A complex issue . . . it may result from over-rapid growth of borrowed funds – the cash generated from trading being more than absorbed in cash-hungry projects which generate little cash return in the short term, necessitating increased borrowing.

3 Overtrading. When turnover rises at a greater rate than the cash flow generated from trading, there is a need to finance the increased turnover.

4 Entering into major contracts, the consequences of which are not fully comprehended. In some respects this is a lack of business discipline, and it may also reflect an unwillingness to spend a few pounds on some professional advice.

5 Major new projects. Taking on projects which are substantial in size in relation to the existing business, in fields where the

company's management has little or no expertise, without allowing for the down side, or without taking steps to control the project and isolate it from the rest of the business.

These mistakes then characteristically lead into the third stage of financial malaise and progressive collapse, which includes the sequences of:

- failure to react to the warning signs;
- low profitability or loss making;
- adverse cash flow;
- extended credit taken from suppliers;
- adverse gearing, where there develops an overdependence on lenders as against the company's own resources;
- increasing losses as the situation deteriorates;
- with the business tumbling out of control, the management becomes totally absorbed in plugging gaps and staving off creditors in order to survive until the following day.

Each initial defect in the above summary is visible to a board which is alive to its responsibilities. If the board is wholly executive, or if its non-executives are of the one-day-per-month variety, then the defects will often go unchallenged until it is too late to challenge or change. But the defects will be visible. The onus lies on any director who sees them to expose his concern, and to require management action. The executive director may do this once or twice, but will seldom keep at it long enough for improvement to be finally effected; it feels too much like destroying the solidarity of the team, and it certainly means upsetting his boss.

The weight falls on the non-executives. They have no boss except the board. Their team is the board. The board as a whole is always responsible.

These characteristics of companies which fail provide a practical checklist against which the responsible board can measure its own company's situation. They are the conclusions of one major international accounting firm, which has viewed company collapse from the inside.

Strikingly similar conclusions were reached by an 'outside' study of a number of failed companies (Argenti, 1976). This study also found that fraud or bad luck were insignificant factors, but that there was always one or more of six basic defects:

1 One-man rule. A chief executive who dominated rather than led. The difference between a successful, dominant leader and an unsuccessful autocrat could be determined by other, more visible features of the company.

2 A non-participating board. Not just non-executives who did not know the company's true situation, but also executives who awoke only when their specialised function was under discussion. Note here the similarity with bad cabinets. Richard Crossman (1975 – 7) wrote in his diaries that, *'We came* [to cabinet meetings] *briefed by our Departments to fight for our Departmental budgets, not as Cabinet Ministers with a Cabinet view.'* A passive board enables the autocrat to suppress discussion, or to prevent controversy coming to the board at all.

3 An unbalanced top team, e.g. where all the directors are engineers. *'If the board does not contain a wide spectrum of skills then the chances of some new threat appearing but going unnoticed is severely increased.'*

4 Lack of management depth.

5 Weak finance function, especially at the very top. John Argenti plays down this feature in comparison with others, though the writer has seen corporate death result from this specific defect.

6 A combined chairman / chief executive. Not all the participants in Argenti's study agreed that this was a basic defect. But it must be self-evident that it is one where any of the other defects also appear.

Again, all these defects are visible to the board that is alive to its responsibilities. Where the board is not sufficiently alive, a number of management weaknesses will arise, which the Argenti study recorded as:

1 Poor accounting information. Poor comparison of 1 – 5 year budgets against actual performance, i.e. poor budgetary control; poor

costing systems; inadequate cash flow forecasting. Top managers know the company is failing, but the lack of an adequate system of information means they can keep quiet, and the board does not detect the growing problem.

2 Inadequate response to change, whether competitive, political, social, economic or technological. Sometimes external constraints were found to have hindered the company's ability to respond freely to change, e.g. the constraint not to increase prices; not to build a pipeline or factory; not to make a merger; or not to do anything very dramatic at all, for example as a result of trade union opposition.

3 Overtrading; increasing turnover at the expense of margins.

4 Launching the 'big project' which the company underestimated or could not handle. *'Companies run by autocrats are much more likely than other companies to adopt grandiose schemes.'*

5 Overgearing to the point that even normal business hazards become a constant threat.

6 Deterioration in various financial performance ratios.

7 'Creative accounting' which hid the true situation or hindered prediction. The reader will be able to think of his own examples of companies which have changed their accounting bases more than once, changed their treatment of taxation, or the percentage of profit taken on work in progress, in order to appear to maintain a barely acceptable reported profit level. It cannot go on for ever.

8 'Non-financial' symptoms, such as declines in morale, service, stock availability, or increases in payment periods, complaints. Management begins to get desperate.

9 The last few months, when suppliers demand 'cash', creditors ask questions, shareholders get restive, the board gets on its knees to the bank, other 'friendly companies, their wives . . .'

Every item on these two very similar summaries becomes a board-level matter when a company is weak. The director who sees the problems, but does not act remorselessly within the boardroom to remedy them, can find the subsequent receivership acutely uncomfortable. First, he might get fired by the receiver, who does not have to honour previously existing employment contracts. No golden handshake. Alternatively, he might be kept on a while to do all the dreary things like signing and sealing documents covering decisions taken by others, without his involvement. The receiver does not have to ask his opinion. Being emasculated is less humiliating than being treated as a eunuch. Second, he might find that the receiver unearths all sorts of strange transactions about which he had no personal knowledge. The humiliation of emasculation is a great deal less than the humiliation of exposed ignorance. Third, he might just find himself enmeshed in the periphery of, or bang in the middle of, a case for misfeasance, or a claim for damages. In the UK he might also find himself found guilty of 'wrongful trading', or he might be disqualified for *at least* two years as 'unfit' to be a director in any other company.

Certainly there will be more actions against individual directors in the future. And rightly so. Few would deny that it has long been inequitable that directors, including both executives and non-executives, could walk away from one disaster into similar roles elsewhere, without public query.

Some helpful American experience from the exercise of Chapter 11 of the federal Bankruptcy Code has been incorporated in the UK Insolvency Act 1985, which enables the appointment of an administrator to a weakening company at an earlier stage than that at which a receiver is normally appointed. This, together with a moratorium on debt repayment, can improve the probability of continuing the company's life. The administrator must be a specialist in corporate insolvency (not in business management), which in practice means an accountant from one of the firms working in this lucrative field. It remains to be seen whether court-appointed administrators will prove more successful than receiver-managers, who had for the most part become a variety of asset-stripper, whose main objective was to divide the organisation as quickly as possible into more easily saleable portions. This was made simpler by the fashion for management buy-outs, which in too many cases are used as an acceptable way of ending a working relationship which has reflected no credit at all on the holding company directors selling the unit, or on the subsidiary company directors who are buying part of it. Most accountancy-based receivers have no experience in managing *healthy* businesses, let alone in reviving weak ones, and have no intention of launching themselves into the full-scale general management of the organisations over which they are given total, exclusive control. The law does not force them to be efficient, or quick, or clever in how they handle the affairs of the insolvent company which is placed in their hands. In practical terms it only requires them to ensure that the debenture holder regains its lendings – in the unlovely words of their trade, to ensure that '*the bank can wash its face*'.

Further, there is no *practical* control over the number of staff from the receiver's own firm who can be brought in to assist him and who, like him, are paid 'from the top of the pot' before anyone else obtains a penny. There is no practical control on the quality, relevance or experience of those supporting staff and there is no check on whether or not the receiver makes use of other, more productive expertise. There is no practical control on whether the receiver has taken good advice on what to sell to whom, at what price, or on whether he has negotiated wisely. The act of placing a company into receivership chops more off the asset value of a company in ten minutes than even the stupidest directors could destroy in months or years; the misjudgements of accountant-receivers, working in markets and industries unknown to them, can double the damage, unseen.

Corporate solvency or insolvency is not simply a question of whether assets exceed liabilities, or vice-versa. Directors must cease trading the moment they judge that the company will not be able to meet any new credit taken when it falls due, and they can be held personally liable for any such credit taken during the period of insolvency. The decisive criterion is the ability, or not, to meet credit at some future date – and *that* depends on the attitude of the funders. If the bankers will allow the overdraft to increase, or will arrange new loans, given sensible evidence that suitable management changes have been made to strengthen the company, then the company is technically able to continue to trade, whatever the present relationship of assets to liabilities. The bankers are dependent on the accountants for advice on whether or not to extend the funding. Accountants can disagree. In the UK in 1984 the Hills family's construction company was put into receivership by Barclays Bank following a report by the well-reputed accounting firm, Touche Ross, which stated that there was a deficit of around £3 million. 'Not so', said the equally well-reputed accounting firm, Thompson McLintock, which stated that the company had still been solvent and could have been managed to trade its way out of its problems. To no avail. The act of receivership is instantly, and often comprehensively, destructive, and the company was by then very dead. By one judgement the company had been destroyed by the directors; by another it had still been viable, and was thus destroyed by the bankers and the perfectly legal actions of another firm of accountants.

The judgement of bankers, and the relevance of accountants, in evaluating such situations can be questioned. In cold-blooded reality, an accounting firm can make 100 per cent certain income, at high rates, out of a nice easy receivership, and it will find *that* more seductive than the uncertainty and stress of trying to revive a weak corporation from the side-lines. Similarly, a banker who has charges on all of a company's assets will find it more seductive to shut the company down while the assets charged are *still* greater than the monies owed to it, instead of agreeing to extend the life of the company for a period in which the assets may continue to decrease – *even though* new directors and managers have been recruited and there are reasonable prospects of trading out of trouble.

Unfortunately, the UK practice is to leave too many kinds of judgement, and too much influence, in the hands of accountants (compared with the American practice of depending too heavily on lawyers). A support function has been allowed to become a 'lead' role. The secondary has been made primary. Apparent, snap-shot performance statements are treated as real-life descriptions of businesses which have to survive in constantly changing environments. Too many businesses have been closed, and too many good people put out on the street, on the basis of such too limited measures of judgement. Of course, there are numerous experienced accountants with business acuity who do help companies. But there are others who, when placed in the position of managing companies, have demonstrated more limited qualifications.

Consider the American federal Bankruptcy Code, which applies in all states. In Chapter 11 of the Code there are provisions which enable a business entity – whether an individual, a partnership or a corporation – to reorganise over a period of weeks under the protection of the bankruptcy courts. The objective is to provide time to restructure the finances of the business so that it may continue to operate, to pay creditors and to produce a return to the stockholders. The reorganisation may be initiated by the voluntary filing of a petition under Chapter 11, or by a petition filed *against* the debtor. The debtor, for example a corporation, may continue in 'possession' of the business, subject to the supervision of the court. However, if the court decides that the debtor is guilty of fraud, mismanagement or dishonesty, it can appoint a trustee; in appropriate cases it can also appoint an examiner to investigate the affairs of the debtor. A Creditors' Committee can be formed to advise the trustee, or the debtor-in-possession, on the management of the business, and the committee can appoint attorneys, accountants or others to perform services for it.

A corporate debtor which remains in possession of the business has the exclusive right to file a reorganisation plan for the 120 days following the filing of the petition; thereafter *any* party can do so. In all cases the plan must provide for the *equal* treatment of the different 'impaired classes' – creditors, lenders, stockholders – and must include details on how it can be carried out successfully. The court decides type and format of information required, and this must be disclosed to all creditors and stockholders so that they can then decide whether or not to approve the plan. If it does receive approval by two-thirds or more of the 'impaired classes', it is still subject to the confirmation of the court. Indeed, the court will on occasion confirm a plan which has not obtained those approvals, and in such cases there are statutory conditions which protect the interests of the 'disapproving parties'.

In Japan, too, a corporation which has become insolvent, but which has good prospects of continuing in business if its current crisis is overcome, may commence corporate reorganisation (rehabilitation, or Kaisha-Kosei) or corporate rearrangement (Kaisha-Seiri) procedures, the objectives of which are to revive the corporation under a court-appointed receiver. The Japanese receiver is usually an attorney, which is also the case in most of Europe.

Receiver, administrator, creditor-appointed or court-appointed, accountant or attorney – all dismal shadows of a good board manned by responsible directors. In the event of corporate insolvency, UK legislation now affects a director's future status and also, as in the USA, his pocket; leading accountants Touche Ross believe that more than 50,000 UK directors a year could now face court action. As financial risks increase, so do indemnity insurance premia, up 570 per cent in the USA in 1986, and up 362 per cent the previous year. Defensive measures also increase. Delaware has led the way by allowing their state-registered companies to seek to alter their bylaws so as to excuse directors from liability for money damages for negligent, but not deliberate, injuries to their company. Directors' potential liability to persons or organisations outside the company will remain. Numerous variations will certainly follow, with possibly increasing conflict between state and federal statutes, court decisions and original objectives (Herzel, 1986). A common objective should, however, be enabled to prevail; that the director who sits on his hands in situations where he should, instead, be thumping the boardroom table with them, has defined his own level of skill and care as being too low to justify his having a seat at that or any similar table.

12 Mechanics of the boardroom

The board's responsibilities are faced and discharged within the boardroom, at meetings of the directors operating collectively, making collective decisions, and carrying collective responsibility. Defined parts of these responsibilities may be delegated, if the articles so permit, to committees, or to individuals such as the managing director, operating effectively as a board 'committee of one'. But actions and decisions of committees or individuals must be confirmed in the boardroom; delegation does not mean abrogation.

Meetings

Meetings of directors are the machinery of the board, indeed are the sole machinery for exercising board responsibility and control. The mechanics of the meetings must be smooth; the meetings themselves need not be. The board should:

- establish a forward programme of board meetings twelve months ahead, and keep it updated. If possible choose 'third Monday in the month' or similar routine which makes planning ahead more simple, especially for the non-executives.
- meet once a month. Skip holiday July and December if it must, but ensure that an ad hoc committee of the board looks at the figures in those months also, and takes appropriate actions. In times of crisis, meet fortnighly or weekly. Charge the executive committee with meeting weekly, even daily, until the pressure eases. Circulate the minutes of boards and committees to all directors without delay – those who were unable to attend can telephone comments. In times of crisis, all corners of the company turn to the board, relying on the speed of its action and reaction.

Even those corners which have studiously avoided talking to it in the past. In times of crisis, the true commitment, and true availability, of the non-executives is exposed, to their credit or discredit;

- charge the company secretary with ensuring that papers, agenda, minutes, management and financial accounts are all collated and despatched to directors by a given date each month, decided by allowing an agreed period for the preparation of routine figures after each month end;
- ensure that a quorum is always present, even at ad hoc meetings. Check the required number in the bylaws or articles, you may get a surprise. An ad hoc meeting can be called at a few moments' notice, assuming that all the directors to be involved agree to it. Minutes of such a meeting must be tabled at the next full board, but it is wise to circulate them immediately, so that all the directors know what is happening. In theory a meeting short of a quorum can also take decisions (for example, an ad hoc meeting of two directors, when the quorum is three), but these decisions only become valid if subsequently ratified by every single member of the board. This theoretical mechanism is fraught with risk, and should never be applied. The writer has seen a company bankrupt itself by commitments entered into by such an ad hoc meeting which did not contain a quorum, which did not inform the other directors quickly enough for the others to countermand the destructive decisions made, and which did not obtain the subsequent ratification of all the directors;
- remember always that voting in the boardroom is by simple majority of the directors, not by shareholding. The chairman may own or control a majority of the shares in a private company, but he does not thereby have authority to determine what the board will decide. He has one vote, plus a casting vote in the event of a tie (if the articles so permit). Very occasionally a company's articles give special, additional, voting rights to one or more directors, or to categories of director. If this is the case in your company, try to obtain the board's agreement to ask the next general meeting to alter that article. If all directors are not truly equal, and are not treated as equal at the board table, then the boardroom process becomes a charade;

- remember that the board should not need to vote frequently. Directors should normally find that a common agreement can be reached on most points. The chairman's role is to steer the board to such agreement when he judges it truly represents responsible unanimity, not weak compromise. Occasionally the board will remain split. The chairman must then judge whether to take a vote and reach a majority decision, or to postpone decision until further information has been produced and the directors have had more chance to weigh the pros and cons. If the matter is not urgent, delay is the best policy. Voting down a minority can be distressing for the minority; it can also mean taking the wrong decision;

Decision by majorities is as much an expedient as lighting by gas.
GLADSTONE

- keep the meetings brisk, but not brusque. While this is primarily the chairman's responsibility, the other directors can greatly help. They can sense when the chairman is seeking to curtail a discussion which deserves more time, and can usually judge the rightness or wrongness of his reasons for doing so. The effective chairman will ensure that all viewpoints are fully and responsibly expressed. He does have the final authority to decide when 'enough' has been said, and it can be difficult for him to let someone press on with a line of argument with which he strongly disagrees. But this is what differentiates a good chairman from a bad one, not how quickly he brings you to Any Other Business. If routine monthly meetings last less than two or three hours, or a great deal longer in times of difficulty, are the directors really in touch? And in control?
- remember that, while a director with a burning passion or a deep-felt concern may 'have said it all a dozen times' to his co-directors outside the boardroom, the only place where he can obtain a board hearing and a board decision on his subject of concern is within the boardroom at a formal board meeting. He has to put his case there. If he does not, he cannot grumble that the chairman is a bully. That is why he is a director, not just a manager;

- ensure that the dissenter is given free air. If his case is bad or irrelevant, this will soon show. If it is not, he will help the company.

The style of the boardroom meeting must be open, equal, impartial, patient. Occasionally also unpredictable, surprising, outrageous. Even the ridiculous has its place. A large loss-making company was once in trouble because, while it was winning a few tenders, it was losing most by being 10–20 per cent more expensive than its competition. One director suggested it should increase all its prices. Ridiculous, apparently, but he had guessed that the company was also *winning* tenders by margins of 10–20 per cent. The board accepted the ridiculous, gave the necessary instructions, and the losses were rapidly replaced by significant profits.

Apart from meetings of directors, the board is also responsible for calling general meetings of members, or shareholders. The annual general meeting (AGM) of even the largest corporations is often a brief affair, sparsely attended, and covering only statutory routines, including:

- declaration of dividend;
- approval of reports and accounts;
- election of rotating directors, or those appointed since the last AGM;
- appointment and remuneration of auditors.

It can also cover special business, such as altering the share capital or the articles, incentive schemes or borrowing powers. Special business may otherwise be covered at an extraordinary general meeting (EGM) called by the directors, or by a given proportion of shareholders, usually 10 per cent.

General meetings, too, can become a charade in those few public companies which retain a combination of voting A shares and non-voting B shares as a hang-over from their private company days. They argue that this enables a few, often family-related shareholders to block unwelcome take-over bids. The counter-argument is that in recent years several companies with this share structure have appeared to become complacent, and have become uncompetitive. Their boards might consider the positive effect on the company's overall capitalisation which could be achieved by changing that share structure.

Minutes of meetings

The company secretary records decisions taken at board meetings, and drafts the minutes. These need only include decisions made, but it is sensible to add a brief record of the main factors, for and against, which led to their making. A decision, all on its own, can prove difficult to interpret after the passage of a little time.

The chairman approves or amends the draft. Normal practice is that he then circulates his version to all directors for their comments, usually in the bundle of papers for the next meeting. He obtains their approval, or occasional suggested amendments, at the beginning of that next meeting. He does not *have* to circulate the minutes, but is clearly wise to make this a routine. In meetings where there is a large measure of dissent, or where an item is complex, the best practice is for the chairman to require the company secretary to draft the eventual decision at the meeting itself, while the directors wait, and then have the wording agreed by all of them on the spot.

If any one director believes that the draft minutes are incorrect on any point, he must say so, and seek his co-directors' agreement that the draft be amended. If they do not agree, but he continues to judge that the matter is important, he should ask that his disagreement also be recorded. Cabinet ministers have often stated that they do not recognise the decisions recorded in the cabinet minutes; company directors frequently say the same. The fault is their own.

The chairman signs the minutes of the meetings which he chaired, and they are entered into a minute book. There must be such a book, and it must be a permanent record. If in loose-leaf format, each page should be numbered and initialled.

Minutes of general meetings are normally signed at the following directors' meeting, to avoid leaving this till next year's general meeting.

The signed minutes become 'evidence' of the decisions taken by the board. Not 'conclusive evidence', unless the articles specifically state that they be 'conclusive'. In subsequent legal action it can be possible to demonstrate by other means that additional decisions were taken by the board, but not minuted. The director involved in such action will, however, feel a little foolish that he has to find 'other means', and did not ensure that the minutes were a proper record in the first place.

The minute book is therefore a document of the greatest importance. The director of a company which is in trouble, either in its external trading or in its internal behaviour, will be wise to ensure that each month's minutes are a true and full record of board decisions, and that any strong objections he has made are clearly recorded, if only to 'protect his back'. A perfectly valid objective where there is a high level of boardroom conflict, or where internal behaviour is questionable. If he does not take this precaution, who will believe him anyway?

The question is not academic. Manipulation of minutes to disguise reasoned dissent is not uncommon, usually just a 'softening', but sometimes worse. In one listed corporation there was incomplete recording of dissent on one item, complete exclusion of another controversial item, and the effective reversal of a decision actually made on a third item – all in the minutes of just one meeting. The chairman was not fired. But beware. Court precedents and tougher legislation now put a heavy onus on the individual director to be able to prove, from the evidence of minutes or other documents, that he had behaved with active responsibility, whatever the pressures from his co-directors to preserve a pretence of calm unanimity. If a company in the UK becomes insolvent, the performance record of a director can be reviewed for 'unfitness' for a period up to three years prior to the date of insolvency – *even if the director resigned and left the company as much as three years before that date*. We have been warned.

Agenda and papers

The board should plan its agenda three to four months ahead, to give time for the production of specific papers by individual directors. Forward programmes should be minuted. If a scheduled paper will be delayed for some good reason, the director concerned should inform his colleagues of this as soon as possible. They should not first learn about the delay at the meeting when the scheduled paper was due to be presented – they may be rushing some preparatory work of their own to meet that deadline.

All directors should participate in the preparation of the forward agenda, particularly non-executives when they believe that questions of importance are being either ignored, or swept under the carpet. The non-executive may have a useful role to play outside the board-room, but it is within the boardroom, in the agenda, and in the minuted decisions, where his primary contribution is evidenced – or not.

Conventional wisdom has it that the executive directors often fear the appointment of a good, active non-executive because he is likely to rootle around and request papers on subjects which he judges the board is not giving enough attention. In practice it can be the *in situ non-executives* who are most discomforted by such an appointment as it can simply expose their own past inertia, or their harmful supporting of inadequate boardroom mechanisms, or worse.

> *Boards of directors have the legal authority to find out anything they want to know . . . But over the years they have grown so soft and ineffectual that most often are a captive of management.*
>
> GENEEN, 1985

Individual directors may, indeed, be prevented from finding out 'anything they want to know'. In one corporation a non-executive director asked for a list of the company's investments, in a year in which profits from the sale of investments would form a significant part of the reported annual profits. *The chairman refused to provide that director with any information at all about the investments*, stating that he had been delegated unlimited authority to buy and sell investments without any reference to the board. The fact that he had not, of course, been delegated such open-ended authority is much less important than the fact that the other directors accepted the chairman's statement without comment or question; yes, boards can be that bad.

The board decides how much or how little information will be routinely provided, though the individual director can make specific additional requests, within reason. Guidelines on basic minima are suggested in the section on Performance. Agreed papers should be short, opened by a summary of recommendations, then a summary of conclusions, then the body of hard facts or assumptions. The director reading them has to be taken through the logic backwards. It is the bit on the front page that the presenting director has to justify. Papers should not be pre-vetted. The man responsible for the paper is responsible for deciding whom he will check it with in advance of circulation. It is not his boss's paper. It should give the board a chance to judge his acuity, not his boss's.

Routines

When the chief executive draws up the job description for a newly appointed manager he includes, among other things:

*   the person's primary roles;
*   his limits of authority in performing these roles; and
*   the routines he is expected to maintain, monthly, quarterly, yearly.

This assists the chief executive to:

*   check later that the manager is doing his job;
*   guide the manager in planning his own activities;
*   induce the manager to do regularly those things which he might otherwise let slip. Everyone lets slip the things they do not like doing.

So also with the board. It draws up its own roles, and describes which directors, or committees, do what in order to fulfil those roles. It defines the limits of each director, or committee, and requires that anything beyond these limits be brought to the full board. It can establish a programme of routines, including those things which it does not like doing, which describes what it will discuss and resolve, monthly, quarterly, half-yearly, yearly. For example:

Monthly

- Review of management and financial accounts, covering performance to date against the year's budget and recommendations for improvement. As with all reports, but particularly this one, it is essential that the board describe in advance the desired content and extent of the subject matter. It needs enough, but not too much detail.
- Finance director's report on cash and related matters.
- Chief executive's report on operations, for review, decisions and recommendations. Again, enough but not too much detail, otherwise the board becomes a management committee.
- Business development director's report on trading situation, competition, overseas expansion, and similar. Many boards rely on a single monthly report from the chief executive. This can place too much of the work, in detail, on one man's shoulders, and he may be of a character which is reluctant to be seen to share responsibilities. Better for the board to decide in advance that instructions are channelled out of the boardroom, and reports are therefore channelled back into the boardroom, by the three separate key directors: the chief executive, the finance director, and the business development director. This does not subtract anything from the chief executive's ultimate operating responsibility. It just ensures that he does not try to do everything himself. Many do.

Quarterly

- a one-by-one divisional review, covering all of them once a year.

- A similar one-by-one functional review, covering all of them once a year (personnel and training, marketing, production, research and development).
- Selected subsidiaries, including the critical ones and the best performers. Invite the MD to lunch afterwards; he may be nervous.

Half-yearly

- Industrial relations. It is hoped that this would not be necessary more frequently. Is the participation mechanism in good working order?
- Performance against long-term plans, not simply against budgets (which is checked monthly in the review of management accounts). Are the policies, objectives and strategies on beam? Is the organisational structure effective?
- Possibly a formal re-budgeting of critical subsidiaries or activities. The alteration of an approved one-year budget should only be agreed if the external environment has significantly changed, not if the managers are failing to perform to par. Maybe they ought to be altered instead.

Yearly

- Decision on, and communication of, any changes to corporate policies, objectives, or strategies.
- Approval of plans and budgets for the coming year.
- Annual performance review, with decisions on how improvements are to be effected.
- Annual review of senior staff performance below the board, and whether any changes should be made.
- Annual board review of its own performance as a board, of the contribution of its individual directors, particularly the non-executives, and of any changes it needs to make to the mix of directors, skills and styles, in the boardroom.
- Election, or re-election, of a chairman.

Committees

There is no limitation on what the board can choose to delegate to committees (assuming that the articles permit their formation), but it has to accept responsibility for the committees' actions and decisions, and therefore has to wade through the committees' reports. It is often just as effective, and at least as quick, to keep most of the deliberating and deciding within the full board. The following are some of the most common committees.

Executive committee

American and British practice differs significantly regarding executive committees. In larger US corporations the committee most commonly contains more non-executives than officers and full-time directors. In a few cases of corporations in difficulty in the 1970s, the desirability of such a weighting of outside directors was confirmed by federal court orders. In the UK, in contrast, many a board is just a façade behind which the real business of the company is controlled by a committee chaired by the chief executive and comprising executive directors and managers, only. This frequently works to its own terms of reference, with little instruction or guidance from the board. The practice can put the directors at risk; it leaves them remote from the decisions and actions for which they are ultimately responsible. However, given proper terms of reference from the board, and with formal reporting routines, an executive committee can be helpful in carrying much of the detailed burden in a larger, diverse enterprise.

Audit committee

All companies with a New York Stock Exchange listing must have an audit committee with a majority of non-executives. (They must also have at least two non-executives to obtain a listing. The London Stock Exchange could helpfully introduce a similar ruling, but preferably with a minimum of three rather than two.) The NYSE definition of an independent outside director, for audit committee purpose, is a director who 'is independent of management and free from any relationship which could interfere with the exercise of independent judgement as a committee member'.

The audit committee in the US is intended:

(a) to increase public confidence in the credibility and objectivity of published financial information;
(b) to assist directors in meeting their financial reporting responsibilities;
(c) to strengthen the independent position of a company's external auditor by providing channels of communication between him and directors other than the executives.

Managements may comment on any adverse conclusions tentatively reached by a US audit committee. (It is sensible policy in any context to let management comment on adverse conclusions regarding their behaviour or performance before the board reacts to them.)

The audit committee:

- discusses problems with the auditors;
- discusses the effectiveness of internal financial controls, staffing, the computer system – and recommends changes where these are found necessary;
- discusses the performance figures;
- checks on possible bribery, and on political contributions;
- approves, or not, the auditors.

In the UK, a Conservative Member of Parliament has tried several times to have a Bill enacted which would require UK companies to establish three-man teams of non-executives to perform similar functions. The Accountants International Study Group Report of 1977, and UK accounting institutions in general, favour the establishment of such audit committees.

But it will be readily apparent that management's cosy relationship with the auditors, which the audit committee is intended to prevent, could quite easily be replaced, after a short passage of time, by a similarly cosy relationship between the auditors and the audit committee – if the latter lets itself become less than ruthless. The British are seldom ruthless for very long.

Each reader may have his own view on the need, or not, for audit committees. The writer (and the Institute of Directors) believes they are *not* necessary, and that the board should be its own audit committee. It can only be this if it contains enough non-executives who are truly impartial, truly 'critical', truly pure-as-driven-snow – as well as being truly able to put in the amount of time which a control activity of this kind demands.

It can be considered a matter of shame that boards have had to have this committee imposed on them in the US, and that the case for a similar committee can, sensibly, be pressed so hard in the UK. The concept of the audit committee can only have grown in an environment where the directors, especially the non-executives, had demonstrated that they were not performing their role with adequate commitment.

Remuneration or compensation committee

The predominantly or exclusively non-executive remuneration or compensation committee determines the pay and perquisites of directors and top managers. It is an 'obvious' committee, which avoids involving the executives in a hassle about each others' salaries, and although very common in the USA only half of the major UK companies have one (rising to 80 per cent in the very largest). But it is also often just a friendly formality:

> *The discussion might take no more than three minutes or thirty minutes; it is all cut and dried . . . But the key question that should be addressed is: What real personal contribution did he make that was sufficiently outstanding to earn that level of compensation?*

> GENEEN, 1985

In one organisation the performance of an executive was good, while the non-executive committee agreed that the performance of his boss, the CEO, was bad. The executive director was awarded X per cent more salary for inflation plus Y per cent more for performance. The CEO was given exactly the same percentage increases because the majority of members felt that one really couldn't give him less of an increase than his subordinates. Which tidily eliminated the concepts of non-executive responsibility and of executive performance, without eliminating the rewards.

Nominating committee

The purpose of the nominating committee is to vet and present potential new directors, especially non-executives. In the US half the boards have one, and the proportion is increasing. In the UK there are very few.

The importance, and suggested composition, of this committee has been argued in Chapter 10. The style and standard of contribution in boardrooms could be greatly improved if a 'professional', methodical, semi-independent approach is made to recruiting directors, instead of simply relying on, or surrendering to, the fancies of the chairman or chief executive.

Finance committee

One-third of US boards have a finance committee, compared with one-sixth in the UK. They commonly include the chairman, chief executive, finance director, and one or two non-executives with financial or banking backgrounds. They commonly consider accounts, both half-year and full-year, and the proposed statements to cover the publication of those accounts; plus or minus the funding mix, the appointment of bankers and financial advisers, and the implications of the cash flow forecasts.

All these activities are so fundamental to the overall deliberations of the board as a whole that it can be argued that they are best left to the full board.

Planning committee

About one in seven of the larger UK companies have planning committees, whereas few smaller companies have even a planning office within their structure. American corporations have even fewer planning committees (none being recorded in the Korn/Ferry Study on which Appendix I is based), though it is becoming more common for planning and competitor comparisons to be itemised for full board consideration. An Australian study (Viljoen/Clayton, 1985) concluded that business situations have become too complex for the chief executive to handle alone; strategic planning requires active pursuit by a committee, if not by the full board.

Companywide planning, leading on the one hand to very detailed subsidiary company plans, and on the other hand to resources-oriented collective corporate plans, needs onerous explanation, exhortation and coordination. It is recommended that the business development director be charged by the board with establishing and chairing a committee to undertake this most vital activity; drawing up formats, defining and explaining contents, assisting with compilation, illustrating how Group policies affect the individual units, highlighting the possible, eliminating the fantastic, organising the annual country-house planning weekend, collating and presenting the finalised whole to the board for approval.

The board, it is repeated, has no more important managerial role than to initiate and maintain a clockwork planning routine which carries through all the company's thinking. Planning is a way of thinking, an attitude of mind.

Other committees

Other committees may be set up as the board judges helpful. For example, a donations and charities committee may seem a nuisance for those who are press-ganged, but it does eliminate some pet causes which have no corporate relevance, or which create avoidable resentment. Establish a committee of two; define what it can spend; instruct all units to send in proposals; give the committee an hour one wet afternoon to divide the budget. Thereafter the company secretary can tell all suppliants that 'sorry, the large budget for this has been spent', which will be true. Otherwise the whole business can get out of hand and consume hours in all corners; otherwise the directors will spend more time arguing about $100 for the Retired Lozenge Wrappers Benevolent Fund than they will spend on the $10 million for the new factory.

More importantly, a training committee may be set up for a year or two if the board decides it has neglected that area. Once routines are well established the committee can be disbanded, and the subject can receive a half-yearly spot on the board agenda. Similarly with technology, production, R & D, or Public Relations.

Be guided, when considering whether or not to establish a committee, by the fact that all committees, apart from the audit and executive committees, can basically help only by digesting a welter of detail, and then presenting a predigested, slimmed-down version to the full board. If the board really needs all the detail to reach a firm, responsible conclusion, it does not need a committee.

Dissent; resignation; removal

The board decides by a majority of the directors. A director who disagrees with the decision of the majority will normally accept it, and help to implement it, but if his disagreement is very strong, either because he believes the decision will lead the company into serious trouble, or because he believes it is not wholly in accordance with the law, he has to express and press his dissent.

He can, and should, have his dissent minuted against his name.

He can call a special board meeting to discuss his dissent, but there is no guarantee that any of the other directors will come to it.

He can circulate his co-directors with his views if he feels they were not given a good airing (which may have been his own fault).

And, if he has convinced himself that he is not just being 'contrary', and that what he complains about really is foolish, illegal, corrupt or immoral, he can arrange to put his case to a general meeting of shareholders, in the form of a resolution of no confidence in the policy of the board. The shareholders cannot reverse any decision taken by the board, nor can they instruct the board on any matter which the board is empowered by the articles to decide, but the shareholders can, if they agree with the dissenting director, choose to remove the rest of the directors.

He can also propose to the general meeting that they request that a Department of Trade Inspector be put into the company.

Or, as an alternative to the usually destructive weapon of a general meeting resolution, and dependent on the exact nature of his concern, he might threaten his colleagues with a chat with the auditors, or with the company's bankers. This can be a practical alternative in a private company where the main shareholders are also on the board.

But he cannot remain quiet. In the Department of Trade Inspector's Report on First Re-Investment Trust Ltd, *all* the directors were castigated in varying degrees for not having stopped a dominant chairman who was doing what he should not. Some of these directors had in fact 'complained'. *But not enough to rid them of all responsibility.*

He might consider court action, if he is also a shareholder. But only if he believes the board is acting fraudulently, or *ultra vires*. Better to use the general meeting, and leave it to them to decide whether to use the court.

He can resign. He must do so if the board is acting illegally, and will not remedy its illegal actions. If he does so, he should explain, publicly, why he is doing so. Otherwise no lessons will be learnt, and the company will almost certainly be harmed, not helped. Resignation must be written, or verbal at a general meeting. It cannot be withdrawn, even if it has not been formally accepted.

He might get himself removed. Normally a board cannot remove a director before the expiry of his term of office, unless the articles say it can. They usually do not.

The board might lobby friendly shareholders to remove him, and they can at any time, given due notice under the special notice rules. In this instance the director concerned has the right to circulate a written statement of his case, and present it at the relevant general meeting. This might do the trick.

Whatever course the dissenter, or dissenters, consider, remember always the presence of groupthink described in Chapter 4. Experience in all groups, including boards, shows that however great their original concern, all except one of the dissenters will usually knuckle under. The rest will rationalise away their lack of courage by deceiving themselves that any real action 'will upset the chaps', or 'will destroy the share price', when what they really fear is either disturbing their own comfortable status quo, or getting into a struggle which they haven't the wit to handle. In judging how to act, remember that: *Two can be made a multitude. One can be made a dog.*

13 Dos and don'ts for directors

The board must decide policies, generate plans, appoint and monitor management, for the benefit of the company as a whole. The directors must work purposefully and collectively towards that objective, without influence from specialist interests, dominant interests within the boardroom, or self-interest. Therefore:

DO propose and pursue the composing of a board which

- is chaired by an independent director who is not also managing the company;
- is business-oriented, not figures-oriented or technology-oriented alone;
- contains a core of executives including a chief executive, who is people-oriented rather than figures-oriented or technology-oriented, alone, plus a finance director and a business development director; contains a balance of part-time non-executives with very varied skills and styles, half of them executive directors in other companies, half of them from among board-experienced consultants, academics and professional directors who provide added width and depth;
- has the maturity of judgement to be able to make productive use of the occasional conflict of strong opinions.

DO ensure that

- the board formally reviews its composition and performance, as a board, once each year;
- the changes to the mix of membership, or to the terms of reference of existing members, are agreed at that formal meeting;

241

- the terms of reference for new directors are matched to the needs of the board and of the company, not to the wishes of any one director or interest grouping;
- the chairman of the board is elected or re-elected at that meeting, election being based on the criterion of who is best able to perform the role, not of maintaining status or status quo, alone.

DO consider appointing professional or hybrid part-time directors, because they can provide more active, more involved and thus more effective contribution, and:

DO require a minimum commitment of two days per month from each non-executive and arrange that some of them overlap onto lower boards, and onto joint venture and associate company boards, if you have such within the Group. This improves the board's vision, understanding and control.

To enable the board to remain, collectively, in control:

DO ensure that the board

- collectively compiles its forward agenda;
- maps out a programme of routines for monthly, quarterly, half-yearly and yearly reviews, so that all functional and line activities are, and are seen by the company to be, regularly evaluated by the board;
- meets ten to twelve times each year;
- calls for and coordinates papers to a defined timetable, so that meetings do not become a shambles or a sham;
- establishes some, but not too many, board committees to smooth the mechanics of the boardroom – especially nominating, remuneration and planning committees;
- decides and communicates company policies;
- maintains formal business planning, allocating resources against a required scale and time-scale of returns;
- considers plans for overseas expansion as a priority. (The UK's home population, for one example, is little more than 1 per cent of the world's population; markets are people);

- reviews regularly the company's performance against the performance of competing companies and countries;
- maintains a clockwork system for communication and participation which parallels the company's control structure;
- reviews once or twice annually the company's control structure, amending it in step with changes in the company's growth. Remember that almost every company leaves structural change too late to avoid people-problems, which are always more onerous than marketing or methods problems;
- defines limits of authority for senior staff and individual units;
- operates as far as possible through largely autonomous divisions and subsidiaries, working within their limits and containing a mix of executives, Group executives and non-executives on their own boards who can ensure that they do not run astray;
- monitors management against budgets; assists where there is a short-fall; then changes management if it still performs below par;
- maintains a routine of cash monitoring in each unit, each day.

When you sense that problems are developing:

DO study the detailed causes and symptoms in companies which collapse, and if one or more is detected, apprise the board, initiate a time-scaled programme of remedial action. Always put 'actions' into the minutes, and 'time-scales' into the actions. Remember 'luck' rarely comes into it; bad results mean bad management, means a bad board.

DO stimulate the board or, through the board, any lower level to engage defined-term doses of outside expertise. Something else which most companies leave late – and some too late.

And always:

DO make better use of those external organisations which benefit from the survival of your company:

- your bankers (they do well on your overdraft, could and would be helpful in many ways, but are strangely shy of volunteering suggestions);
- your main institutional shareholders (they know how others view your company, which may be nearer reality than your own viewpoint);
- your industrial associations and spokesbodies (they are only as good as the guidance they receive from member companies).

DO meet external responsibilities to time, as a habit. Delay does not remove debt, and it may only disguise the depth of the hole down which you are continuing to fall.

DO read your company's memorandum and articles, and the local Companies Acts. Ask the company secretary to circulate copies. Badger him to ensure he has discovered and circulated all other relevant legislation, too – you may get some surprises.

DO keep the board well within the limits of all the laws, and keep morality a notch above legality.

DO keep at the front of your mind that:

- you are responsible to the company. If the company prospers, so do the employees, shareholders, creditors;
- you are supposed to ask 'searching questions';
- the board is a 'group', and groups thrive on diversity, stagnate under conformity, and suffocate under domination.

Each director is just one vote. Each vote can be a helpful voice, or a hollow echo of some more dominant voice. When a board is dominated by a chairman or chief executive, it can be very difficult for the individual director to find his voice. When a board contains no truly independent, or no truly committed, non-executives, it can become impossible. Therefore:

DON'T allow the board to be dominated. Lobby your colleagues, prepare a combined case, present it diplomatically outside the board-room. If this does not do the trick, vote in combination in the boardroom to effect a change or two. You, too, may have to bully. You may lose the case. You may feel you have to quit. As a director, you are responsible to the company, not to your career. That's the 'consideration' you pay for joining the board of a Company Limited. But if you do not play the director's role responsibly, and with courage, how can you expect a lathe operator to give a damn, either?

DON'T delay either when you conclude that the chief executive is abusing the managers or management procedures. You have to confirm that your co-directors have reached the same conclusion, and you then have to act together with them or things will get worse.

DON'T vote for a combined chairman/chief executive. That is often what creates the problem in the first place.

DON'T let the chairman do everything. Don't let him do very much. The role of chairman is the most important position in commerce and industry. The chairman is chairman of the board. But he is not chairman of the company. There is no such position as chairman of the company.

DON'T vote for a new chairman who is at present chief executive. The roles are entirely different. The characteristics and personalities required are mutually exclusive.

DON'T let the chairman decide who will be the next chief executive. He may propose someone he can man-handle. Or he may indeed propose the best man – but the board as a whole decides.

DON'T elect a chief executive who does not carry the votes of all, or of almost all, the executive directors. The non-executives may be in a majority on the board, but if there is such strong disagreement about an internal candidate there must be good enough reasons – so the non-executives should call for external candidates to be considered.

DON'T elect joint MDs, except just occasionally in the largest holding boards where the men head divisions which are quite discrete.

DON'T elect managers to be executive directors as a reward for being good managers, when they are not able to contribute productively to most items on the agenda. If they are really valuable managers, give them a much better remuneration package to demonstrate they are valued.

DON'T appoint or promote anyone to the board as an executive director without applying a professional recruitment process, including a board committee, advertising the position, obtaining support from a recruitment consultant, psychological testing, full board vetting. Don't leave 99 per cent of this key responsibility in the hands of a head-hunter, alone, even if you choose to use one, also. Don't use head-hunting in countries where it is not wholly sanctioned by the local laws. Don't use it at all if you have staffed your personnel department responsibly.

DON'T appoint non-executives who are retired executives from your company. They cannot be truly independent. Nor retired executives from any other company unless they retired early to become professional directors.

DON'T appoint non-executives who represent specialist interests, e.g. consumers, employees, unions, ethnic minorities, sexes. Just appoint 'contributors'.

DON'T appoint non-executives because they are your bankers, lawyers, business associates of any kind, or members of 'the family'. Or civil servants (retired), admirals (retired), lords, MPs, big names who are happy to passively make weight. Or chums. Or anyone who cannot give your company a minimum of two days per month, and more when you really need it. Directorship is more serious, more responsible, more critically important than a short sharp trot through a bundle of monthly papers.

DON'T be afraid of the maverick, the court jester, the critical director, the uncomfortable director. They are performing what the role entails, their way. *And they are performing*.

DON'T apply any qualifications to board membership which have nothing to do with business performance, e.g. schooling, clubs, religion, Freemasonry, nationality, natural tendencies. Many do.

DON'T let Humphrey leave again, before item 4. Or William doze off, again, before item 3. If that really is the best they can do, it is not good enough.

DON'T agree to associate or alternate directors. There are better alternatives.

DON'T give inflated golden handshakes when you have to part company with an executive. Soon enough that grossly abused practice will stimulate even the shareholders to complain. What are you actually paying for, and why do you have to? Should he instead be paying something back to your company?

DON'T lead the race to push up pay and perquisites, and don't let the remuneration committee be just a feeble formality where everything goes 'up' regardless.

DON'T get fevered by the frenzy to buy, buy, buy. Don't let the board give lengthy consideration to any potential acquisition which is not already described, if not named, in the agreed corporate plan for expansion, or which you feel the board or the chief executive will not be able to handle.

DON'T let the board spend longer on choosing pictures for the corridor than on choosing a site for the new factory. If you tease the chairman once or twice he will take the message.

DON'T, ever, let a vote go by on the nod when you disagree. Say you disagree. You do not have to make a big issue out of every second-order item, but your voice might trigger two or three others who also disagree, and together you might develop a conclusion which moves the company forward, even if only a little. The 'silly' question or silly comment is seldom as silly as you think it may sound.

Regarding the company itself:

DON'T get involved in restrictive trade practices, such as collusive bidding. It only helps to hide bad management, or bad marketing, and only slightly prolongs the time that these inadequacies can be hidden. After which time the damage to your company will have increased.

DON'T maltreat your environment with effluent, noise, or ugliness. But don't, either, get charity-minded. The need for charity in your community is greater than your company can handle.

DON'T create or maintain:

- subsidiaries just to create directorships;
- funnies;
- minorities in your subsidiaries if you can buy them out;
- associate companies, unless their return on capital (ROC) is markedly greater than that of your subsidiaries;
- joint ventures, unless essential, for example overseas;
- any subsidiary, division, committee or other organisation which does not have clear terms of reference and measured and time-scaled objectives, which it has a reasonable chance of meeting.

DON'T leave the chief executive to chair the divisional or subsidiary boards. Use non-executives.

DON'T leave the linking of the board and the shopfloor to a one-man chain of chief executive and direct line subordinates. Use multiple linkages for better communication, better control. 'Control' is not solely a line-management matter. The chief executive and his managers control operations. The board needs to control how well its policies, objectives, plans are attuned to the company's needs and abilities. These are not exclusively line-management matters.

DON'T forget, however difficult this may occasionally be, that:

- you are responsible to the company;
- you have to analyse it, plan it, structure it, ensure that it is properly managed;
- whenever you sense that it is less than perfect, you have to DO something about it.

14 Dos and don'ts for institutions, bankers and accountants

Now that the long bull stock market of the 1980s, which followed the long inflation of the 1970s, has run out of breath and collapsed in a heap, the institutions and bankers will need to become more interested in the real, rather than the apparent strengths of companies. Already accounting firms, now smarting under expensive court actions brought by disadvantaged shareholders and others, have begun to probe more deeply behind the 'face' which companies carefully present.

All three categories stand in positions of potential influence and actual responsibility in relation to their client and investee companies. Closest of the three, in law and theory, are the institutions, because they own the shares and elect the directors. Yet:

> *I doubt whether the institutions have fully realised the tremendous responsibilities they now hold. They ought to be well informed about the companies they invest in, and base their policies on two factors: first, long term plans and strategies in different sectors and industries, and second, the strength and composition of management . . .*
>
> LORD BENSON, 1986

They should be looking at market share, R & D, and all the other factors which affect long term performance, because: *'Earnings per share are not the most important factor'* (Ibid.).

All three categories are empowered to ask the same kinds of questions, and *they are flying blind if they do not*. Therefore:

DO ask the combined chairman/chief executive precisely how he arranges for his board to monitor and amend the performance of the chief executive half of him. Is there a routine spot on the agenda for this? Or a special committee? Or does he pass the chair on this item and leave the room? Based on his answers, can you conclude that the management's performance is being properly reviewed? Is it being reviewed at all?

DO ask precisely what the non-executives contribute within the boardroom, and outside it. How much time does each devote to the company? Do they visit the subsidiaries? The factories? How often do they meet down-line managers? Ask the non-executives themselves if they feel they are able to contribute from their (long) experience in the (short) time expected of them. Many do have great experience, do want to contribute actively, and will reply quite honestly that they often feel they cannot contribute enough. Perhaps the chairman will hear their replies and learn from them, too.

DO ask how often the board reviews its own performance, and considers the mix and contribution of individual directors. How many years have the non-executives been *in situ*? And the chairman? Probe the composition – retired executives? merchant bankers? family members? irrelevant politicians? Determine from this how many of the non-executives are likely to be active within the boardroom, and *how many are truly independent in judgement*. Decide what this tells you about chairmanship and leadership in the company. Are the chairman and chief executive capable of handling actual contributors, or are they packing the board with passive make-weights?

DO ask about board committees, what they do, who sits on them.

And accountants:

DO remember that you have the authority, as auditors, to read all the minutes of board and committee meetings. Some accounting firms make this a standing instruction to all their staff, but not all. All should. Look for 'gaps' in the record; is anything being excluded?

DO ask how planning is handled. How many years forward in the holding company? In the subsidiaries? How far down the organisation does the process reach? Or how far up? Who is in charge of the mechanics – chairman, chief executive or a specialist executive director? If not handled by a well-routined mechanism, why not? Has the company found a better way?

DO ask how the company plans and controls its R & D programme. Is a director in charge of the mechanics? Does he report regularly? What are the R & D expenditure trends year-on-year; up, down, static? Make sure that the answer relates to total company size. Acquisitive companies may evidence an increase in absolute amount when there's a steep decline in proportion to total turnover; some cut R & D programmes as a post-acquisition routine. Search them out. Ask how the expenditure-to-turnover ratio compares with their competition, and with the Germans and Japanese – if they cannot answer precisely, immediately, then you've learnt a lot.

DO ask exactly the same about the evaluation of new technologies, which is, naturally, quite closely related to the question of R & D.
  But then:

DO ask exactly the same about the evaluation of production techniques. This is probably the greatest single strength of Japanese manufacturers. The odds are that the directors can give you a fair answer about R & D, possibly even a very precise answer, but will be flummoxed when you ask about production. Make time when going through the factory to have a look at the production control system. You won't understand every step, and don't need to, but you will be able to see at a glance whether the company administers this process with ancient or modern methods. Large investment in new machinery can be wasted if the production control system cannot catch up.

DO ask how and how often the board reviews its competitive situation: full board? within subsidiary boards? monthly? quarterly? Can the directors, including the non-executives, reel off the names of their main competitors in each of their main business sectors, and can they tell you just where the company stands in relation to them?

DO pick up any single weakness admitted to you and ask what the company is planning to do to overcome it. Similarly pick up any single strength claimed and ask how the company plans to capitalise on it.
Then:

DO ask about the company's market share in each of its main business areas, in the home market and main overseas territories. If they can't answer quickly and precisely, *then they are flying blind*.
You will have surmised that this demands that you, too:

DO make sure that you yourself know the company's main areas of business before you visit.

DO believe that 'services' are just the same as 'manufacturing' in requiring constant evaluation of competition and market share, consistent company-wide planning, the analysis and adoption of suitable new technologies and techniques, and a continuing review of 'production' or administrative methods.

Turn closer attention to the tightness or looseness of everyday ethics:

DO ask, for example, who uses the company facilities, such as apartments, country houses, yachts, jets. How often? Is that cost-effective compared with alternatives? Who controls usage – a main board director? Is that usage reviewed from time to time by the board? Why not – these are resources, too?

DO, at this point, slip in a question whether family members also use those facilities. You may get a surprise at the response, or no response at all.
And accountants:
Is it recorded? And paid for? Should it be?

DO ensure that your firm has a small pool of potential non-executives to name to boards which say they need, or which seem to need, some strengthening. The chairman may react against the names, any names, with an almost automatic reflex – which enables you to recommend that he advertise without delay. If you have already established the initiative by putting forward specific names, then your second initiative, that the company now advertise, cannot also be brushed aside.

DO make sure that you meet all, or as many as possible, of the directors, particularly the non-executives. You can get yourself invited to a post-board lunch or two if you are diplomatically persistent. Ask to meet a few of the senior managers below the board. Directors themselves are well routined in 'playing' the institutions and bankers, but the senior managers are not. They may let their guards or their tongues slip a little, consciously or unconsciously. *You may learn a great deal from that.*

As institutions, shareholders and accountants you are entitled to ask questions. You are entitled to express concern if the company evades your questions, or cannot answer them.
The company may learn a great deal from that.
  But:

DON'T confine your questions to the contents of handouts, press releases or Annual and Interim Accounts.
  You know from your own daily activities that the relative success of individual investment funds depends on the qualities of the individual fund managers concerned. So also with the long-term success of companies and the qualities of the individual directors concerned.

DON'T be too shy to rootle around for signs of their characters and personalities, because these do affect morality, morale and performance. Some practitioners swear that having personalised number plates on the company car is 'a bad thing'. It probably is not, by itself. Having a portrait of the chairman in the corridor, or in the boardroom before he is dead, may not be either, even if he put it there himself without asking the directors if they agreed. But look for the signs of balance or instability; what do they tell you about the chairman – and what do they tell you about the quality of the directors?

Look for the relationships; are they a team or just a collection of passive subordinates, the non-executives included? Is the chief executive a superstar, and all the other directors bright stars in their own right – or are the others just cheer-leaders and pom-pom girls?

DON'T be impressed if the chief executive or other directors are frightfully busy, couldn't see you for three months, and then kept leaping up from the table to take phone calls or give instructions. This could be because they fear delegating even petty authority, which means that there are frustrated and restless managers below them. Or it could be because there are inadequate managers below them. Or that they cannot manage their timetables, which suggests that they cannot manage the company, either.

Frantic activity and overlong hours are not laudable, except in short spasms. Whatever the cause, they lead to avoidable stress, and then to unbalanced judgement.

DON'T assume that the last acquisition, or the one currently afoot which is causing all the leaping from the table, is part of an elaborate corporate plan. Ask how long it had been planned. Was it in the annual budget? In the five-year plan? Ask about the last three to four acquisitions. Are they fitting in? What problems are being met? Were they expected? Try to decide for yourself whether the sequence of acquisitions demonstrates a methodical, logical, calculated plan, or just a boardroom enthusiasm for size. Size serves the directors themselves very well, because it affects directly their pay and perquisites – but can the directors handle the resulting size and diversity? Can they contribute anything to the acquisitions? Ask precisely what they do plan to contribute to them.

Similarly with divestments:

DON'T assume that a programme of divestment is part of a corporate plan. What went wrong with the companies sold? Why weren't they producing adequate returns? Who was managing them at board level? Is he now in charge of the acquisitions? Many divestments were, once, enthusiastic acquisitions. You have to determine whether the new acquisitions will be handled any better than the divestments. You have to determine the quality of the company's management and the board's control, and a programme of divestment can provide useful information.

DON'T assume that the latest large acquisition is a sign of 'muscle' or that a big lift in reported profits is a sign of improved 'performance'. Ask how much the company has gained in the last two to three years from pension contribution 'holidays' (which result primarily from the behaviour of the market, not from the performance of the company). Such pension holidays are currently swelling company profits, which pleases the taxman, and the party in power in parliament, and the directors, who get bigger bonuses. Meanwhile, the employees lose out.

> *Companies are milking pension funds to boost profit figures and finance take-overs . . . employees find their pension expectations dramatically cut and the secure funding of their benefits undermined because of abuse of pension funds.*
>
> IRVING, 1987

'Asset stripping' of pension funds began in America, with acquisitions being made by extracting money from the acquired company's pension funds – often greater sums being extracted than the original acquisition price. As the employing company's contributions to such funds is a form of deferred post-retirement pay to employees, and as non-executives in America can receive deferred post-retirement payment of fees, then this practice can be seen to be unacceptable, or worse.

DON'T forget to then ask how much of the reported profits in the last two to three years came from sale of investments. In a long bull market, the proportion is often substantial. You need to determine the real performance level; a camel doesn't consume its hump when it lives in an oasis.

DON'T assume that a company's rapidly increasing share price is a sign of a rapid increase in performance, reported or hinted; is there any good reason for a rise in its P/E, or are you, or the directors, just 'talking it up'?

DON'T be put off by jargon. It may be used just to check your flow. Everything can be expressed in everyday terms. The chemicals going through the factory may have frightfully long technical names, but they end up in packets in the kitchen.

DON'T be satisfied by speaking with the Public Relations Officer, or with the financial PR consultant. They want to believe everything is marvellous, and they don't probe deeply.

DON'T be worried if you can't follow it all, and can't remember very much. That is not expected. Your objectives are to determine, by the very process of questioning, if: the board is planning ahead; is thoroughly informed; is clearly in control of all aspects of its business; is realistically confident; and if: the board works as a productive, balanced team, led with mature understanding, not with macho or mad autocracy.

There are many more detailed questions which you can ask if you and the company have the time. They are indicated through the chapters of this volume, including the 'causes' and 'symptoms' of company collapse. Search to see if you can find one or more of those causes and symptoms. You have great potential influence on company performance. Most of you are not yet exercising it.

Good companies respond to stimulus and react quickly to eliminate any exposed weaknesses, or to close an exposed gap in their knowledge or control. Good companies will make sure that they have all the answers next time, and will invite you again soon to demonstrate this.

Bad companies . . . well that's why there's one more chapter in the book.

15 Legislation needed

Certainly many of the institutions, bankers and accountants will become more thoughtful about company characteristics, and will begin to exercise a more productive influence for change. Equally certainly, many of the companies which most need to make changes will not do so. Their controlling directors will feel well served by the status quo.

Some gentle Codes of Practice have been produced by semi-official organisations to record a few of the changes which they consider desirable. But it has been shown, time and again, within a great variety of different collective-interest groupings, that Codes don't work. Codes pull their punches, and therefore don't hit their targets.

The PRO NED Code on Non-Executives, for example (PRO NED, 1987) records that '*the Non-Executive Directors will need to enjoy the full support of the Chairman*'. But it was the Guinness directors who forced the resignation of the Guinness chairman; it is, in law, the directors who elect or dismiss the chairman; it is the chairman who needs to enjoy the full support of the directors. The Code is upside-down. It records 'how things are', not how they should be – legally and in common sense: it illustrates how little directors understand their roles, either in law or in common sense.

The Code also avoids any direct comment on the most critical question of separating the roles of non-executive chairman of the board from that of chief executive. So does the Institute of Directors' Code for Non-executives (IoD, 1986). This begins by 'realising' that companies may appoint non-executives who are not independent, but then lists that '*the non-executive directors should be independent*'. Looks as though they had trouble in the drafting committee, which they decided to resolve by facing both ways.

If these organisations, with their dedicated staff and most influential sponsorship cannot do better than that, then the case for introducing 'no arguments legislation' seems soundly made.

Legislation forces attention on reality. Consider the following proposals. Each would help greatly to improve board behaviour and company performance. The arguments behind each have been debated through the chapters of this volume.

We should legislate that:

re chairmanship

1 *The chairman of the board cannot hold any management position within the company.*

Civilised Denmark, and others, already have such legislation. It would emphasise that managements, steered by the chief executive, manage the businesses of the company while the board, steered by the chairman, manages the company. The roles, and the personalities required to perform them well, are very different.

2 *The chief executive cannot be elected chairman of the board in the company in which he was chief executive.*

The chairman should be independent of present management, and independent also of the hierarchies which he used to control.

3 *The chairman must be elected or re-elected annually.*

The CBI made this proposal in 1973.

re non-executive or outside directors

The most important single requirement in a non-executive is that *he is able to be truly independent in judgement*. The best way – indeed the only way – of ensuring that this qualification can be met would be to legislate that

4 *Persons with prior professional or social relationships with the directors of a company cannot become non-executives in that company.*

The logic is inarguable. The arguments would, nonetheless, be numerous, because most non-executives are chosen precisely *because* they are known to the directors.

Considering a number of very specific relationships:

5 *Executives from subsidiaries, the parent company or any of its acquisitions cannot become non-executives on the parent company board.*
Any continuing contribution they may be able to make after retiring can be absorbed via consultancy arrangements.

6 *Persons with full-time employment in one organisation cannot hold more than two non-executive directorships elsewhere.*
'One' would be a more responsible figure, but let's allow-off slightly for wind.

7 *Persons without full-time employment in one organisation* (independent professionals, professional directors, consultants), *cannot hold more than eight non-executive directorships.*
The arithmetic places a workable maximum at around seven; French law says eight is the limit; German law says ten.

8 *Suppliers, customers and other trading associates of a company cannot become non-executives of that company.*
The need for confidentiality, alone, makes this a sensible provision.

9 *When a provider of services to a company* (attorney, independent accountant, consultant, banker) *is proposed for appointment as a non-executive*
or
where an existing non-executive is charged by the board to undertake such services (specific consultancy, development project) *then the relationship must be specifically described for approval by the shareholders at the next general meeting.*
The objective is to ensure that it can be demonstrated to the shareholders that he, in particular, is best placed to provide the

services concerned alongside, and without inhibiting, his responsibilities as a director. The routine will enable some to de-select themselves.

10 *A minimum of twenty-four days per annum must be provided to the company by each non-executive.*
Current efforts to get more non-executives appointed onto UK boards are, in themselves, no help at all. They can be harmful. Effort should be directed instead towards obtaining more contribution, not just more directors.

11 *Time spent per annum by each non-executive must be recorded against his name in the Annual Report.*
Shareholders have a legal right to know that the company is properly controlled. To do this they need relevant information. Worthy names on the letterhead may be a deception if those names are not an active, productive part of the team.

12 *Each board is required to hold an annual review of directors' performance and board performance, within one of the scheduled board meetings.*
The minutes of that meeting will be available to the accountants, but not to the shareholders and bankers. Therefore 13, below:

13 *The Annual Report must include a separate non-executive directors' report, signed by all the non-executives, confirming that the board is functioning properly in the responsible management of the company.*
This proposal has been raised from time to time; let's now enact it.

14 *The board must contain non-executives totalling at least one-third of the board, with a minimum of two in all companies and three in all public companies.*
Similar proposals have also been raised from time to time. There has been hesitation to pursue the proposals because they might induce some boards to stuff in make-weights; this would be avoided by the other proposals, above.

re all directors

15 *The Annual Report must record details of all forms of remuneration and benefits of all directors, including family-obtained benefits.*
All forms. This would highlight, and help to remove, the unreasonable excesses. The shareholders might conclude, when faced with the bizarre details for the first time, that we should revert to the old, old patterns of a decade-and-a-half ago when top men received top salaries, and that was that.

16 *The Annual Report must record progress in remuneration and benefits, in all forms, over a five-year period.*
This would enable shareholders to weigh the observed gains against personal performance, or at least against corporate performance. Do the directors have anything in this area which they don't want to expose to the shareholders? Should they have?

17 *When persons related to the founding family or to any director are appointed to the board of a public company, the shareholders must be advised of the specific relationships and why he, in particular, has been appointed, for their approval* (or rejection) *at the next general meeting. Existing relationships of this kind must also be advised to the shareholders.*
Some may de-select themselves in the face of this requirement. We are concerned with preserving independence of judgement in the boardroom, with ensuring that election is based exclusively on potential contribution, and with avoiding possible abuses. One-third of British *public quoted companies* have executive directors related to the founders, and almost the same proportion have non-executives with similar relationships.

re recruitment

18 *All positions in a company must be publicly advertised by the most suitable local means for the level concerned; for manager and director positions, executive and non-executive, by advertisement in traditional trade or national journals.*

We must eliminate secretive, limited, protective recruitment and we must maximise the pool of potential quality candidates. We can learn from Sally Ride, who was chosen after tough tests and tougher competition to be the first American woman astronaut; in her words: '*I didn't know NASA wanted women until I saw an advertisement*'.

19 *Recruitment for all board positions must be controlled by a board committee of at least three directors, at least one of whom is non-executive.*
We need to ensure that we get the most productive men, not the most pliable.

20 *When recruiting, no limitation may be applied on age, unemployment, self-employment or present employment.*
If we don't remove the shibboleths we waste resources. Several European and other advanced countries already outlaw such discrimination, alongside existing laws against sex and race discrimination. The whole recruitment process, with the above three clauses as a trigger, needs detailed legislation, both to avoid ease and comfortable conformity for the employing company and to remove the numerous open abuses of candidates and potential candidates which commonly occur. The head-hunters have tried to introduce their own Codes of Practice, but they, too, don't always work.

re take-overs

The take-over process also now clearly needs detailed legislation. Experts in the field (for example, see Millstein, 1986) can produce many proposals, but in the terms of reference of this volume, concerned with the effect which this 'fashion' is having on corporate behaviour and on professional and institutional 'vision', there is one overriding need that:

21 *Bidder companies must demonstrate precisely, in terms of money and future corporate strength, how the take-over will benefit the shareholders, the employees and the national interest.*

We saw in the opening chapters that these benefits seldom result, though the executives, particularly the chief executive, always gain generously.

It has become conventional wisdom that our nations gain strength if we leave rugged individuals to run and reshape our corporations. But there's an anomaly. Individual power can only derive from the holding of positions within organisations. It can be used productively within those organisations, or abused to serve individual interests. The exercise of individual power has to be directed to the exclusive benefit of the organisation if there is to be any eventual national gain. It will be clear to all who work in company boards, or in government cabinets, or in the President's team, that business and government life has become so complex that the days of effective dominant control, the days of the effective one-man band, have long gone. If, indeed, they ever really existed. It is part of fondly believed American mythology that their nation's frontiers were opened by rugged individuals breaking into the unknown and building empires from nothing. There were just a few such cases, but for the most part:

> *The history of the Frontier West was ever one of defeat for difference, separation and individuality . . . The victory went continuously to the traditions of the East.*

And to the established corporations of the Eastern states, with which the frontiersman could not compete:

> *The frontier gave more to those that had than to those that had not.*

> BURCHELL/GREY, 1981

Nations are built by corporations. Checks and balances on corporations today, internally in the form of non-executive directors, or externally in the form of institutional shareholders, bankers and accountants, have failed to control the abuse of individual power within corporations, which has limited potential corporate power.

They have failed to prevent comparative corporate decline in the USA and the UK, when viewed against the strengthening international competition.

There remains just one more form of external control: national interest, expressed through national legislation, defined by those elected to govern through law.

Appendix I   Composition of unitary boards in the USA and UK

This appendix contains a summary of data on unitary, or single-tier boards in the USA and UK. These are status quo data, and do not represent ideals. The sources used are the two excellent Korn/Ferry Studies of 1987 (see Appendix III), which themselves contain much more detailed information about remuneration in the USA and UK, and about director profiles and shareholdings in the UK.

Japanese unitary boards were described in Chapter 7. The culture, history and environment in which Japanese companies have evolved are so different from those of the USA, UK and Europe that, while comparisons are thought-provoking, they cannot in themselves be very helpful.

US boards

Sample
532 companies; 66% NYSE, 5% AMEX, 19% OTC, 10% private, mutual.

Industrials:	under $200m t/o	23	4.3%	
	$200m–$1 bn	114	21.4%	54.3%
	$1 bn–$5 bn	97	18.3%	
	over $5 bn t/o	55	10.3%	
Banks, financial		83	15.6%	
Insurance		51	9.6%	
Retailers		24	4.5%	
Service companies		85	16.0%	

		Average no. inside directors	Average no. outside directors
Industrials	under $200 t/o	2	6
	$200m–$1 bn	3–4	7–8
	$1 bn–$5 bn	3–4	10
	$5 bn +	4	11

Banks, financial	4	14
Insurance	3	12
Retailers	4	9
Service cos.	3	8
Average	3	10

The figures show an increase in proportion of outsiders from two-thirds to three-quarters in recent years, at least in these larger corporations.

Meetings p.a. (%) for all companies:

Under 5	16.1	
5–6	31.7	An average of 8 meetings p.a.
7–9	18.8	has remained unchanged for
10–12	28.4	several years
13+	1.7	
No response	3.3	

Committees	*% with*	*Average number inside/outside dirs.*	*Meetings p.a.*
Executive	80.4	2/3	5
Audit	97.5	0/4	4
Compensation/personnel	90.5	0/4	4
Nominating	57.9	1/4	2
Finance	34.6	2/4	7
Benefits	25.0	0/4	3
Public affairs	9.9	1/5	3
Corp. ethics	7.2	1/4	3
Science/technology	3.7	1/4	4

All corporations listed on NYSE must have an audit committee. Nominating committees are most common (80%) in the largest and least common (37%) in the smallest sampled companies. The chairman (80%) and other directors are the main source of suggestions for new outside directors, though the Study records that 58% are located by the nominating committee, suggesting that the committee is vetting names provided by the chairman and directors.

Combined chairman/CEO: 77.3% with; higher in largest corporations.
Combined chairman/COO: 38.3% with.

Boards containing one or more of the following (%)

CEO/COO of other companies	74.2 ⎱	higher in
Retired exec. (other cos.)	67.4 ⎰	largest cos.
Retired or previously employed exec., own co.	40.2	decreasing
Academician	49.7	
Senior exec. (other cos.)	46.0	
Attorney (not providing services to co.)	35.2	
Attorney (providing services)	23.7	decreasing
Major shareholder (not officer)	30.9	
Former government official	27.6	
Commercial banker	25.0	decreasing
Investment banker	24.3	
International exec. (US)	6.2	
Professional director	25.0	increasing over 5 years
Woman	42.9	
Ethnic minority member	29.5	increasing slightly
Non-US citizen	13.0	decreasing
Consumer group representative	1.4	
Employee representative	1.0	

Women and ethnic minorities are drawn from academicians, senior executives in other companies, former government officials, CEO/COO of other companies, major shareholders and attorneys (not providing services).

In retailers, banks and financial institutions women (60%) and ethnic minorities (c. 53%) have higher representation.

Time spent on board matters (review/preparation/meetings/travel) (%)

Under 40 hours p.a.	4.7 ⎫	i.e. 48.8% spend less than the
40–70	19.8 ⎬	equivalent of c. 12 days p.a.
71–100	24.3 ⎭	
101–130	20.1	
131–160	10.1	
161–190	5.4	
191 +	7.6	
no response	8.0	(too ashamed?)

Average time spent = 114 hours, or c. 14 days p.a. Least time (ave. 94 hrs) is spent in the smaller companies, most in the larger (ave. 153 hours in $5 bn +), equivalent to 19 days p.a.

Chairmen devote an average of 175 hours (say 22 days p.a.), again higher in the largest companies.

Fees:
Average $20, 462; c. 20% under $14,000; c. 25% over $25,000.

Thus $20, 462 for 114 hours, or 14 days p.a., equates with an average per diem of $1,500. Rates are highest in retailing, lowest in insurance.

Outside directors commonly receive additional benefits:

directors' liability insurance 84.1%; deferral of fees until retirement 66.8%; matching educational gifts programme 47.2%; accident insurance 41.2%; pension plan 25.4%; life insurance 23.3%; *travel expenses for spouse* 22.7%; medical insurance 12.6%; stock options 8.2%.

A quarter of the Study's respondents have outside directors who receive special consulting fees, a proportion which appears to be increasing.

Board compensation is determined by: chairman 58.8%; compensation committee 37.7%; nominating committee 11.3%; executive committee 10.7%.

Ages
Average age of CEO is 57; of outside directors is 59; of chairmen is 69.
Average retiring age for outside directors is 70; average range for outsiders is 48–69.

UK boards

Sample (nos.)	*t/o above £500m*	*£1–500m*	*up to £100m*	*all cos.*
UK quoted	44	66	48	158
Private		8	9	17
UK subsidiary	1			1
Foreign subsid.	5	12	20	37
Nationalised	4			4
Total	54	86	77	217
Average t/o	£1837m	£211m	£66m	£558m
Average employees	38,420	5,482	1,424	12,278

The Study covered a broad range of industrial, services and financial companies.

Board numbers (% with)

5 or less	7	12	26	16
6–8	11	44	57	40
9–11	43	37	13	30
12 +	39	7	4	14

Board *structure (%)*	t/o above £500m	£1–500m	up to £100m	all cos.
No non-executives	9	7	27	15 (was 10 5 years ago)
Non-exec. majority	22	24	9	19 (was 21 5 years ago)
% non-executives	42	40	25	36 (unchanged in many years)

Meetings p.a. (%)

5 or less	13	14	25	18
6–8	20	26	12	21
9–11	37	28	19	25
12	27	21	38	29
12 +	3	11	6	7

Committees (% with)

Executive	74	63	50	62
Audit	59	27	15	32
Remuneration	80	69	42	62
Advisory board	6	16	20	16

Combined chairman / chief exec. (% with)

	56	35	41	42

From the time spent (see below) it would appear that many chairmen have some executive responsibilities.

Full-time roles of non-execs. (%)				
Lawyer	2	3	8	4
Banker	3	5	2	4
Politician	2	3	3	3
Accountant		2	6	2
Main board director	54	31	32	41
Parent co. director	2	6	7	5

Roughly similar breakdowns were seen for non-executive chairmen and non-executive deputy chairmen.

The Study figures above add up to only 59% of non-executives. As it is unlikely that the remainder are retired or professional directors with no other full-time roles (though 44% are older than 60), it could be that the proportion with 'main board director' from elsewhere is higher. Indeed the Korn/Ferry Study for 1982 showed that 70–75% of non-executives were full-time executives, MDs or chairmen elsewhere.

Time spent by non-execs. (%)	*t/o above £500m*	*£1–500m*	*up to £100m*	*all cos.*
Up to 6 days p.a.	11	8	24	12
7–12 days	23	40	41	33
13–19	30	20	16	24
20	10	10	4	9
Above 20	26	22	15	22

More than half the non-executives had been in that position for more than five years.

Median base fee (non-executives)	£10,000	£7,500	£5,000	£7,500
Range of fees	£5–13,000	£5–10,000	£450–10,000	£4–12,000

Earlier Korn/Ferry Studies indicated that only 60% of smaller public companies would allow their executives to take non-executive posts elsewhere, and that only 30% of this category would allow them to keep the fees received, rather than to pay them into their employing company. While this seemed rather 'mean' at the time, executive remuneration has since risen so rapidly that it now seems eminently reasonable.

For *non-executive*
chairmen

Spend 20 + days p.a.	77	84	65	79
Median base fee	£45,000	£25,000	£15,000	£25,000
Range of fees	£11–94,000	£8–50,000	£1–45,000	£5–64,500

Almost half had been in that position for more than 5 years.

For *UK quoted cos.*

% with executives related to founders	23	29	50
% with non-execs. related to founders	27	30	21

Information about boards of smaller or private companies in the UK is limited and ageing, but it is believed that they continue to show wider variation in composition and procedures than the above.

Broadly: they have 2–10 directors, average 5–6; there are far fewer non-executives, and a high proportion have none; boards therefore consist mainly of functional directors, and a high proportion have 'executive chairmen'.

Appendix II   Two-tier boards in West Germany, Denmark and France

In the autumn of 1979 the Legal Affairs Committee of the European Parliament rejected, by thirteen votes to nine, the European Commission's proposal for the appointment of worker directors to company boards in the EEC member countries. British Conservative members of the committee, who had been joined in this vote by the Liberals and Christian Democrats, stated then that it was vital that any proposals for a common format throughout the EEC *'shall represent a fair compromise of the essential features acceptable in the member States and should not blindly follow the German form of company organisation'*.

It will be seen by comparing the following outline of current West German company organisation with alternative two-tier systems, such as those of Denmark and France, and then by comparing any one of these with the unitary board system of the UK, that a compromise which really does include the *'essential features'* of all of them will not be possible. Or necessary; or desirable.

West German boards

The West German two-tier system evolved without disharmony from its introduction by Bismarck over a hundred years ago till the Codetermination Act (*Mitbestimmungsgesetz*) of 1976. Employer organisations instituted legal proceedings in the German constitutional court to have this Act declared unconstitutional, though pending resolution of this major disharmony the Act remains in force. Its main provisions are as follows.

1 A private limited company (*Gesellschaft mit beschränkter Haftung*, GmbH) with less than 500 employees may retain a single-tier board, with shareholder-elected directors alone, unless the company and the employees voluntarily agree that they want a two-tier structure and worker directors. There are 150,000 GmbH in Germany, compared with 2,500

public limited companies (*Aktiengesellschaft*, AG). Most maintain the single tier, in which the manager (*Geschäftsführer*) or managers are appointed by the general meeting, or specifically by the articles. The shareholders may give instructions to the managers at meetings, or if the managers are not also members, outside of meetings. Managers must act jointly unless the articles allow (as they normally do) sole action, or dual action by two managers or one manager and a procuration holder (*Prokurist*).

2 Non-business organisations, such as political, religious, charitable, educational, artistic or opinion-disseminating groupings may also maintain a single-tier structure.

3 A GmbH with more than 500 employees, and any public limited company outside of the mining, iron and steel industries, must adopt the two-tier structure. The supervisory board (*Aufsichtsrat*) appoints or removes members of, and supervises, the management board (*Vorstand*), determines their remuneration, and can reduce such remuneration in times of severe financial stress, irrespective of existing contracts. It determines company policy, but cannot manage, or represent the company to third parties. It receives regular reports from the management board on performance, trading, problems, and related matters, and can request information at any time from the management board on matters it considers of importance. It can specify which transactions, or types of transaction, require its prior consent. The management board manages the company, represents the company to third parties, and is bound by resolutions of the supervisory board, though not by resolutions of a general meeting. Members of the management board may not become members of boards of other companies without permission. In companies with between 500 and 2,000 employees the supervisory board contains from three to twenty-one directors, dependent on the size of the company's capital, the total being required to be divisible by three. Two-thirds are shareholder representatives (often bankers, in larger companies) and one-third are employee representatives elected by ballot of the employees. One or two of the employee representatives must be actual employees of the company. A person cannot be a member of a supervisory board if he is already a member of ten other supervisory boards, or if he is a member of the management board or the board of one of the company's subsidiaries.

4 More complex rules apply to companies with more than 2,000 employees, which explains why many larger corporations are seeking to reorganise into visibly smaller units. There are around 1,000 companies in this size

category. Half of the directors are shareholder representatives, half are employee representatives:

(i) for 2,000 – 10,000 employee companies, there must be twelve directors – six representative of shareholders, four employees, two union nominees;

(ii) for 10,000 – 20,000 employee companies, there must be sixteen directors – eight representing shareholders, six employees, two union nominees;

(iii) above 20,000 there must be twenty directors – ten representing shareholders, seven employees, three union nominees.

The rules require that 'employee' representation include wage-earning 'blue-collar' men, salaried 'white-collar' men, and executive staff. All companies with more than 2,000 employees, and all companies in the mining, iron and steel industries, irrespective of size, must have a labour director (*Arbeitsdirektor*). He is appointed by the shareholders, but he cannot be removed against the votes of the employee representatives on the supervisory board. Despite the apparent arithmetic, the shareholders maintain a marginal advantage in companies with more than 2,000 employees. The chairman has a casting vote. He is elected by the members of the supervisory board by a two-thirds majority, or by a simple majority if two-thirds is not attained. If no simple majority can be attained either, then the chairman is elected solely by the 'shareholder' directors, and the vice-chairman, who has no casting vote, is elected by the employee directors. This marginal advantage extends also in theory to the appointment of the management board, which is again by a two-thirds majority or, failing that, by a simple majority.

Note: the 'exoneration' or relief (*Entlastung*) of both the supervisory and management boards is decided annually in general meeting. It is intended to signify confidence, but it does not provide any waiver of liability.

5 Companies in the mining, iron and steel industries are governed by a separate set of very complex rules. Broadly, they have supervisory boards with eleven to twenty-one members – equal numbers of shareholder and employee directors, plus one 'further' member who must not come from a background related in any way to either shareholder or employee interests.

In practice, any system which is so delicately tuned will in time begin to cough and splutter – as the German system is already doing. It will end up with bronchitis, which is infectious if you get too close. The only valuable lesson from German practice is that works councils can play a productive role. These can be formed, if the employees wish, in all companies with more than five employees. They act as a watchdog over employer – union agreements, and must be consulted or informed on matters such as safety, manpower and investment plans, production changes, and the general situation of the company. More controversially, they also have powers to give or withhold approval on working conditions, hours, wage scales, holidays, rules for engaging and dismissing employees, specific dismissals, new work methods, closures or reduced working, takeovers and mergers.

On the whole, common sense, and collective sense in the balancing of overall company interests with specifically worker-oriented interests, prevailed in West Germany until the politically oriented Codetermination Act of 1976 introduced unnecessary new stresses, of which we have certainly not heard the last.

Danish boards

The two-tier system applies if the company's capital exceeds Danish Kroner 400,000 (= £36,000 or $58,000) or if there are more than fifty employees. The two types of company are the public limited company (*Aktieselskab*, A/S) and the private limited company (*Anpartsselskab*, ApS).

With two tiers, the board (*Bestyrelse*) ensures that there is a suitable organisation for the activities of the company, produces guidelines and instructions for management, and appoints the management.

The management (*Direktion*) conducts the daily management, and refers significant decisions to the board. Division of functions between the two levels is loosely defined, and varies widely in practice. It may be defined in the articles. Both levels can represent the company to third parties, and can bind the company.

The articles may provide for a shareholders' committee, which supervises the administration of the company by both the board and the management, and may take responsibility for appointing the board away from the general meeting. Such committees are still rare.

The board has a minimum of three directors. Where there are more than fifty employees, which is the case in around 3,000 companies, those employees can appoint two directors only to the board, irrespective of how many other directors have been appointed by the shareholders. (In Sweden the limiting size is twenty-five employees.) These two directors must have been employed by the company for at least a year, and are appointed for two years.

They may be removed during that period by the employees. They may not participate in board discussions on wages, labour relations or labour conflicts, which makes one wonder just what they can contribute. As voting for these two directors is by simple majority of all employees, 'blue-collar' workers will tend to predominate. When the worker director reform was first introduced, the blue- and white-collar categories commonly agreed to share the seats, one apiece; latterly the blue category has tended to take both. The board is empowered to co-opt a white-collar nominee if it feels such would be helpful, even when two blue-collar representatives have been elected. The white-collar nominee is then appointed by the shareholders.

Not all companies with more than fifty employees have chosen to elect worker directors. Many, particularly the smallest, prefer the kind of consultation available through cooperation committees, where management and employees are equally represented. By an agreement between the Danish equivalent of the Trades Union Congress and the Employers' Federation, such committees can be formed in any company with more than fifty employees where either management or workers want it.

The board may contain managers as directors (in contrast to West German law) and about one-third do so. The chief executive of United Breweries, the Carlsberg/Tuborg combine, for example, is not a board director. The majority of the board must be non-executive if the capital is over Danish Kroner 400,000. When the board itself does not contain managers as directors, it is quite common to find that the chief executive is 'co-opted' to attend board meetings, though without a vote. Managers in general have the right to attend and address the board if they so request.

The chairman of the board (*Formand*) can be full time, i.e. effectively executive, but he cannot be a member of management.

Directors or managers who wilfully or negligently inflict loss on the company are liable for damages. Similarly with founders or auditors. Decision on taking such action is made by the general meeting, or by shareholders with at least 10 per cent of the equity.

The flexibility with which the Danes may apply their legislation has enabled them to operate their system smoothly, to date. In practice it lies half-way between the German two-tier structure and the UK's unitary system, in some aspects closer to the former, in others to the latter. In a strictly business sense, the Danes have long demonstrated exceptional skill in overcoming the severe disadvantage of having no native natural resources whatever, apart from their wits and professionalism. Alas, here too politically oriented pressure for changes to shareholding structures is introducing unproductive new stresses to an economy already under siege.

French boards

The articles of a French company determine whether a two-tier or unitary structure is applied, the latter being called the 'classical' system.

A limited company (*Société anonyme*, SA, and broadly though not precisely the same as the British plc and German AG) most commonly maintains a single tier. Similarly with a private limited company (*Société à responsabilité limitée*, Sàrl). There are 370,000 Sàrl and 128,000 SA.

1 The single-tier SA has a board (*conseil d'administration*) of directors (*administrateurs*) and is managed by a *président* elected by the board from among its members. The board delegates most of its powers to him, and he represents the company to third parties. He cannot be president of more than two French SAs, excluding affiliated companies. A general manager (*directeur général*) can be appointed to assist the president, and he may or may not be a director. His powers are the same as those of the president, and there can be two general managers if the capital exceeds 500,000 francs. There are three to twelve directors, and none may hold more than eight directorships. Up to one-third of the directors may be employees (of any level) and they must have been employed by the company for at least two years. Directors are appointed in general meeting; general managers are appointed by the board on the suggestion of the president. Directors are liable for damages in cases of mismanagement, and action can be brought by shareholders representing only 5 per cent of the equity. They can also be held responsible for the entire excess of liabilities over assets if the company becomes bankrupt as a result of demonstrated mismanagement.

2 In the two-tier alternative there is a supervisory board (*conseil de surveillance*) and a directorate (*directoire*). The supervisory board appoints and supervises the directorate, and may appoint general managers to assist the president. It contains three to thirteen members, with the same limit on number of directorships, and the same range of liabilities, as in the single-tier system. The directorate, or 'management board', acts as a body, with one to five members. It has a president, but no special powers are delegated to him. No person can be a member of the directorate of more than two French SAs, and no member of a directorate can be a member of the same company's supervisory board. The directorate must report at least once every three months to the supervisory board.

3 The Sàrl is managed by managers (*gérants*) rather than by a board, but they have similar powers and duties to those of directors.

4   The French also permit the formation of an economic cooperation group (+ § + groupement d'intérêt économique), which is a loose grouping of persons, companies and/or other organisations composed to serve the economic interests of its members. It is a legal entity, not just a grouping of bodies tied to each other by a contract, though there will normally be such a contract defining the objectives and operations of the grouping. It is mainly used for cooperation between companies to assist them in exporting, research, materials processing, or similar, and it may not operate for outsiders, or itself operate for profit. It is managed by *administrateurs*; multiple votes are possible (a more influential or more interested member may have more votes than a lesser member); there is unlimited liability for debts incurred within the grouping's objectives.

A decade ago the French Committee on the Reform of the Enterprise produced a report, known as the Sudreau Report (1975). This proposed a large number of changes to French corporate structures, including:

an extension of employee representation on single-and two-tier boards;
full voting rights for employee representatives;
an extension of employee participation schemes;
a reduction in the number of directorships which can be held;
a more frequent renewal of board membership;
the separation of the roles of chairman and chief executive;
planned successions from the age of 60 years; and
far-reaching rights for information and consultation for works councils,
    especially in holding and multinational companies.

The report received an understandably varied reception, and its proposals have been largely left on the shelf, *pro tem*.

Acknowledgement: The major source of legal data for Appendix II is Meinhardt (1981). The writer, however, is responsible for operational details, and for opinions expressed.

Appendix III Recommended reading

Legal

1 Your company's charter and bylaws (USA) or memorandum and articles (UK).
2 Your local Business Corporation Act or Law (USA) or Companies Act. In the UK also the Insolvency Act 1985 which overlapped with, and partly altered the almost contemporaneous Companies Act 1985.
3 A good commentary on your local Corporation Act and related legislation which extracts and describes the key points for practical consideration. The ABA Guidebook of 1978 (USA) needs updating, but there's the helpful: Mattar, E.P. and Ball, M., *Handbook for Corporate Directors*, McGraw-Hill, 1985.
   For the UK there's: Loose, Peter and Yelland, John, *The Company Director*, Jordans, 1987.

Statistics

Annual *Board of Directors Study*, Korn/Ferry International, Los Angeles (for US boards) and London (for UK boards).
Both are compiled from questionnaires to larger companies.

General

1 The chapter 'The Board of Directors' in Geneen, Harold S. and Moscow, W. Alvin, *Managing*, Avon/Granada, 1985.
2 The chapter 'The Boardroom Mafia' in Heller, Robert, *The New Naked Manager*, Hodder & Stoughton, 1985.
3 The chapter 'Needed, an Effective Board' in Drucker, Peter F., *Management, Tasks, Responsibilities, Practices*, Harper & Row/Heinemann, 1974.
4 The chapter 'Conclusions' in Mace, Myles L., *Directors, Myth and Reality*, Cambridge, Mass., Harvard University Press, 1971.

Japan

Franko, Lawrence, G., *The Threat of Japanese Multinationals – How the West Can Respond*, John Wiley, IRM Series on Multinationals, 1983.

Lawrence Franko is Professor of International Business Relations at Tufts University, Mass., USA.

Non-executive/outside directors

1 Barr, Joseph W., 'The Role of the Professional Director', *Harvard Business Review*, May–June, 1976.
2 Chandler, Marvin, 'It's Time to Clean Up the Boardroom', *Harvard Business Review*, Sept–Oct 1975.

These two ageing articles remain worth reading. There have been changes in boardrooms, but they have been small, and some have been retrograde. Many of the articles listed in the References section of this book are also worth reading in full.

Take-overs and buy-outs

1 Law, Warren A., 'A Corporation Is More Than Its Stock', *Harvard Business Review*, May–June, 1986.
   The article lists other reports and articles recommended to the reader.
   Warren Law is Professor of Banking and Finance at Harvard Business School, is a director of several American companies, and has participated in both sides of take-over battles.
2 Lowenstein, Louis, 'No More Cozy Management Buy-outs', *Harvard Business Review*, Jan–Feb, 1986.
   Louis Lowenstein is Professor of Law at Columbia University where he teaches corporate finance. He has experience both as a director and, particularly, as a lawyer engaged on mergers and acquisitions for a NY law practice and as counsel for a leading leveraged buy-out banking firm.
3 *The Times* newspaper article, 'Counting the Cost of Merger Mania', 7.4.86.
4 *The Sunday Times* article, also entitled 'Counting the Cost of Merger Mania', 20.7.86.

Again, a number of the articles on these subjects in the References section are worth reading.

Company collapse

Argenti, John, 'Discerning the Cracks of Company Failure', *The Director*, Oct 1983.
Read the 'A-score Table' and do the sums for your own company. You may not get past line 2 before feeling faint.

References

Abegglen, J. G. and Stalk, G. (1986), 'Kaisha – Growth, Not Profits', *FE: The Magazine for Financial Executives*, April.

Abernathy, W. J. (1982), 'Competitive Decline', *Research Management*, Sept.

The Accountant (1981), 'Survey of Professional Opinion', 30.4.81.

Aggarwal, S. G. and Aggarwal, V. S. (1985), 'The Control Gap at the Top', *Business Horizons*, May–June.

Albrecht, Willian and Jhin, Philip (1978), 'The Million Dollar Men', *Business Horizons*, August.

Alderfer, Clayton P. (Professor at Yale School of Organisation and Management) (1986), 'The Invisible Director on Corporate Boards', *Harvard Business Review*, Nov–Dec.

American Bar Association, Section on Corporate, Banking and Business Law (1978), *Corporate Directors' Guidebook*, Chicago, Jan.

Argenti, John (1976), *Corporate Collapse*, McGraw-Hill.

Argenti, John (1983), 'Discerning the Cracks of Company Failure', *The Director*, Oct.

Argyris, C. (Professor of Education and Organisational Behaviour, Harvard University Graduate School of Education) (1986), 'Skilled Incompetence', *Harvard Business Review*, Sept–Oct.

Barr, Joseph W. (1976), 'The Role of the Professional Director', *Harvard Business Review*, May–June.

Benson, Lord (1986), quoted in 'A Tilt at the Short-sighted Institutions', *Financial Times*, 3.12.86. (Lord Benson was a distinguished accountant who became Industrial Adviser to the Governor of the Bank of England.)

Bierce, Ambrose (1911), *The Devil's Dictionary*.

British Institute of Management (1970), *Boards of Directors in Small/Medium Sized Private Companies*, BIM Information Summary no. 149.

British Institute of Management (1972), *The Board of Directors*, Management Survey Report no. 10.

Brown, Malcolm (1987), 'The Hunt is Hotting Up for Money Managers', *The Sunday Times*, 10.5.87.

Brown, Lord Wilfred (1980), in personal communication.

Bullock Committee (1977), *Report of the Committee of Inquiry on Industrial Democracy*, Cmnd 6706, HMSO.

Burchell, R. A. and Grey, R. J. (1981) 'The Frontier West', in *Introduction to American Studies*, Longman.

Burns, Paul (Professor of Small Business Development, Cranfield) (1985), 'Are Small Businesses Being Oversold?' *The Director*, Oct.

Carroll, Daniel T. (1981), 'Boards and Managements: Ten Challenges and Responses', *Harvard Business Review*, September–October.

Castaldi, R. and Wortman, M. S. (1984), 'Boards of Directors in Small Corporations', *American Journal of Small Business*, Autumn, 9/2.

Chandler, R. F. and Henshall, B. D. (1985), 'The Changing Roles of the Board of Directors', *Singapore Management Review*, vol. 7, no. 1.

Clough, W. S. (1981), 'Sweeping Away the Amateurs on the British Board', *The Director*, July.

Collins, Neil (1986), 'The Inside Story', *The Sunday Times*, 9.3.86.

Confederation of British Industry (1973), *A New Look at the Responsibilities of the British Public Company*.

Crossman, Richard (1975–7), *The Diaries of a Cabinet Minister*, Jonathan Cape.

Cyert, R. M. and March, J. G. (1973), *A Behavioral Theory of the Firm*, Prentice-Hall.

Davey, Douglas Mackenzie (1980), in personal communication.

Dayton, K. N. (1984), 'Corporate Governance: The Other Side of the Coin', *Harvard Business Review*, Jan–Feb.

Dixon, Michael (1986), 'How Many Heads Can Be Dafter Than One?', *Financial Times*, 3.4.86.

Dixon, Michael (1987), 'Stupidity of Barring Unemployed Applicants', *Financial Times*, 7.1.87.

Drucker, Peter F. (1974), *Management, Tasks, Responsibilities, Practices*, Harper & Row/Heinemann.

DT: *Daily Telegraph* (1983), '£19m. Debtor Discharged for £10,000', 3.2.83.

DT: *Daily Telegraph* (1983), *'Bankrupt Property Chief "never put a penny into business",'* 25.3.83.

Eales, Roy (1987), 'Secrets To Be Learned From the East', *The Independent*, 25.4.87.

The Economist (1987), 'Definitely Not World Class'; and 'Of Crooks and Cartels', both 14.2.87.

Festinger, L. (1957), *A Theory of Cognitive Dissonance*, Row Peterson.

Festinger, L. (ed.) (1964), *Conflict, Decision and Dissonance*, Stanford University Press.

Financial Times (26.11.1982), 'Row looms over proposal for top Lloyds executive'. See also the *Financial Times* of 14.1.83, 'US Insurance Chief Calls for British Action on Fraud' and 3.9.83, 'Lloyds Accused of Lack of Control.'

Financial Times (1985), 'Men and Matters', 7.11.85.

Fleet, Kenneth (1979), 'Qualities of Non-Executive Company Directors' in *Financial Weekly*, no. 41.

Foster, Geoffrey (1987), 'The Legacy of Harvey-Jones', *Management Today*, Jan. (Comments confirmed also in personal communication.)

284   *Controlling Companies*

Fox, H. W. (1982), 'Quasi-boards: Useful Small Business Confidants', *Harvard Business Review*, Jan – Feb.

Fox, H. W. (1984), 'Quasi-boards – Guidance, Without Governance, *American Journal of Small Business*, Summer, 9/1.

Franko, Lawrence G. (1983), *The Threat of Japanese Multinationals – How the West Can Respond*, John Wiley, IRM Series on Multinationals.

Geneen, Harold S. and Moscow, W. Alvin (1985), *Managing*, Avon/ Granada.

Gilbert, Nick (1985), '(American) Banking on the Rocks', *The Sunday Times*, 14.4.85.

Hall, William (1982), 'A Jolt to the City's Status', *Financial Times*, 16.4.82.

Harris, Anthony (1986), 'The Long View', *Financial Times*, 22.2.86; 22.11.86; 7.3.87.

Harvey-Jones, Sir John, then chairman of the board of ICI, in the BBC Dimbleby Lecture, 1986.

Heller, Robert (1985), *The New Naked Manager*, Hodder & Stoughton.

Heller, Robert (1986), 'The Agonies of Agglomeration', *Management Today*, Feb.

Henderson, Bruce (1980), in personal communication.

Henke, J. W. (1986), 'Involving the Board in Strategic Planning', *Journal of Business Strategy*, Autumn.

Herriot, Peter (Professor of Occupational Psychology, Birkbeck College, London) (1986), quoted in 'Setback for Recruitment', *The Independent*, 6.12.86.

Herzel, Leo (1986), 'Business Law: Relief for Directors (American)', *Financial Times*, 17.7.86.

Institute of Directors (1986), *Code of Practice for the Non-executive Director*, London.

Irving, Joe (1987), 'Guarding the Pension Funds', *Sunday Times*, 31.5.87, quoting a Union leader and Sir Brandon Rhys Williams, Conservative MP.

Janis, I. L. (1972), *Victims of Groupthink*, Houghton Mifflin.

Janis, I. L. and Mann, L. (1977), *Decision-Making – A Psychological Analysis of Conflict, Choice and Commitment*, The Free Press.

Jay, John (1987), 'Foreign Banks Criticised for Risky Loans', *Sunday Times*, 12.7.87.

Johnson, R. J. (1974), 'Conflict Avoidance Through Acceptable Decisions', *Human Relations*.

Kaletsky, Anatole (1983), quoted in his article 'Chile's Economic Experiment', *Financial Times*, 9.3.83.

Katz, D. and Kahn, R. L. (1978), *The Social Psychology of Organizations*, 2nd edn, John Wiley.

Kelvin, P. (1970), *Bases of Social Behavior*, Holt, Rinehart & Winston.

Kets de Vries, M. F. R. and Miller, D. (1984), 'Neurotic Style and Organisational Pathology', *Strategic Management Journal*, Jan – March. *See also*: Kets de Vries, M. F. R. and Miller, D. (1984), *The Neurotic Organisation*, Jossey-Bass. (Manfred Kets de Vries is Professor of Management at INSEAD, Fontainebleau; Danny Miller is a management professor at McGill University, Montreal.)

Klein II, William (a lawyer writing in *Institutional Investor*) (1984), quoted in Thackray (1984).

Kolb, D. A., Rubin, I. M. and McIntyre, J. M. (1979), *Organizational Psychology – A Book of Readings*, 3rd edn, Prentice-Hall.

Korn/Ferry International (annual), *Boards of Directors Study*, London.

Korn/Ferry International (annual), *Board of Directors*, Los Angeles.

Law, Warren A. (1986), 'A Corporation Is More Than its Stock', *Harvard Business Review*, May – June.

Lawson, Gerald (1980), 'Company Profits, the Grand Illusion', *The Sunday Times*, 30 July.

Lawson, Gerald (1980), 'The Measurement of Corporate Profitability on a Cashflow Basis', *International Journal of Accounting*, vol. 16, no. 1.

Lee, T. and Tweedie, D. P. (1981), *The Institutional Investor and Financial Information*, The Institute of Chartered Accountants, London.

Lester, Tom (1985), 'The Corporate Buying Spree', *Management Today*, Sept.

Linaker, Paddy (MD of M & G Investment Management) (1986), quoted in 'Counting the Cost of Merger Mania', *The Times*, 7.4.86.

Lindblom, C. E. (1959), 'The Science of Muddling Through', *Public Administration Review*, vol. 19, Spring.

Lloyd, John (1983), 'The Strains Begin to Show', *Financial Times*, 6.4.83.

Lowenstein, Louis (1986), 'No More Cozy Management Buyouts', *Harvard Business Review*, Jan – Feb.

Luffman, G. and Reed, R. (1985), 'The Giant Company Comeback', *Management Today*, June.

March, J. G. and Simon, H. A. (1958), *Organizations*, John Wiley.

Meinhardt, Peter (1981), *Company Law in Europe*, Gower.

Millstein, Ira M. (1986), 'Take-over Reform: Common Sense From the Common Law', *Harvard Business Review*, July – Aug.

Mizruchi, M. S. (1983), 'Management and Boards in Large Corporations', *The Academy of Management Review*, July.

Monks Publications (1984, 1986), *Boardroom Pay and Incentives in Growth Companies*, and *Board and Senior Management Remuneration*.

Moore, John (1987), 'Risk-takers Run for Cover as Shake-up Looms', *The Independent*, 5.5.87.

Munn, N. L. (1972) *Psychology*, 5th edn, University of Adelaide.

Murray, Angus (1980), quoted in *Financial Times*, 3 March.

Nachiro, Amaya (Special Adviser to MITI) (1982), quoted in Wilson, Dick, 'Japan: The Trade Challenge', *The Banker*, May.

Oram, Rod (1987), 'SEC Chairman Backs Harvard Ethics Course', *Financial Times*, 1.4.87.

Ozawa, Terutomo (1983), quoted from his Foreword to *Franko*.

Pickens, T. Boone, quoted in Law (1986), from interviews in *Barron's*, 23.9.85 and *Chief Executive*, Fall, 1985.

Porter, Professor Sir George (President of the Royal Society and winner of the Nobel Prize for Chemistry) (1987), quoted in *The Independent*, 23.3.87.

PRO NED (1987), *Code of Recommended Practice on Non-executive Directors*, London.

Prowse, Michael (1987), 'The Long View', *Financial Times*, 21.3.87.

Questor column, *Daily Telegraph*, 10.8.84.

Richardson, Gordon (1978), 'The Joint Stock Company', 10th Annual Lecture to the Institute of Directors.

Roberts, Eirlys (1980), in personal communication.

Ross Jr., Wilbur (of Rothschild Inc.) quoted in Thackray, (1984).

Scotese, Peter G. (1985), 'Fold Up Those Golden Parachutes', *Harvard Business Review*, March–Apr. *See also*: Muckley, J. E. (1984), 'Dear Fellow Shareowner', *HBR*, March–Apr.

Shellard, David (1986), quoted in 'More Firms Employ Headhunters', *The Times*, 8.1.86.

Simon, H. A. (1977), *Administrative Behavior. A Study of Decision-Making Process in Administrative Organizations*, 3rd edn, Free Press.

Smallwood, Christopher (Economics Editor) (1986), 'Counting the Cost of Merger Mania', *The Sunday Times*, 20.7.86.

Sorkin, Ira (1985), quoted in 'Accountants Face a Double Indemnity', *Financial Times*, 10.4.85.

Spencer Stuart (the executive search company) (1986), *Point of View No. 10*, London.

Sudreau, Pierre (1975), *La Réforme de l'entreprise: rapport du Comité*, Documentation Française, Paris.

Swedish Institute (1979), 'Labor Relations in Sweden', Swedish Information Fact Sheet F3.

Sylvester, Tony (solicitor advising Institute of Directors on employment matters) (1986), quoted in 'Going for Gold in a Company Handshake', *The Sunday Times*, 8.6.86.

Tarrant, J. (1985), 'Can Loyalty be Locked up?,' *Across the Board*, May, 22/5.

Thackray, John (1983), 'America's Amazing Executive Wealth', *Management Today'*, July. *See also*:

Thackray, John (1984), 'The Great American Buy-out Binge', *Management Today'*, Aug.

Thackray, John (1985), 'America's Management Mischief', *Management Today*, Feb.

Thorne, Paul (1986), 'On the Prevalence of Madness in Businessmen', *International Management*, Sept.

Thorne, Paul (1987), 'Pay As an Incentive: The Road to Ruin?', *International Management*, Feb.

US Supreme Court, Trustees of Dartmouth College v. Woodward, in vol. 4, Wheaton's United States Supreme Court Reports 1816–27.

Viljoen, J. and Clayton, B. M. (1985), 'Strategy and the Role of the Board of Directors,' *Management Forum* (Australia), Dec.

Weidenbaum, M. L. (1986), *The Journal of Business Strategy*, Summer.

Whitley, Richard (1974), 'Commonalities and connections among directors of large financial institutions', Manchester Business School.

Williams, Ian and Stelzer, Irwin (1986), 'Insider Trading Soars', *The Sunday Times*, 12.10.86.

Woolf, E. (1986), 'The Hazards of Being a Director', *Accountancy*, Nov.

Index